Equality, Diversity and Discrimination

A stu...

Kathy Daniels teaches Employment Law and Employee Relations at Aston Business School, and tutors and authors on a range of HRM and Psychology topics for ICS Limited. She has written a textbook published by CIPD Publishing in the area of Employment Law. She is a lay member of the Employment Tribunal, sitting in Birmingham. She is also a tutor on the Advanced Certificate in Employment Law, and a Regional Certificate Moderator – both for the CIPD. Prior to these appointments she was a senior personnel manager in the manufacturing sector.

Lynda Macdonald is a self-employed freelance employment law trainer, advisor and writer. She is a panel member of the Employment Tribunal Service in Aberdeen, where she lives.

The Chartered Institute of Personnel and Development is the
leading publisher of books and reports for personnel and training
professionals, students, and all those concerned with the effective
management and development of people at work. For details of all
our titles, please contact the publishing department:
Tel: 020 8612 6204
E-mail: publish@cipd.co.uk
The catalogue of all CIPD titles can be viewed on the CIPD
website:
www.cipd.co.uk/bookstore

Equality, Diversity and Discrimination

A student text

Kathy Daniels and Lynda Macdonald

The Chartered Institute of Personnel and Development

Published by the Chartered Institute of Personnel and Development
151 The Broadway, London, SW19 1JQ

First published 2005
Reprinted 2006, 2008, 2009

Typeset by Ferdinand Page Design, Surrey
Printed in Great Britain by The Cromwell Press Group, Trowbridge, Wiltshire

British Library Cataloguing in Publication Data

A catalogue of this manual is available from the British Library

ISBN 1 84398 112 2
ISBN 13 978 1 84398 112 1

Chartered Institute of Personnel and Development
151 The Broadway, London, SW19 1JQ
Tel: 020 8612 6200
Email: cipd@cipd.co.uk   Website: www.cipd.co.uk
Incorporated by Royal Charter   Registered Charity No. 1079797

CONTENTS

List of Tables

List of Acts, Regulations and Directives

Anti-Terrorism, Crime and Security Act 2001
Asylum and Immigration Act 1996
Code of Practice for the elimination of discrimination in the field of employment against disabled persons
Code of Practice for the elimination of discrimination on grounds of sex and marriage and the promotion of equality of opportunity in employment
Code of Practice on age diversity in employment
Code of Practice on equal pay
Code of practice on the protection of the dignity of women and men at work
Crime and Disorder Act 1998
Criminal Justice and Public Order Act 1994
Data Protection Act 1998
Data Protection Code of Practice
Disability Discrimination Act 1995
Disability Discrimination Act 1995 (Amendment) Regulations 2003
Employment Act 1989
Employment Act 2002
Employment Act 2002 (Dispute Resolution) Regulations 2004
Employment Equality (Religion or Belief) Regulations 2003
Employment Equality (Sexual Orientation) Regulations 2003
Employment Relations Act 1999
Employment Rights Act 1996
Equal Pay Act 1970
Equal Pay (Amendment) Regulations 1983
Equal Pay Directive (Council Directive 75/117)
Equal Treatment Directive (Council Directive 76/207)
Equal Treatment Framework Directive (No. 2000/78)
European Convention on Human Rights 1950
European Employment Directive (Council Directive 2000/78/EC)
Fair Employment (Northern Ireland) Act 1976
Fair Employment (Northern Ireland) Act 1989
Fixed-Term Employees (Prevention of Less Favourable Treatment) Regulations 2002
Flexible Working (Procedural Requirements) Regulations 2002
Flexible Working (Eligibility, Complaints and Remedies) Regulations 2002
Human Rights Act 1998
National Minimum Wage Act 1998
Part-Time Workers (Prevention of Less Favourable Treatment) Regulations 2000
Protection from Harassment Act 1997
Public Disclosure Act 1998
Race Directive (Council Directive 2000/43)
Race Relations Act 1976
Race Relations (Amendment) Regulations 2003
Race Relations Amendment Act 2000
Race Relations (Statutory Duties) Order 2001
Sex Discrimination Act 1975
Sex Discrimination (Gender Reassignment) Regulations 1999
Trade Union and Labour Relations (Consolidation) Act 1992
Treaty of Rome 1957
Working Time Regulations 1998

List of Cases

List of Abbreviations

CRE	Commission for Racial Equality
DDA	Disability Discrimination Act 1995
DDP	Dismissal and disciplinary procedure
DRC	Disability Rights Commission
DTI	Department of Trade and Industry
EAT	Employment Appeal Tribunal
ECHR	European Court of Human Rights
ECJ	European Court of Justice
EEA	European Economic Area
EOC	Equal Opportunities Commission
ERA	Employment Rights Act 1996
GOQ	Genuine occupational qualification
GOR	Genuine occupational requirement
HRA	Human Rights Act 1998
LIFO	Last in, first out
RRA	Race Relations Act 1976
RRAA	Race Relations Amendment Act 2000
SDA	Sex Discrimination Act 1975
SOSR	Some other substantial reason
TUC	Trades Union Congress

The CIPD would like to thank the following members of the CIPD Publishing Editorial Board for their help and advice:

- Pauline Dibben, Middlesex University Business School

- Edwina Hollings, Staffordshire University Business School

- Caroline Hook, Huddersfield University Business School

- Vincenza Priola, Wolverhampton Business School

- John Sinclair, Napier University Business School

Preface

There has been legislation relating to discrimination in the UK since 1970. The first piece of legislation related to equal pay and benefits for men and women. Since that initial legislation, the range of areas covered has been gradually extended, with discrimination on the grounds of religion and belief or sexual orientation being added in 2003. In 2006, we will see a further addition of legislation, relating to age discrimination.

This rapid growth in legislation reflects the fact that many people are starting to realise the benefits of having a diverse workforce. Diversity brings a broader range of ideas and experiences to an organisation, and also improves motivation by allowing all employees an equal chance to join and progress within an organisation.

Despite the many examples of organisations that have embraced diversity and seen huge benefits from it, discrimination still occurs in the workplace. Some employers remain unclear about the requirements of the law and the implications of this.

The benefits of diversity, and the need to understand discrimination legislation, have made this area an important topic for those studying a business- or human resource-related degree. It has become a fundamental part of learning for those who wish to move into general or human resource management.

This textbook has been written for students studying such a degree. It looks in detail at the relevant legislation, and considers how this is applied in the workplace. It also looks at a range of psychological and organisational issues associated with diversity and equality. The textbook specifically covers the syllabus for the CIPD elective in Managing Diversity and Equal Opportunities.

Included within the textbook are the following key features:

- All legal cases are summarised in some detail to aid learning and understanding.

- There are 'tasks' throughout the text, suggesting activities the student can do to further their understanding of the topic area.

- There is a list of key points to facilitate revision.

- There are examples to work through to test the student's ability to apply the material that has been taught.

Kathy Daniels
Lynda MacDonald

Introduction to Equality, Diversity and Discrimination

CHAPTER 1

> **OBJECTIVES OF THIS CHAPTER:**
> - to understand what diversity, discrimination and equality are
> - to evaluate why problems occur
> - to analyse current statistics
> - to consider ways to promote a diverse workforce.

WHAT ARE DIVERSITY, DISCRIMINATION AND EQUALITY?

Diversity within an organisation is having a range of differences among the people. These might be differences relating to such things as gender, ethnic origin and disability. If these differences are valued within an organisation, there is a positive diversity belief, which is defined by the CIPD as:

> **" Valuing everyone as individuals – as employees, customers and clients. "**

In the CIPD bulletin, 'Diversity: stacking up the evidence' (2004), three different types of diversity were described. They are:

1 social category diversity – relating to differences in demographic characteristics such as age and race
2 informational diversity – relating to differences in background such as education and knowledge
3 value diversity – relating to differences in personality and attitudes.

Social category and informational diversity are known as surface level diversity. These aspects of diversity describe the make-up of the particular group. Deep level diversity is the value diversity – the attitudes, beliefs and values.

These different categories are an important consideration because it is easy to think of diversity purely in terms of social categories. When we think of the differences between people, we have to understand that the range of areas where difference can occur is very broad.

Diversity within organisations is about recognising this range of differences in people and valuing people as individuals, respecting their differences and their differing needs. It is also about accommodating differences wherever possible so that an individual can play a full part in the working environment.

1

In acknowledging the range of differences that exist, we also need to consider that range against the use of teamwork within organisations. Is there a dilemma between the need to treat people as individuals and the desire to promote teamwork?

It is also important to acknowledge that implementing diversity practices is not always easy. Taylor (2002) notes that managing a more diverse workforce places new demands on government, employers, employees and trade unions. Such people do not always realise why an existing working practice might not be encouraging diversity and, indeed, can find that the increasing demands of trying to meet a wider range of needs is difficult.

There are many different groups that a person can belong to by virtue of their differences (eg male, black, university-educated, manager).

Discrimination is the favouring of one of these groups over another for no justifiable reason. This discrimination is an acting out of the prejudices that people hold. Prejudice is described by Brown (1995) as:

> **" The holding of derogatory social attitudes or cognitive beliefs, the expression of negative affect, or the display of hostile or discriminatory behaviour towards members of a group on account of their membership of that group. "**

We see, therefore, that prejudice is a mix of cognitive aspects (stereotypes that we believe in), affect (a decision that we do not like a particular group) and behavioural aspects (actions that result from the dislike of the group).

Discriminatory behaviour comes, therefore, from the negative stereotypes and decisions that people have made about other groups. It is interesting to note that prejudice is usually something that comes from a group – it is typically a group of people that forms a negative attitude towards another group; it is not typically a reaction of an individual towards an individual.

Discrimination can be evident in the representation of different groups in specific sectors, types of job or levels of management. This is known as occupational segregation. Horizontal segregation is when certain jobs of a similar level are dominated by one group (for example, chambermaids being primarily female and porters being primarily male). Vertical segregation is when one group is dominant at a higher level within an organisation than another group – for example, there being primarily men among senior executives and primarily women in administrative and clerical positions.

Discrimination can be intentional, or it can be deliberate. Deliberate discrimination is often the result of prejudicial attitudes that are held by the discriminator. This leads to one of the challenges that makes achieving a diverse workforce a difficult task – how can people work together if they hold prejudicial attitudes about the group from which each other come?

In the UK there is a wide range of anti-discrimination legislation that we will look at in detail in this book. However, alongside the implementation of the law, there are also benefits for organisations in promoting equality – and we will look at these benefits in more detail later in this chapter. This opportunity for equality was classified by Straw (1989) as operating on three levels.

Straw suggested that there needs to be *equal chance* (ie everyone having the same chance to gain from any opportunities that arise in the workforce [eg promotion]), *equal access* (ie everyone having the same opportunity to enter the organisation) and *equal share* (ie there being a representation of all groups at each level within the organisation).

Later in this book we will look at different ways in which organisations can achieve this equality. This can involve the writing of equal opportunity policies, taking positive action, equal opportunity monitoring and training, and education for all employees.

TASK

Think about the way that diversity is managed in your organisation, or an organisation with which you are familiar. Do you think that the organisation has succeeded in promoting a truly diverse workforce? If not, why not?

CASE STUDY

A small manufacturing company in a rural area of England had a workforce composed almost entirely of employees from a white ethnic origin. This was a reflection of the local population, and the company did not see it as evidence of any discrimination in its recruitment process.

A manager's post fell vacant and the best person to fill the job was a lady of Asian ethnic origin – she was duly appointed. This left the company with two problems – a number of employees reacted negatively to a female manager (there being none other in the organisation), and there was also a negative reaction from some employees to her ethnic origin. Although the issue of racial prejudice had never been raised as a problem before, the management now realised that definite prejudices did exist.

A decision was taken to run a number of focus groups asking employees to explain their concerns about the appointment. Each focus group ran twice – once without the new manager present, to allow the employees to feel free to talk openly, and once with the manager present (at her suggestion) to allow her to address some of the issues. It was soon found that the employees actually had no real issues – in fact, most were unable to think of any reasons for their concerns.

At the end of the focus groups many of the employees apologised to the new manager, saying they were surprised to find that they had no reasons for their reactions. She was well accepted into the organisation and went on to become one of the most effective managers.

This case study gives a clear example of a situation where prejudice had occurred – probably on the grounds of stereotypes developing. When challenged, the prejudicial views had no grounds.

WHY DO PROBLEMS OCCUR?

In understanding why discrimination occurs, it is useful to start by thinking about how people react within different social or work groups. Research by Sherif (1956) has shown that we quickly develop a great loyalty to a group that we belong to, and in doing so develop a negative attitude towards other groups. Sherif worked with boys aged 11 and 12 years in a summer camp setting. The boys were unknown to each other at the start of the camp. After a few days, staff divided the boys into two groups and observed that the groups quickly developed their own identities, with special jargon and secrets, leaders emerging and all members being forced to pull their weight. Sherif then introduced conflict between the two groups in a series of games. The boys in one group were refused contact with the other group, and gave negative ratings to boys in that group. Sherif had shown that, simply by separating people into two groups and introducing some conflict, hostilities could be produced. In the next stage he introduced tasks that required the two groups to work together, and he found that the boys did work together and form new friendships with those in the opposing group. He had shown that the hostility that had been created could be made to disappear just as easily.

Further research by Tajfel (1970) has shown that merely being *categorised* as a group member can produce a negative attitude towards other groups. Tajfel worked with 64 boys aged 14 and 15 years old, who all knew each other well before the experiment. In the first experiment the boys were told that the experiment was about visual estimation. They were shown a series of pictures with a number of dots, and they were asked to estimate how many dots appeared. The boys were then divided into two groups – they were told that one group were the 'over estimators' and the other were the 'under estimators', whereas the allocation to groups was actually completely random. They were then asked to offer rewards of small amounts of money – to any boys. Tajfel found that a significant majority of boys elected to give more money to boys in their own group, rather than to boys in the other group. Tajfel concluded that it was actually very easy to provoke negative attitudes towards other groups.

This has an interesting impact on our understanding of why discrimination occurs. If we belong to a group (eg male, white), then we develop a sense of loyalty and pride in that group. In doing so, we can develop a negative attitude towards other groups (eg female, non-white) and that negative attitude can lead to prejudices. Once those prejudices have developed, they become deeply held attitudes and can be difficult to change.

Discrimination also occurs because groups have a lack of understanding about each other. This is probably particularly evident in tensions between different racial groups. Here there are often outward signs of differences (eg dress, diet, language, religion), and a lack of understanding of the reasons behind these differences can lead to misconceptions developing about the other group. Hence, education about different groups is an important part of the fight against discrimination.

Another important factor in the fight against discrimination is the amount of contact that people have with the 'out' group. Research by van Dick et al (2004) showed that the negative attitudes towards other groups significantly decreased if those with the negative attitudes had opportunities to have acquaintances and make friends with those in the 'out' group. This is an important factor because, if people discover for themselves that negative views are wrong, this is much more powerful than simply being told that they hold wrong views and beliefs about others.

Education is also useful to challenge attitudes and prejudices that people hold. To understand how this education needs to operate, it is important to understand how attitudes develop. Michener et al (2004) suggest that attitudes form in three primary ways: instrumental conditioning, classical conditioning and observational learning.

Instrumental conditioning is learning through direct experience or through interaction with a third party. Hence, if a person has a negative attitude towards a person of another race, this could be because of a negative experience with people of that race, or it could be as a result of information about that race that has been supplied by family or friends. If the attitude has formed as a result of information from a third party, it could have been formed as the result of prejudicial information – and hence prejudices are passed down from person to person and reinforced. The reinforcement is an important part of this conditioning. If a person displays the negative attitudes that they have been taught by the third party, and that third party praises or rewards the negative attitudes, then those attitudes will be further reinforced.

Classical conditioning is the forming of an attitude as a result of associating a response with a stimulus on a number of occasions. So, if we are told that one racial group has a negative attribute, and we hear that information often and regularly, we will come to believe that negative attribute.

Observational learning is learning through watching others. If we are exposed to ideas from the media or other sources that consistently portray a group in a negative way, we will come to adopt that negative attitude. This type of learning has led to the criticism of many books that were written for children several years ago and adopted the stereotypes of the time – for example, with women subservient to men. Increasingly, educationalists have removed such books from reading lists for children.

Education, therefore, needs to return to the reasons why people hold particular attitudes and challenge those attitudes. Unless the underlying attitudes change, it is unlikely that any discriminatory behaviour will change.

The outward signs of discrimination are often illustrated by statistics that show differences between two groups in areas such as rates of pay, or levels of seniority in a job. Such statistics are important, but we should be aware that data can be affected by external factors or causes which are not necessarily discriminatory.

A good illustration of this is the percentage difference in the workplace of men and women. In the UK in 2003, 79 per cent of men and 69 per cent of women between the ages of 16 and 64 were in employment (Labour Force Survey 2004). This might seem to show discrimination against women; however, we have to note that women are more likely than men to take time out from employment for childcare reasons. This is shown in statistics from the Equal Opportunities Commission (EOC) website (www.eoc.org.uk) for 2005:

- 52 per cent of mothers of under-fives are in employment
- 91 per cent of fathers of under-fives are in employment.

So long as we have the social tradition of women taking time out of work to care for children, there will be a disproportionate number of men in employment.

However, there might be evidence of discrimination against women when we consider the statistic, also from the EOC, that in 2005 average hourly earnings for women working full-time are 18 per cent lower than earnings for men working full-time. (The difference in part-time earnings is 40 per cent lower for women). Again we have to consider external factors such as women taking time out from their careers for childcare reasons, but we cannot use those external factors to deny that any deliberate discrimination is taking place.

Diversity has both negative and positive effects. Research by Watson et al (1993) has shown that increased diversity leads to increased creativity and improved decision making. Research by Tsui et al (1992) has shown that there is reduced interpersonal liking, psychological commitment and intergroup communication as a result of diversity. Further research has shown that diversity can have a negative effect on group cohesion (Smith et al [1994]) and increased group conflict (Jehn [1995]). However, research has shown that these negative impacts of diversity decrease as time passes.

Social categorisation suggests that we are more likely to identify with groups of people who have similar backgrounds to ourselves. There is also evidence that more conflict occurs in groups that are more diverse. However, research by Van Knippenberg and Haslam (2003) has also shown that diversity beliefs (viewing everyone as individuals, and accepting differences between people) can reverse the negative effect of diversity on group identification.

If an employer is aware of these negative effects, it is more likely that there will be some reluctance to change an existing team, notwithstanding the positive effects that a more diversified team might achieve. Although an organisation might operate within the law, which we will define in some detail, this does not necessarily mean that it is gaining the full benefits of diversity – because so many differences between people are not the subject of any legislation.

TASK

Think about the way that diversity is managed in your organisation, or an organisation with which you are familiar. Do you think that the organisation has succeeded in promoting a truly diverse workforce? If not, why not?

FACTS AND STATISTICS

It is very important that our concerns relating to discrimination are based on facts, and not on our perceptions. Hence, the purpose of this section is to present current statistical evidence and discuss the possible implications of this.

Ethnic origin

According to the Labour Force Survey (2004), the breakdown of employment by ethnic group is:

Table 1.1 *The breakdown of employment by ethnic group*

Ethnic group	Percentage employed
All origins	74.5
White British	75.9
Other White	71.6
Asian/Asian British	58.2
Indian	68.0
Pakistani	45.2
Bangladeshi	42.5
Other Asian	65.4
Black/Black British	62.8
Black Caribbean	70.7
Black African	55.7
Chinese	55.2
Other	57.2

Source: Labour Force Survey 2004

(Note: Definitions of ethnic groups are as defined by the Office for National Statistics.)

Why is the employment level for some ethnic groups so low? One reason could be that a considerable percentage of people in the ethnic groups with lower employment levels have traditionally been working in the manufacturing, transport and communications sector. As the manufacturing sector has declined, particular ethnic groups could have been disproportionately affected by loss of employment.

Another reason could relate to education level. However, according to research by Modood et al (1997), the Chinese, African Asians and Indians are the most well-educated ethnic groups, with Caribbeans and Pakistanis being less well qualified, and Bangladeshis being least well qualified. The low employment levels of the Chinese in the above statistics are not explained by this reason.

A further reason could be related to language fluency. Research by Modood et al (1997) has shown that more than three-quarters of Asian men speak English fluently, although fluency among women is not so uniform. Although there are distinct differences in fluency between genders among Indian, Bangladeshi and Pakistani groups, the extent of fluency is not really seen to be a reason for the lack of employment in a significant number of situations.

The Parekh report (2000) attempted to address some of these issues. The report was from the Commission on the Future of Multi-Ethnic Britain and was the result of research conducted by 23 individuals, chaired by Bikhu Parekh. The report looked at all aspects of a multi-racial society, not just employment, and made a series of recommendations. The recommendations that relate to employment were:

- The government should 'place a statutory duty on all employers to create and implement equity employment plans' and do so as a matter of priority.
- The award of 'Investors in People' status should be made conditional on the creation of these equity employment plans.
- If an organisation is involved in the New Deal schemes (schemes run by the government primarily directed at reducing unemployment among young people), they should show that they are positively addressing issues relating to employment equity.

The report also has many recommendations that are not related to employment. However, what is particularly important to note is the conclusion that there is active discrimination on the grounds of ethnic origin occurring in this country. We might try to give explanations for the statistics relating to employment, but one of the reasons we cannot ignore is that there is discrimination still occurring.

An article in *The Guardian* dated 9 November 2003 reported that 32 per cent of those surveyed had observed discrimination happening in the workplace. 15 per cent had actually experienced discrimination themselves. This report suggests that discrimination is a reality.

As well as there being differences in the levels of employment, there are also significant differences in the types of work that people from different ethnic origins most typically do. According to data from the Commission for Racial Equality (CRE), 52 per cent of Bangladeshi males work in the restaurant industry (compared with a national average of 1 per cent of white males), and one in eight male Pakistani workers is a taxi driver or chauffeur, compared with a national average of one in 100 workers. These industries are typically lower paid than average, and offer limited opportunities for career progression.

This, inevitably, has an effect on average income. The following table, also from the CRE website (www.cre.gov.uk), shows average income analysed by ethnic origin, in comparison to the national average income and before housing costs have been taken into consideration:

Table 1.2 *Percentage of ethnic group whose average income falls below the national average income*

	National average income		
	Below 40%	Below 50%	Below 60%
Before housing costs			
White	7	14	22
Black Caribbean	9	18	27
Black Non-Caribbean	14	28	42
Indian	13	24	35
Pakistani/Bangladeshi	37	58	76
Other	16	25	33

We clearly see from this table that there is a significant difference in income between different ethnic groups.

Why do these differences in levels of income occur? On its website the CRE goes on to suggest a number of possible reasons:

Human capital
Human capital is the combination of the skills, knowledge, experience and qualifications that an individual possesses. As it is really describing the attributes of the person that the employer is looking for, it clearly is a strong determinant of success in employment. Children of Pakistani, Bangladeshi and African-Caribbean descent have a significantly lower human capital level than average. This results, therefore, in their being less likely to be successful in finding employment.

Geographical
About 70 per cent of the ethnic minority population lives in the 88 most deprived districts in the UK. In four out of five local authorities where there is a significant proportion of residents from ethnic minority groups, there is also a higher than average rate of unemployment. In essence, there are a significant proportion of people from ethnic minorities living in areas where there are fewer jobs available.

Health
The CRE report suggests that Pakistani and Bangladeshi groups in particular are likely to self-report that their health is poorer than average. This means that a higher than average proportion of these groups are not actively looking for work because of health problems.

Childcare
In disadvantaged areas (where, we have already noted, a significant proportion of people from ethnic minority groups live) there are fewer childcare places available (six to eight places

per 100 children, compared with a national average of 12–14 places). This makes it particularly difficult for women to work.

Transport

The CRE reports that people from ethnic minorities are more likely to be reliant on public transport, and less likely to travel long distances to work. Given that a significant proportion live in areas where there are not many job opportunities, this is an additional factor explaining the lower levels of employment and income.

Racial discrimination

The last point is one that we cannot ignore – there is discrimination against people from minority ethnic groups. Discrimination tests by the CRE found that people of white origin were twice as likely to get an interview for a job as someone of African-Caribbean or Asian origin.

From this information it is obvious that there are differences in employment between different ethnic groups. Although we can clearly see some of the reasons why these differences might have occurred, it is difficult to conclude that we are not observing some evidence of discrimination.

CASE STUDY

An interesting study by Klink and Wagner (1999) gave evidence that discrimination is still occurring. This study was based in Germany, where 14 different experiments took place. Examples were a woman dressed as a typical German stopping passers-by and asking for directions to the station, with the same requests for information being made later by a woman dressed in typical Turkish clothes. The helpfulness of the passers-by was recorded for each condition. Other experiments included dropping, in telephone boxes, letters that were stamped and ready for posting – some with a German address and some with an address for another country – and seeing how many were posted by whoever found them. In none of the 14 experiments was any discrimination found towards Germans. However, in 9 of the 14 experiments significant discrimination was found against other ethnic groups.

This is an interesting study, because of the range of experiments that was carried out. As explained, there were situations when people actually met someone of a supposed ethnic origin, and also a situation where the only link to an ethnic origin was the address on an envelope. Is the discrimination so deep-rooted that a simple trigger such as an address on an envelope is sufficient to elicit discriminatory behaviour?

Gender

We have already noted that 79 per cent of men between the ages of 16 and 64 are in employment, compared with 69 per cent of women, and that some of the differences are linked to childcare responsibilities. However, there are other statistics that are important to note.

Women are more likely to work part-time than men. The percentages shown below are the number of employees who work part-time as a percentage of all working employees in each category:

Table 1.3 *The number of employees who work part-time as a percentage of all working employees*

Age (years)	Female	Male
16–24	45	29
25–34	33	4
35–44	47	3
45–54	42	4
55–64	56	13
65+	89	69
All ages	44	10
		Source: Labour Force Survey 2003

The reasons for part-time work are often associated with balancing childcare (or other caring responsibilities, such as elderly relatives) and work responsibilities. However, the differences in type of employment cannot be explained as easily:

Table 1.4 *Employment by occupation (2003) (percentages)*

	Female	Male
Taxi cab drivers	8	92
Security guards	12	88
Software professionals	14	86
ICT managers	16	84
Police officers, up to Sergeant	22	78
Marketing and sales managers	25	75
IT operations technicians	32	68
Medical practitioners	39	61
Solicitors, lawyers, judges and coroners	42	58
Shelf fillers	48	52
Chefs and cooks	49	51
Secondary school teachers	55	45
Sales assistants	73	27
Waiters and waitresses	73	27
Cleaners and domestics	79	21
Retail cashiers	82	18
General office assistants and clerks	83	17
Primary and nursery school teachers	86	14
Care assistants and home carers	88	12
Hairdressers and barbers	89	11
Nurses	89	11
Receptionists	96	4
		Source: Labour Force Survey 2003

The statistics in this table show us that there are some clear demarcations between men and women in some jobs. In this country there are still jobs that are traditionally 'female' (eg nurses, hairdressers and care assistants). The EOC reported that, in 2002, 75 per cent of working women were in the five lowest paid sectors. There are areas where the stereotypical gap between men and women is narrowing (eg solicitors), but in some occupations there is still a very clear divide.

In addition to these statistics we should note that 97 per cent of modern apprenticeships in engineering and construction, paying £115 per week on average, are held by men, whereas 89 per cent of apprenticeships in social care, paying an average of £60 per week, are held by women. Women are also under-represented in more senior jobs. Women hold fewer than one in ten of the top jobs in the FTSE's top one hundred companies, the police, the judiciary and the trade unions. Only 18 per cent of the Members of Parliament are women. (Source: EOC 2004, www.eoc.org.uk).

Apart from the issue of childcare responsibilities, why are these differences occurring?

Stereotyped jobs
There are still jobs that are typically seen as female jobs. Although a lot of effort has been made in schools to remove these stereotypes, girls and boys, when making career choices, are still drawn to jobs that are stereotypically relevant to their gender. This is partly because it is difficult to go against a stereotype – it might be more difficult to find work, and it is more likely that there will be some teasing and prejudice during training.

Jobs of parents
A significant influence on career choice is the career of parents. These are jobs that the child is familiar with, and there is often the opportunity to gain some work experience in the job. If the child does decide to take the same job as their parent, then the statistical trends that we have reported will be perpetuated from generation to generation.

Flexibility of working
There are some jobs where it is easier to get part-time work or flexible working. These types of jobs will be more attractive to someone who is needing to balance childcare responsibilities.

Aptitude
One of the most comprehensive studies investigating differences between genders was by Macoby and Jacklin (1974). They concluded that there were four significant differences between boys and girls:

1   Girls have greater verbal ability than boys.
2   Boys have greater visual and spatial abilities than girls.
3   During adolescence there is evidence that boys have developed greater mathematical abilities than girls (this difference is not evident at an earlier age).
4   Boys are more aggressive than girls, physically and verbally.

Some commentators would suggest, therefore, that the differences seen in occupations are a direct result in the different abilities of boys and girls. However, recent research from the EOC into results at GCSE and A level has shown that girls outperform boys in every subject. The difference between genders in mathematics and science is small – but girls did achieve better results than boys. It is not clear, therefore, what impact aptitude really has on the differences that we observe.

Roles in society

There is the assumption that women want to have the jobs that are traditionally male, and in particular there is the assumption that women want to have more senior roles. However, there are women who want to have the role of staying at home, caring for the family and being a homemaker. It is important to recognise this choice, but not to use it as an excuse to justify discrimination against women.

Discrimination against women

A final reason that we need to consider is that some employers discriminate against women. This might be because they believe that women will not do a job as well as men, or because they fear that women are more likely to take lengthy periods of time off due to maternity leave which would be difficult for them, as employers, to manage. However, we have to accept that discrimination does still occur.

The current Labour government has introduced measures to make it easier for women to work. As part of the Employment Act 2002, maternity leave was extended to include a potential period of leave of 52 weeks (not all of which is paid). Although this does give women more flexibility, it could also result in some employers being more reluctant to employ women. Discrimination against women in this way is unlawful; however it might still occur.

In addition, the Act introduced the right of either parent to *request* flexible working (if they have a child under the age of six years (or 18 years if the child is disabled). The flexibility can relate to the hours that the person works, the time they work or the place where they work.

The employer must give the request serious consideration, and can only refuse the request on one or more of the following grounds:

- burden of additional costs
- detrimental effect on the ability to meet customer demand
- inability to reorganise work among existing staff
- inability to recruit additional staff
- detrimental impact on quality
- detrimental impact on performance
- insufficiency of work during the periods the employee proposes to work
- planned structural changes
- any other grounds the Secretary of State may specify by regulations.

The purpose of this legislation is to make it easier for parents, especially women, to work. However, it is too early to determine whether it will really have any impact on the statistics that we have looked at in this section.

CASE STUDY

A solicitor's firm employed a group of people to carry out general administration duties such as typing, filing, booking appointments and copying legal documents. The group worked collectively for all solicitors, rather than the solicitors having personal secretaries.

The group of 12 were all women, nine of whom had young children. In advance of the Flexible Working Regulations being introduced, the solicitors worked out an approach they would take if all the nine women exercised their rights to request flexible working, which basically involved a rather complex shift pattern.

Once the legislation was introduced, all the nine women who were eligible made the request for flexible working, as had been expected. After a series of discussions, a range of shifts similar to that which had been thought up in advance was agreed. However, the one constant was that the three women who did not have young children had to keep their current working patterns.

The three women saw this as grossly unfair, and protested strongly. However, legally they had no right to request flexible working. As they were a team of all women, they were unable to claim sex discrimination had occurred.

Due to the strength of their feeling, and the friendships within the team, the women eventually agreed a way of working that suited everyone in the team, allowing the three without young children some level of flexibility. As this met the needs of the firm, it was accepted by the solicitors.

This is an interesting case study because it shows how legislation that is introduced to help people with a particular issue can negatively impact on others.

Throughout this section we have viewed discrimination on the grounds of gender as being in favour of men. It is definitely true that, in the great majority of cases, sex discrimination claims that are brought to the Employment Tribunal are brought by women claiming that they have been discriminated against in favour of a man or men. However, there are occasions when a man has brought a claim. One such example is the case of Thompson v Department for Work and Pensions:

Department for Work and Pensions v Thompson v (2004)

Thompson worked in a Job Centre. The Job Centre introduced a new dress code which required all men to wear a shirt and tie, whereas women were required to dress 'appropriately'. In reality this meant that women could dress much more casually than men. Thompson did not come into direct contact with the public, and considered that the dress code was unnecessary and unfair; hence he chose not to abide by it. He was given a formal warning. As a result of this, he made a claim of direct sex discrimination to the Employment Tribunal.

At the hearing before the Employment Tribunal he was successful in winning the claim. However, the employers appealed and the Employment Appeals Tribunal overturned the decision of the initial tribunal. They determined that there was not discrimination because the requirement to wear a collar and tie was just a means by which the required dress standards for men could be achieved. The requirement was not resulting in a higher standard being expected of men, in comparison to women.

Disability

The legal definition of disability (from the Disability Discrimination Act 1995) is a person who has:

" a physical or mental impairment that has a substantial and long-term adverse effect on a persons ability to carry out normal day-to-day activities. "

Although there might be some variations in this definition among different organisations which research into the issues of disability, this is the definition that we will be referring to in this section.

The following table from the Labour Force Survey 2003 shows the economic activity status of working age people by sex and disability:

Table 1.5 *Economic activity status of working age people by sex and disability (percentages)*

	Men		Women	
	Disabled	Non-disabled	Disabled	Non-disabled
Economically active				
In employment	51	86	46	75
Unemployed	5	4	3	3
Economically inactive				
Wants a job	15	2	15	5
Does not want a job	28	7	36	17

Source: Labour Force Survey 2003

(Note: Economically active means that the person is either employed or actively seeking employment. 'Wants a job' when economically inactive means that the person would ideally like a job, but is not actively seeking employment at this time).

These statistics show us that there is a significant difference between the employment status of disabled and non-disabled people.

As we noted earlier, one of the indicators of the likelihood of finding employment is human capital – the qualifications, knowledge, skill and experience of an individual. It is interesting, therefore, to look at the qualifications of people with disabilities:

Table 1.6 *Percentage of people with no qualifications, by age group*

Age group	Long-term disabled	Non-disabled
16-24	24	14
25-34	17	8
35-49	24	11
50-64	33	19
All ages	27	12

Source: Labour Force Survey 2003

Those who are long-term disabled are significantly less likely to have qualifications than those who are non-disabled. If we follow the line of argument based on human capital, we can conclude that there is an increased difficulty for people with disabilities in securing employment.

If we look at the types of jobs that disabled people have, we do not see a really significant difference between disabled and non-disabled. The following table shows the number in each occupational group as a percentage of the total group (either disabled or non-disabled).

Table 1.7 *Percentage of disabled and non-disabled employees by occupation group*

	Disabled	Non-disabled
Managers and senior officials	13	15
Professional occupations	9	12
Associate professional and technical	14	14
Administration and secretarial	12	13
Skilled trades	12	12
Personal service occupations	8	7
Sales and customer service assistants	8	8
Process, plant and machinery operatives	10	8
Elementary occupations	14	11

Source: Labour Force Survey 2003

Why are fewer disabled people qualified and in work, compared with non-disabled people?

Lack of understanding about disability

There is often an assumption that a disabled person is very limited in the type of work that they can perform. It is true that a disability results in some limitations, but disabled people are not always given the opportunity to show what they can do – rather, there is the negative focus on what they cannot do. Typically, there is also a rather narrow understanding of what disability is – people often think of a wheelchair and then think no further. However, in reality there is a wide range of disabilities, meaning that a limitation faced by one disabled person is not necessarily a limitation faced by another.

Human capital

As already noted, human capital is the sum of knowledge, qualifications, skills and experience. We have already seen statistics showing a significant difference between disabled and non-disabled people in terms of qualifications. In addition, if there is prejudice against employing disabled people, they will find it more difficult to gain experience and knowledge, and hence they will have a low human capital. As human capital is directly linked to the ability to find work, this has an obvious impact.

The age of the legislation

Legislation prohibiting the discrimination against people on the grounds of their disability was introduced in 1995 (we will examine this in more detail later in the book). This is a lot more recent than legislation relating to sex and race discrimination. Although many years have passed, there is still a certain amount of learning that is going on about disabled people in the workplace.

Discrimination

As with ethnic origin and gender, one of the reasons for the differences in employment levels for disabled people can be linked to discrimination. Some employers do not want to employ disabled people because they fear the additional costs associated with any adjustments they might need to make, and because they fear that disabled people are likely to be absent from work more frequently than non-disabled employees. However, these fears are largely based on ignorance. As already noted, disability covers a vast range of problems – from motor impairment to deafness, blindness, mental illness and other chronic illnesses. It is not practical to have a general view about employing disabled people because the nature of disability varies so greatly.

According to the Disability Rights Commission (DRC), disabled people have an annual spending power of £50 billion. There are 9.8 million people in the country who are disabled – which is one in seven of the population. Hence, disabled people are a significant group of people that employers cannot afford to ignore.

PROMOTING DIVERSITY AND ELIMINATING DISCRIMINATION

A major focus of this book is the legislation that exists in this country to eliminate discrimination. At present in the UK, discrimination on the grounds of race, sex, marital status, disability, transsexuality, sexual orientation and religion or belief is unlawful. From 2006 discrimination on the grounds of age will be added to this list. However, as we have seen from the statistics in the last section, the legislation has not been completely successful in eliminating discrimination. What else can be done to promote equal opportunities for all?

There are a number of organisations that exist to promote the rights and needs of groups who suffer discrimination. We will take a brief look at the objectives and activities of three of these groups:

Equal Opportunities Commission (EOC) *(www.eoc.org.uk)*

The EOC is an independent statutory body, although it reports to the Equality Minister. It is funded primarily by the government. It was set up as a direct result of the Sex Discrimination Act 1975, and its main aim was to work towards the elimination of discrimination on the grounds of sex or marriage. Its main aims are to:

- promote equality of opportunity for women and men
- keep under review the Sex Discrimination Act 1975 and the Equal Pay Act 1970
- provide legal advice and assistance to individuals who have been discriminated against (it runs a helpline and also has a range of useful advice on its website).

Specific activities to support these aims are to:

- provide up-to-date advice on rights to both employers and employees
- run campaigns and lobby decision makers at every level
- carry out relevant research, and publish and promote the results
- represent employees in specific landmark cases under the Sex Discrimination Act 1975 and the Equal Pay Act 1970.

Commission for Racial Equality (CRE) *(www.cre.gov.uk)*

The CRE was set up under the Race Relations Act 1976 to tackle racial discrimination and to promote racial equality. It is a publicly funded, non-governmental body. Its main aims and activities are to:

- work in all sectors of employment to encourage fair treatment and to promote equal opportunities for everyone, regardless of their race, colour, nationality or national/ethnic origin
- provide information and advice to any person who believes that they have suffered racial harassment or discrimination
- promote policies and practices that will ensure equal treatment for all through working with public bodies, businesses and a range of other organisations
- run campaigns to encourage organisations and individuals to contribute to the creation of a just society, and to raise awareness of race related issues
- make sure that all new laws take full account of the Race Relations Act 1976 and the protection it gives against discrimination.

Disability Rights Commission (DRC) *(www.drc-gb.org)*

The DRC was established by an Act of Parliament in April 2000 to eliminate discrimination against disabled people and promote equality of opportunity. It is an independent body. Its main aims and activities are to:

- provide advice and information to disabled people, employers and service providers
- support disabled people in exercising their rights under the Disability Discrimination Act 1995
- support legal cases, particularly those setting new precedents, and test the limits of the law through representing and/or advising applicants

- campaign to improve and strengthen legislation so that it better protects more disabled people
- organise campaigns to educate people about disability issues, hoping to change policy, practice and awareness as a result
- put on events and conferences to raise awareness of disability issues
- write and produce publications about rights for disabled people and good practice for employers and service providers
- research issues and publish policy statements on issues that affect disabled people.

TASK

Access the websites of all three of these organisations and gain a better understanding of their work.

A common theme in the aims and activities of all these groups is to raise awareness of the issues, to research into the issues and publicise the results, to lobby relevant groups and to give advice to people who are affected (both employees and employers). In doing this, the groups help to challenge prejudicial views that stop the development of diversity within organisations.

On 30 October 2003 the government announced plans to bring together, in a single body, all the organisations concerned with promoting equality of opportunity and eliminating discrimination. In addition to the areas currently covered by these organisations, the new single body would also cover issues relating to sexual orientation, age and religion/belief, and would provide institutional support for human rights.

The single body was provisionally known as the Commission for Equality and Human Rights (CEHR). Its main aim was to promote equality for all in society, as well as working to eliminate discrimination against specific groups. A project team known as the Single Equality Commission was set up to research this proposal. It consists of experts from the current equality commissions, a range of communities, representatives from human rights groups, trade unions, business and academia. The task force is chaired by the Deputy Minister for Women and Equality

The clear advantages of a single body would be a central point of contact for all issues relating to discrimination. It also has the potential to strengthen campaigns and lobbying, as there is a wider range of expertise and interests represented. However, there is also the concern that some of the specific issues faced by particular groups could be lost in the breadth of areas that the Commission would be addressing.

TASK

As you study this course, keep aware of any reports from this Task Force. They will be reported in the personnel and business press – and you can also access more information on the website of the Women and Equality unit (www.womenandequalityunit.gov.uk).

As well as the various bodies that focus on the issues of equality of opportunity and the elimination of discrimination, the government has a section within the Department of Trade and Industry that is responsible for equality issues. The section is called the Women and Equality Unit and is headed up by the Minister for Women (who is also currently the Secretary for Trade and Industry) and the Deputy Minister for Women and Equality. Although the title of the unit would suggest that the primary issue is equality for women, the unit addresses equality across all areas of society.

THE COSTS OF DISCRIMINATION AND DIVERSITY

When considering the costs we need to look at three separate issues:

1 the cost to the individual
2 the cost to the organisation
3 penalties for non-compliance with legislation.

The cost to the individual

The statistics that we looked at earlier in this section showed that there is a significant difference in income between minority and majority groups. Hence, for the individual, there is a direct cost associated with being a member of a minority group.

It should also be noted that, if a person is a member of more than one minority group (eg a woman from an ethnic minority group), they are likely to suffer even greater hardship.

There is also the potential for a spiral of low pay to exist. If people are struggling to find employment, they are more likely to take any job – and any job might mean a low-paid job. They then gain knowledge and experience of that job and employers tend to see them as only suitable for that type of work. Therefore, they never have the opportunity to move out of the poorly paid job and into a job with better pay and more prospects. It should also be noted that many of the poorly paid jobs do not have career prospects associated with them, and hence it is difficult to find a way to move on.

The cost to the employer

When unemployment is relatively low, employers can find it difficult to fill vacancies. In finding the right person for the job, they need to look at a wider pool of candidates than they might do when unemployment is high. If the employer makes a decision (albeit unlawful) to reduce that pool by excluding people from minority groups, they have less choice in filling the vacancy. This could result in recruiting someone for the job who is not really suitable. There is then the cost of having a worker who achieves low productivity, costs more to train and is potentially more likely to leave the organisation because of dissatisfaction with a job that they cannot do well.

There is also the cost of reduced creativity that could result in a competitor taking a greater share of the market. If a group of employees is not drawn from a diverse background, there is likely to be a restricted range of ideas. Indeed, if the group is not representative of the range of customers, then there is potential for the products and services being developed to be unsuitable for the needs of all customers. Hence, there is a potential economic cost to the business in restricted or irrelevant development of products and services.

Penalties for non-compliance with legislation

If an employee makes a claim of discrimination against an employer on any of the grounds currently protected by legislation, the employee is entitled to compensation if they win the case. That compensation is unlimited and will address any actual loss or damage that has occurred; it will also include a sum relating to injured feelings (if appropriate). In 2002–03 the average awards imposed by the Employment Tribunals were:

- sex discrimination   £8,787
- race discrimination   £27,041
- disability discrimination   £10,157.

KEY POINTS FROM THIS CHAPTER

- Positive diversity beliefs is the valuing of everyone as individuals.
- Discrimination is the treating of one group of people in a negative way for no logical reason.
- Discrimination often occurs through learnt attitudes that are prejudicial.
- Managing diversity has benefits to the organisation, but also some difficulties in the early stages.
- Statistics show that there are fewer people in employment from minority ethnic groups.
- Statistics show that there are fewer women in employment than men.
- Statistics show that the percentage of disabled people in employment is less than the percentage of non-disabled people.
- There are three main bodies that exist to promote equality – the Equal Opportunities Commission, Commission for Racial Equality and Disability Rights Commission.
- The government has made proposals to create a single equality body.
- There is a cost associated with discrimination.

EXAMPLES TO WORK THROUGH

1   You are a manager of a department that has recently recruited someone from an ethnic minority group. You are surprised to hear some negative views expressed about this recruitment. Thinking about why people might hold these negative views, how might you address them in order to promote diversity among the group?

2   You have been asked to give a presentation about the advantages and disadvantages of setting up a single equality commission. List the main points that you would cover in the presentation.

3   Choose any of the main equality groups and consider what they can do to try to address some of the issues that have been raised by the statistics we have studied.

Diversity and the Organisation | CHAPTER 2

OBJECTIVES OF THIS CHAPTER:

■ to understand the benefits to an organisation of embracing diversity

■ to understand the specific impact of diversity in the boardroom

■ to evaluate the type of organisational culture that promotes diversity

■ to consider the relevance of the attitude of the organisation to sexual harassment

■ to investigate the concept of institutional racism

■ to examine the influence of Trade Unions

■ to consider future trends in diversity.

THE BENEFITS OF EMBRACING DIVERSITY

In the last chapter we looked briefly at some of the benefits of embracing diversity in the workplace. We noted that there is an increase in creativity and an improvement in decision making. However, we also noted that there are difficulties with managing diversity, and some potential problems with doing so. We are going to start this chapter by considering the benefits of diversity in more detail.

Goss (1994) suggests that there are two primary ways of considering diversity:

Human capital perspective

As we have already noted, human capital is the sum of knowledge, experience, skills and qualifications that an individual possesses. This is the human resource that each organisation draws on in order to achieve its objectives. If this human capital is not allowed to reach its full potential because of discrimination, then the logical conclusion is that the organisation is not making full use of the resources available to it. Therefore, it can only be of benefit to the organisation to promote diversity and to ensure that it gains the full benefit of the human capital of each employee.

Social justice

This is a more principled approach to diversity that suggests that an organisation should have a moral or ethical interest in social equality. To promote any practices that do not allow everyone equality of opportunity is to be immoral and unethical. Employees are often attracted to organisations that have a good ethical record, and hence to promote social justice should help to attract a wider range of potential employees.

Ross and Schneider (1992) suggest that there are clear benefits of this principled approach. They are:

■ The diverse workforce produces a wider range of ideas and can think from a broader range of perspectives than a workforce that is not diverse.

■ Total quality management requires innovation and creativity. This is more easily achieved through a diverse workforce.

■ If all people are treated equally, then people will be recruited and promoted on the basis of their skills and abilities. This will mean that it is more likely that the most capable people will achieve important positions in the organisation.

■ If an employee is working in an organisation where they experience discrimination, or perceive that others are not treated equally, they are more likely to leave that organisation. Not only is this a drain of talent, it is also costly because of the significant expense of recruiting and training a new employee.

■ If employees are treated fairly, they will be more motivated and committed to the organisation. This is likely to lead to an increase in productivity, and a deeper commitment to the mission and goals of the organisation.

Motivation

The relationship between motivation and diversity is an important factor for an organisation to consider. There are three components to motivation:

1   direction – what a person is trying to do
2   effort – how hard the person is trying
3   persistence – the length of time that the person keeps trying.

If employees consider that they are not being treated fairly, it is likely that they will try less hard and will have less persistence in their efforts. This can be explained further by examining two motivation theories.

Herzberg's two-factor model

Herzberg's model, as described in Herzberg et al (1957), is based on the theory that there are two distinct groups of factors – one that gives rise to job satisfaction and the other that gives rise to job dissatisfaction.

The first set of factors are known as the hygiene factors. They have the potential to dissatisfy if they are not met but, once they are met, they become reasonably irrelevant to motivation because increasing them further will not increase motivation. They are things like supervision, working conditions, status, security and relationship with peers. The other set of factors are known as satisfiers or motivators. They are things which are intrinsic to the job, such as achievement, the work itself, responsibility and growth. As they increase, so will motivation increase.

Although there has been criticism of this theory, primarily because of the somewhat limited research (the theory was based on research conducted solely with engineers and scientists), it offers a useful insight into how motivation could be affected by a lack of diversity, or by discrimination. If employees perceive that they are not being given equality of opportunity, this could impact on hygiene factors such as status and relationships with peers. Because the required equality is not being achieved, the factor will become a demotivator. Herzberg's model suggests that demotivation will persist, even if there are satisfiers present, until the issue is addressed. Hence, one could draw the conclusion, using this model, that a person who is not allowed equality of opportunity within an organisation will never be fully motivated at work.

Adam's equity theory

Adams (1965) suggested that people will be better motivated if they perceive that they are being treated equitably (fairly), and they will be demotivated if they perceive that they are being treated inequitably. This perception of fairness is gained by making comparisons between the treatment that the individual sees that they are receiving, and the treatment given to comparable groups. It is important to emphasise that it is based on comparisons. It is not presuming that everyone should be treated equally – because there might be good reasons why, for example, one person is paid more than another. However, motivation decreases if the perception is that people are not being treated fairly.

This has a direct relevance to understanding motivation and diversity. Achieving diversity is not about everyone achieving the same status and pay levels – it is about everyone having equality of opportunity to achieve their full potential. It is about treating everyone fairly. If a person perceives that another group of people are having advantageous treatment, they will perceive that the treatment is inequitable and hence their motivation to perform will decrease.

TASK

Test out these two theories from your own experience. First, identify hygiene factors in your job. Is it true that, if these factors are not in place, then you are demotivated? Can you think of any examples of this? Second, think about your perceptions of fair treatment within your organisation. Have you ever perceived unfair treatment and been demotivated as a result?

The career and self-esteem

In considering diversity within the context of an organisation, it is important to remember that an organisation is a group of individuals. Within that organisation individuals have different expectations and needs that largely drive the careers of the individuals. Michener et al (2004) define a career as a sequence of roles, each with its own set of activities that a person enacts during his or her lifetime. The most important careers are family and friends, education and work. Each person's career will differ in the roles that make up the career, the order in which the roles are performed and the duration of role-related activities.

As the individual is operating within each role activity, they develop a role identity. As a result of this, they develop self-esteem. That self-esteem is heavily influenced by the achievements made within different roles.

Concentrating on the career at work, individuals will develop a role within that career. Psychological theory would suggest that self-esteem is directly linked to that role. Hence, if the employee is frustrated by the role level that they have been able to achieve in an organisation, they are likely to have lower self-esteem.

People with low self-esteem tend to be anxious and ineffective. They see interpersonal relationships as threatening, and hence are not comfortable with teamworking (see later in this chapter). They are also easily hurt by criticism and less likely to suggest ideas and act creatively. They readily expect their ideas to be rejected and have little faith in their ability to achieve.

It is probable that an organisation that does not promote diversity, or that actively discriminates against certain groups, inhibits the development of an individual's career – particularly with regard to the work career. That will lead to a low level of self-esteem and an employee who is not contributing to the organisation to the full extent of their potential. It is important to remember that the approach an organisation takes to diversity has a direct and specific effect on individuals.

DIVERSITY IN THE BOARDROOM

The attitudes and behaviours that are expressed at the most senior levels in an organisation are often indicative of the attitudes and behaviours that will influence the management of the organisation. Hence, if the boardroom is not diverse and non-discriminatory, then it is likely that the organisation will not be diverse.

The Women and Equality Unit, within the Department of Trade and Industry, makes the following suggestions as to why a diverse board is important:

■ The organisation is more likely to be able to recognise potential new markets and, as a result, attract a much wider customer base.

■ An organisation with a diverse board is likely to have a competitive edge. Research has shown that organisations with high quality human resources, in which equality plays a part, deliver better products and services, and hence better shareholder value.

■ A more diverse board results in a wider range of skills at the top of the organisation, and this has to be positive for the organisation.

■ A more diverse board means that the needs of a broader range of customers can be understood, and hence services and products can be developed that are more applicable to individual needs.

■ If younger, more junior people can see a diverse range of role models, they are more likely to be encouraged to stay with an organisation and to become future leaders.

■ By promoting and developing people according to their skills and abilities, rather than according to irrelevant factors, there is more chance of having the best people at all levels of management.

As a result of the benefits that are perceived from having a more diverse boardroom, the Secretary for Trade and Industry commissioned two reports to consider how diversity in the boardroom could be promoted further. The main findings from the first report (Higgs 2003) were:

■ Personal contacts should be avoided when recruiting non-executive directors. People tend to have contacts who are the same race, gender, disability status, etc. as themselves. Hence, relying on personal contacts adds more people of a similar background to the board, and restricts the diversity of that board.

- There should be a direct attempt to recruit non-executive directors from groups where women are strongly represented. These are groups such as human resources, change management and customer care.

- If an organisation operates in international markets, there should be at least one international non-executive director in the organisation.

The second report (Tyson 2003), commissioned by the Department for Trade and Industry, concluded with these main recommendations:

- There should be a more rigorous and transparent selection process. This should allow for equality of opportunity, and this equality should be clearly visible.

- There should be more investment in training for board members, and this should include a relevant induction programme.

- There should be more measurement of the diversity of boards.

The consistent theme throughout both reports is that the diversity of an organisation is directly influenced by the diversity of the board. If the board has not embraced diversity, then the organisation will not either.

TASK

Read the full reports by Tyson and Higgs at www.womenandequalityunit.gov.uk.

CASE STUDY

The Commission for Racial Equality (CRE) commissioned a report into racial equality in football. As many football followers will know, most premiership teams (and other league teams as well) have a significant number of players of a non-white ethnic origin. However, the CRE was concerned that there did not seem to be a similar representation of non-white ethnic origin employees within the boardrooms of football clubs, and in other positions of senior management.

The report found that this was definitely the case, and also that people of Asian ethnic origin were very poorly represented among both the players and the management.

Why had this occurred? The report found that the vast majority of football clubs do not give their staff any equal opportunities training, and do not have an equal opportunities policy. There is very little monitoring of promotion and training opportunities in most of the football clubs that were surveyed. It was also found that no national football organisation followed the CRE guidelines of best practice in recruitment and selection.

This report was published in 2004, and it will be interesting to see if any action is taken as a result of the findings. (It can be accessed at www.cre.gov.uk/pdfs/football_report_full.pdf.)

THE CULTURE OF AN ORGANISATION

The culture of an organisation is made up of the attitudes, beliefs, norms and values of that organisation. Some of the culture is unwritten and the only way to identify it is through observation. Some of the culture is written – for example, through mission statements and the publications of values. Further indications of culture are observable through actual manifestations of the ways that people behave.

Behaviours

Behaviours can be prescribed by an organisation in order to promote specific values that they want to communicate to a customer. A good example of this could be McDonald's, where the sales assistant looks the customer in the eye and says 'Enjoy your meal' once the order has been served. This is not necessarily a sentiment that is promoted by the employer, but it is a behaviour that has to be shown as part of the job. That approach to customers has become embedded in the culture of McDonald's.

It is unlikely that an organisation will actively prescribe discriminatory behaviours, but the culture of an organisation could be such that discriminatory behaviours are accepted and not challenged. This is probably particularly true of some financial organisations in the City of London, where claims have been made by women that a macho culture is predominating. There have been complaints made by women, who have worked in such a culture, of sexual banter and innuendo, where an attitude to women in the workplace is of a sexual nature. Such behaviours do not promote equitable treatment for men and women, and hence do not promote a diverse workforce.

Values

Some organisations specifically reference diversity in their mission statement, or the statement of their values. However, it is a lot easier to write down a value than it is to act in accordance with it. The organisation is also reliant on employees to work according to the values. According to Cox (1994), individual employees who have different values to those promoted by the organisation can affect the whole culture of the organisation. Potentially this could lead to problems such as institutional racism that we will examine later in this chapter.

Another approach to values is to assume that they have been adopted by the whole organisation, and hence there is no need to keep talking about differences because they are not relevant (the statement of values having determined that the organisation does not see differences in factors such as ethnic origin as being relevant to the workplace). Richard and Johnson (2001) comment that in such a situation the value of the different ideas and perspectives that the different groups can bring can be unnoticed, or not sought after – because there is no recognition that the different groups exist.

Attitudes and beliefs

We have already considered the development of attitudes and beliefs and how they can affect the behaviour of the individual in the workplace. However, they are worthy of mention again because, without addressing the negative attitudes and beliefs held by employees, there will be no change in the culture of the organisation.

ATTITUDE TO SEXUAL HARASSMENT

When considering the behaviours that might indicate the culture of an organisation, we made reference to a culture where sexual innuendo and banter is acceptable. The attitude that an organisation takes to sexual harassment can have a direct impact on the gender diversity within an organisation.

Although most cases of sexual harassment are brought by women, it is important to note that men can also suffer sexual harassment in the workplace.

According to research from the Equal Opportunities Commission (EOC), 90 per cent of claimants bringing cases of sexual harassment to the Employment Tribunal have either lost their job or resigned from their job as a result of the harassment. Only 5 per cent of employees who suffer sexual harassment make a complaint, and only around 10 per cent of these claims ever proceed to the Employment Tribunal. Hence, we can see that the actual impact in the workplace is considerable.

It should be noted that sexual harassment covers a wide range of issues. At the most extreme it is the demanding of sexual favours, typically by a manager more senior than the person being harassed. However, other manifestations of sexual harassment are banter and jokes of a sexual nature, language that refers to sexual acts and inappropriate pictures of naked/semi-naked women being displayed in the workplace.

If the organisation allows a culture to persist where this sort of behaviour is allowed, then it will have less success in promoting a diverse workforce.

INSTITUTIONAL RACISM

CASE STUDY

The phrase 'institutional racism' became widely publicised as a result of an investigation into the handling by the Metropolitan Police into the murder of Stephen Lawrence. The MacPherson report (1999), set up to investigate this incident, concluded that there was evidence that the Metropolitan Police were institutionally racist. The report defined this as:

" The collective failure of an organisation to provide an appropriate and professional service to people because of their colour, culture, or ethnic origin. It can be seen or detected in processes, attitudes and behaviour which amount to discrimination through unwitting prejudice, ignorance, thoughtlessness and racist stereotyping which disadvantage minority ethnic people. "

The definition suggests that racism had become part of the culture of the organisation. It is not suggesting that there is necessarily any deliberate racism, rather that the practices and attitudes towards racism are disadvantaging people, probably without anyone being truly aware of these disadvantages.

In some ways this concept can be compared with the concept of the glass ceiling. This is the reference to minority groups hitting a 'ceiling' in their career prospects, and finding that they are unable to progress any further. Again, it might not be because of any intentional decision on the part of the organisation to stop the progress of an individual's career, rather it is a result of attitudes and practices that have just become accepted as part of the culture of the organisation.

In the MacPherson report, 70 recommendations were made for changes to the Police Force in order to combat institutional racism. Some of the recommendations that are of more general interest are:

- to recruit a workforce that reflects the cultural and ethnic mix of the area in which the organisation operates
- to monitor statistics relating to equal opportunities in order to identify any examples of unintentional discrimination
- training for employees in the understanding of discriminatory practices and how to prevent them occurring
- making the use of language that is specifically offensive to a minority group a disciplinary offence.

When trying to prevent anything from occurring, it is useful to consider why the problem is happening in the first place – it is often more effective to address the causes rather than just try to change the outward manifestations. So, why does institutional racism occur?

To answer this, one approach might be to return to the three primary ways that attitudes develop that we looked at in Chapter 1 (Michener et al 2004).

Instrumental conditioning would suggest that the negative attitude is learnt because of a negative experience with a particular group, or as a result of information about that group that has been supplied by other people. This attitude is reinforced by praise or reward from the group when an individual expresses attitudes or displays behaviours that fit with the negative attitude. It is this second approach that is of particular interest here. Applying it to the Police Force, if a new police officer joins the Force and hears a regular message that a particular ethnic minority is a problem, they will eventually learn this attitude. If they are praised or rewarded by their colleagues when they express this attitude, the learning will be reinforced. If this attitude is widely held throughout the Force through instrumental conditioning, it will become an attitude held by the whole Police Force – and now we have institutional racism.

Classical conditioning would suggest that there is some form of stimulus and response. So, if the new police officer learns that the rest of the Force react in a certain way to an ethnic minority group, then the officer will learn that response to the group. As the stimulus and response are linked more regularly, then the learning will become stronger.

The other approach to the development of attitudes is observational conditioning. If a new officer sees people of certain ethnic groups being treated in a particular way, or being spoken of in a certain way, that officer will learn that this is the way that the force behaves towards the ethnic group. The new officer then learns the behaviours and attitudes of their peers, hence reinforcing institutional racism.

From this analysis we can see that the way to address institutional racism is to challenge the attitudes and behaviours that are being learnt by new entrants to the Police Force. If officers learn a different way of thinking about and interacting with ethnic minority groups, this learning will not be passed from officer to officer, hence becoming indicative of the 'institution'.

It should be noted that, since the MacPherson report, the Metropolitan Police have made huge efforts to address the problems that were raised. They have developed a diversity strategy, with the main intentions being defined as to:

- ensure that victims and their families have a clear understanding and certainty regarding the standards of service that they will receive
- build fair practice and no prejudice into the Force through training, management and measurement
- increase the number of officers from ethnic minorities through new approaches to retention and recruitment
- increase the transparency of what happens in the Force by the greater involvement of lay people
- make it very clear to all employees of the Force that there is no room for racism, and to actively target and address any examples of poor performance or bad behaviour.

TASK

Read the full diversity strategy developed by the Metropolitan Police at www.met.police.uk.

DIVERSITY AND TEAMWORK

Teamwork is an approach that has been adopted by a lot of organisations. It is favoured as an approach to organisational design because it widens the content of the job of individuals, which improves motivation. It is seen to improve the quality of working life by making it more interactive, and by giving groups greater empowerment to make decisions than is typically given to individuals. Teamwork also allows the strengths and weaknesses of individuals to be matched so that overall the team is stronger than the individuals who are within it.

Research by Riketta and Van Dick (2004) has shown that people tend to have a stronger attachment to their workgroup than to the overall organisation. This research emphasises the importance of the teamwork, and the effective development of teams. A further study by Richter et al (2004) found that the more individuals identified with their organisation, the less conflict their group developed with another group that they worked most closely with.

However, we have already noted that diversity can lead to a reduced group cohesion and greater levels of conflict within the group. We have to question, therefore, whether the reliance on teamworking actually has a positive impact on diversity.

In Chapter 1 we briefly touched on research by Sherif (1956) and Tajfel (1970) into social identity and social categorisation. We will return to this research to try to understand what might happen within a team.

Sherif and Tajfel both suggested that people quickly become loyal to the group of which they are part – and see that group as superior to any other groups. This would suggest that, if people are placed in a work team, they will quickly develop loyalty to that work team, and see it as superior to other groups. As stated by Van Dick (2004), the more an individual identifies themselves with a group, the more their attitudes and behaviours will be governed by the group membership.

However, that conclusion ignores the loyalty that the team members might have to other groups to which they belong. For example, if the team is composed of men and women, the men in the team already belong to a 'gender group' and might have the attitude that their gender group – men – is better than the other gender group – women. Hence, there is potential for a split within the team between men and women. This could lead to a reduced cohesion in the overall team. The same explanation can be given to explain sub-groups that can be formed within a team relating to racial groups, disability and other less obvious issues such as status within the organisation.

West (2002) suggests that one of the results of such a split within a team is that individuals do not have the psychological safety that is needed in order to contribute creative ideas without the fear of ridicule (ie a member of another sub-group might deride a contribution). This would suggest that there is a negative correlation between diversity in teams and team innovation.

However, another theory is that diverse teams actually perform better than non-diverse teams because they have a greater range of knowledge and cognitive skills to draw on. Polzer et al (2002) found that diverse teams have a greater variety of information, perspectives, knowledge, abilities and skills to draw on, and hence are more likely to produce innovative ideas. This theory would suggest that there is a positive correlation between diversity in teams and team innovation.

Williams and O'Reilly (1998), Webber and Donahue (2001) and Richard and Shelor (2002) have proposed that the relationship between diversity and teamworking might actually have a U-shaped form. This would mean that small increases in diversity would have small positive effects on the overall group problem solving and innovation, with small impacts on the functioning of the group. However, large levels of diversity would offer little improvements in group problem solving and innovation, but have a large effect on the functioning of the group. Somewhere in between would offer a balance between the advantages of increased problem solving, with the impact on group problem solving and innovation not being too great.

We can understand this theory more clearly by returning to our understanding of social identity and social categorisation theory, and by considering the theory that groups perform better when they have a greater range of knowledge and experience to draw on.

If there are small levels of diversity, then the inter-group conflict is low. This is because the people within the team are not from a large range of other groups, and hence have not developed negative attitudes towards each other. However, because the groups that the team has drawn from have similar backgrounds and experiences, the range of knowledge, skills and experiences that can be drawn from innovation is low. When the team has high levels of diversity, there is increased conflict because people are drawn from a range of different groups, and hence there is increased tension between those groups. To balance this, there is a wide range of experience, knowledge and skills to draw on – but, if this is not employed effectively because of the inter-group conflict, there will not be effective innovation.

This suggests, therefore, that when composing a team there needs to be careful consideration of the level of diversity within that team. Some diversity will improve the innovation, but too much could be detrimental to performance.

It should also be noted that a team needs to be managed effectively, regardless of the level of diversity within that team. Tuckman and Jensen (1977) suggested that all groups go through five stages in their development. We can apply this to the particular stresses that a diverse team might experience:

Forming

This is when the team is getting to know each other and developing an identity. Team members are finding out about each other and establishing ground rules. It is at this stage that different members will be finding out who has a similar background to them, and groups within the team will also be established. Here is where inter-groups can be formed that might affect the overall performance of the team.

Storming

This is the stage at which conflict occurs in the group. People are making individual goals and objectives clear, and there can be conflict as a result. This could also be the time when conflict occurs between different inter-groups, and the successful resolution of these conflicts is key to the ongoing success of the team.

Norming

The team now works out ways to work together and agreed expectations are sorted out. It is possible for some teams never to reach this stage because they never resolve the conflicts.

Performing

This is also a stage that some teams might never reach (although they might successfully reach the norming stage). This stage is when the team starts to get on with the job. However, if the team is still stuck in conflict and has not worked out a way to work together, then they will never successfully perform.

Adjourning

This is when the team disband, typically because the task they were set has been completed.

We can see, therefore, that diversity can have a positive effect on the performance of the team. However, if that diversity is too great – or if the team is badly managed – diversity can actually have a negative impact on the team performance.

CASE STUDY

On a degree course within a university, about 50 per cent of the students were of a UK-white ethnic origin, and the other 50 per cent were from a range of overseas countries. A crucial part of the course was for students to carry out some research in individual groups, and then present their findings. The presentation was an assessed piece of work.

The lecturer decided to divide the students into groups with an equal balance of UK and overseas students. Immediately difficulties occurred. These included:

- UK students dominating the group discussion, because they could speak English (the working language of the group) more fluently than the overseas students
- ideas of some students being dismissed because they did not express them clearly enough – again a language issue
- some students, who came from a culture where speaking out was not encouraged, being too shy to contribute.

It was realised that the students had not taken time to understand the different cultures within the groups, and the expectations of behaviour that came from these cultures. It was questioned whether the groups were too diverse, and whether they would ever be successful. With some guidance from the lecturer, the group did work more effectively, but there remained some difficulties and it was never felt that the group really operated to full efficiency.

TASK

Take time to think about the television programme, Big Brother. Whether you watched it avidly or never saw it at all, it is unlikely that you have never heard about the show! In the 2004 episode, there was criticism that the programme makers had deliberately chosen a diverse group of people to increase the potential conflict in the house – to make the viewing more interesting. It is true that the group was certainly diverse – gender, race, sexual orientation, transsexuality and different career status were all represented. Do you think that the huge range of diversity had a negative effect on the overall performance of the group?

THE EFFECT OF LEGISLATION

There has been legislation relating to sex discrimination in the UK since 1975 and legislation relating to race discrimination since 1976. However, the statistics we have examined have shown us that there is not equality between genders and between ethnic groups. We have to question, therefore, whether legislation is really working.

A presumption is made, of course, that employers know and understand the law. Whereas large employers with effective HR departments have little excuse for not knowing the law, smaller employers do not necessarily have the same access to specialist advice. Although ignorance is no defence in the eyes of the law, it could be a reason why discrimination still occurs.

It should also be noted that much discrimination law has become increasingly complicated, with amendments affecting such points as the burden of proof. As the law becomes more complex, employers might be less inclined to take time to try to understand it.

If employers are aware that legislation relating to specific areas of discrimination exists, there is next the question of whether they understand that legislation. The actual legislation can be quite complex, as we will see when we examine it in more detail in the next three chapters. For example, an employer might not realise that carrying out an act that discriminates against one group of people, but without any intention to discriminate, is unlawful.

The next point to consider is that not all people who have suffered discrimination use the law to address the problem. This might be because of fear of the consequences (for example, the impact on working relationships) or because the employee is ignorant of their rights. So, not all occurrences of discrimination will be addressed by the law. It is also possible that there are certain groups who are more likely to use the law – and it is possible that some minority members are less likely to take legal action. This could result in the unfair treatment of certain groups perpetuating without any action being taken to stop it.

The success rate of taking action against an employer also needs to be considered. According to the CIPD Executive Briefing, 'Discrimination and the Law' (Leighton 2004), only around 4 per cent of claims of discrimination that are brought to the Employment Tribunals result in success for the employee (note that a significant number will be settled or withdrawn before a hearing takes place). Given that rate of success, employees will not be encouraged to take claims to the Employment Tribunals.

It is also important to remember that the law will not change attitudes, although it might curb behaviours. Some employers might have discriminatory attitudes, but the manifestation of these is difficult to address through legislation. For example, if an employee of an ethnic minority group is not selected for a job, it might be because that person has suffered discrimination. However, if the employer can show that a fair selection process has been used and can give a convincing explanation of why another candidate was chosen, it can be very difficult for any discrimination to be proven.

Although this is a very negative view of discrimination legislation, it must be realised that without the legislation the workplace would be a very different place. There have been significant improvements for minority groups even if there are still further improvements that can be made.

DIVERSITY AND TRADE UNIONS

The primary purpose of the trade unions is to protect employees' interests and to promote their interests in the workplace. Trade unions are based on a collectivist approach – they are concerned with the needs of the group as a whole. However, the support and advice that they give to individuals is also an important part of their role. The Trades Union Congress (TUC) defined a series of objectives for all trades unions back in 1966:

- improved terms of employment
- improved workplace environment

- security of employment and income
- industrial democracy
- a fair share in the national income and wealth
- full employment and national prosperity
- improved social security
- improved public and social services
- a voice to government
- public control and planning of industry.

Although diversity is not specifically mentioned in this list (probably indicative of the date of the objectives), we can see how areas that are affected by diversity are part of these key objectives of the TUC. Issues such as improved terms of employment, improved workplace environment and full employment are all areas where we need to see improved equality.

The TUC does have an equality unit and campaigns for equal rights for all its members. It lobbies government and researches into diversity issues.

There is some concern, however, that the trades union movement is not truly representative of the diversity in the workforce. The following statistics all come from the Labour Force Survey published in 2002.

First, it should be noted that only 29.1 per cent of employees in the UK belong to a trade union.

The proportion of those members according to different classifications are as follows:

- male   53 per cent
- female   47 per cent.

In the period 1991–2001, the membership of men within the trade union movement fell by 13 percentage points. In the same period, the membership of women fell by 4 percentage points – with the result that there is no significant difference in the membership between genders.

Age	Percentage of members
Under 20	1
20-29	13
30-39	28
40-49	30
50+	27

It has been of concern to the trade union movement for some time that young people entering employment are not joining a trade union at the rate that this age group once did. This is probably reflective of the changing employment profile of the workforce – particularly the decline of the manufacturing sector and the growth of the service sector. The manufacturing sector has always had a traditionally strong union membership and, as fewer people enter this sector, it is likely that there will be less union membership.

In addition, there are fewer young people taking jobs that involve manual work – another area of employment that has traditionally been strongly represented in the trade union movement. There is also increased legislation protecting the individual, and people are more aware of these protections – and hence might feel less of a need to join the trade union movement.

Ethnic origin	Percentage of members
White	95
Asian/Asian British	2
Black/Black British	2
Chinese/Other	1

In interpreting these statistics we have to remember that there are significantly more people of white origin in the workplace, and hence it is probably inevitable that there will be a greater trade union membership from this origin. It is important, therefore, to look at the percentage of employees from each ethnic origin that are in a trade union:

Ethnic origin	Percentage of ethnic group
White	29
Asian/Asian British	25
Black/Black British	30
Chinese/Other	22

This shows us that there is some variance in the likelihood of people from different ethnic backgrounds joining a trade union, but the difference is not large.

Highest qualification	Percentage of members
Degree or equivalent	23
Other higher education	15
A level or equivalent	23
GCSE or equivalent	18
Other	11
No qualifications	9

This is interesting and might not display the findings you would expect. Trade Unions are often perceived as only representing blue collar workers; however, the comparison by qualification clearly suggests that this is not the case.

Work status	Percentage of members
Full-time	82
Part-time	18

The difference between those who work full-time and part-time is probably less surprising. It is possible that those who work part-time are less concerned about issues associated with their employment, because it is not such a large part of their lives. Alternatively, it could be that part-time jobs are more typically found in organisations where trade union membership is low.

What these statistics show us is that the trade union membership as a whole is not fully representative of the working population. It is important, therefore, that when promoting the interests of their members, trade unions do not unintentionally favour particular groups within society – because they are the most strongly represented in their movement.

TASK

Access the TUC website (www.tuc.org.uk) and read its section on equality to become more familiar with the activities that are taking place to improve equality in the workplace.

FUTURE TRENDS IN DIVERSITY

Legal trends

At present there is only one proposed change in discrimination legislation – and that is the introduction of age discrimination legislation in 2006. When that legislation is in place, the UK will have put into place the requirements of the European Employment Directive (Council Directive 2000/78/EC).

There is no notification at this stage that there will be any further areas of diversity covered by legislation.

Globalisation

Globalisation is the expansion of organisations into global markets. It is typically associated with large organisations – but it is not true to say that all large organisations are global.

One impact of globalisation is that organisations will have a more diverse workplace, because they will be operating in a greater range of countries. This needs careful management. It is important that the dominant characteristics of one country are not imposed on the workforce of another country when it is inappropriate to do so. One way to address this concern is to ensure a representative group of senior managers.

There is also the concern that globalisation can lead to a loss of individualism – although opinion on this is divided. Steeten (2001) suggests that globalisation sharpens differences between countries, rather than leading to a sameness across all countries. However, Herriot and Scott-Jackson (2002) suggest that globalisation leads to the growth of individualism. What is the impact of this argument on diversity?

If globalisation leads to sameness, then this implies that either the differences between groups are being ignored or groups are being put together of people who have similar experiences, skills, knowledge and background. If the latter is true, then there is a real possibility that some form of discrimination is occurring. It is possible that people are being recruited to work in an organisation because they 'fit' with the type of employee who has been deemed to be most suitable.

If the differences are being ignored, then there is the potential for conflict within the team at some stage. If we refer back to our section on teamwork, we can remember that an increased level of diversity can result in poorer operation of the team – depending on the extent of the diversity. If employees are encouraged to ignore their differences, it is still possible that they will emerge at some time.

If globalisation sharpens the differences between employees from different countries, it could make it much more difficult to work together as a harmonious team. We have already seen that the greater the diversity the greater the impact on the innovation and problem solving – but this is coupled with the potential difficulties that the team might have in operating effectively.

Another way that globalisation can cause divisions between groups, and hence negatively impact on diversity, is in the competition for resources. The International Labour Organisation raised this issue at its 2004 conference in a paper entitled 'Towards a fair deal for migrant workers in the global economy'. There is the possibility that globalisation can cause countries to compete against each other to attract jobs to the country. This is particularly true for underdeveloped and developing countries. In trying to be competitive, there is the possibility that pay rates are cut and compromises are made in health and safety.

Education and training

It should be remembered that there has been legislation forbidding discrimination against people on the grounds of gender since 1975 and on the grounds of race since 1976. However, the statistics that we have examined show that there is still evidence of discrimination occurring in both these areas – despite nearly 30 years having passed since the legislation was introduced.

This would suggest that legislation alone is not sufficient to address the issue of discrimination and diversity, and that more needs to be done to promote diversity. One of the ways that the government is proposing to achieve this is through the single equality body that we considered in Chapter 1. A purpose of this is to focus the education and training that is given to employers and employees in order to stop discrimination.

KEY POINTS FROM THIS CHAPTER

■ There are definite benefits to an organisation of having a more diverse workforce; these include increased productivity, innovation and retention.

- There is a link between diversity and motivation of employees, as shown by the two-factor model and equity theory.

- There needs to be diversity in the boardroom to promote diversity at all levels within the organisation.

- The culture of an organisation is evident in the behaviours and values of employees.

- The attitude that an organisation takes to sexual harassment can be indicative of its attitude towards gender equality.

- Institutional racism is an overall failure of an organisation to treat people of all races appropriately.

- Diversity can affect the success of teamwork. If there is low diversity, the group will operate efficiently but have reduced innovation. If there is a high level of diversity, the group will have high levels of innovation but lower levels of effective operation.

- Legislation has had some success in addressing discrimination, but it has not been fully effective.

- The Trades Union movement lobby for equality of treatment for their members, although the membership is not fully representative of the diverse workforce.

- Future trends in diversity include the impact of globalisation on the workplace.

Note: In this chapter there are a number of statistics representing a breakdown of the population measured in percentages. Clearly the totals should add up to 100 per cent. In some cases this is not so, and it is presumed that this is due to rounding up and down of the percentages. However, the authors have had to quote statistics as they are published by the original source, due to copyright restrictions.

EXAMPLES TO WORK THROUGH

1 You have been asked to assemble a group of employees to work on a special project. It is important that the group works together effectively as the project is of major importance to the organisation. How will you ensure that the group fully represents the workforce, while ensuring the effective operation of the group?

2 Your managing director has expressed a reluctance to recognise trade unions in the organisation. One of his objections is that the trade union is not representative of the members of the organisation. How would you address these concerns? (In answering this question, do not concern yourself with the legislation relating to trade union membership – concentrate on the issues of diversity and representation.)

3 Someone describes the culture of your organisation as being 'institutionally racist'. What would you consider in determining whether this was fair criticism?

The Scope and Structure of Discrimination Legislation in Britain

OBJECTIVES OF THIS CHAPTER:

- to understand the current legislation relating to discrimination
- to understand who is covered by this legislation
- to explore the difference between direct and indirect discrimination
- to evaluate the concepts of victimisation and harassment
- to understand the penalties relating to breaches of discrimination legislation.

So far in this book we have looked at issues surrounding the concepts of diversity, equality and discrimination. We have focused primarily on the advantages and disadvantages of diversity and the implications of this for the organisation. However, it is important to realise that there is a range of legislation that determines how diversity, equality and discrimination are managed in employment – and that is the topic we will now turn to.

THE SCOPE OF DISCRIMINATION LEGISLATION

Currently there are nine pieces of anti-discrimination legislation in Great Britain (England, Wales and Scotland). These are:

- the Sex Discrimination Act 1975 – covers unfavourable treatment on grounds of gender, gender re-assignment and marital status
- the Equal Pay Act 1970 – covers equality of treatment as between men and women in pay and contractual terms
- the Race Relations Act 1976 – covers unfavourable treatment on grounds of colour, race, nationality, ethnic origins and national origins; was amended in July 2003 in line with the EC Race Directive (Council Directive 2000/43)
- the Disability Discrimination Act 1995 – covers discrimination that is in any way related to an individual's disability
- the Employment Equality (Sexual Orientation) Regulations 2003 – protects people against discriminatory treatment on grounds of sexual orientation, whether gay, lesbian, bisexual or heterosexual
- the Employment Equality (Religion or Belief) Regulations 2003 – prohibits discrimination on grounds of religion or belief

- the Part-Time Workers (Prevention of Less Favourable Treatment) Regulations 2000 – confers the right to equality of treatment to part-time workers as compared with equivalent full-time workers engaged on the same type of contract

- the Fixed-Term Employees (Prevention of Less Favourable Treatment) Regulations 2002 – confers the right to equality of treatment to fixed-term employees as compared with equivalent permanent employees

- the Trade Union and Labour Relations (Consolidation) Act 1992 – prohibits discrimination on the grounds of trade union membership.

In addition to this, legislation relating to age discrimination will come into force on 1 October 2006. The EC Equal Treatment Framework Directive (No. 2000/78) required all Member States of the European Union to introduce legislation outlawing age discrimination. At the time of writing (Autumn 2004) the detail of the legislation that will be brought into the UK is still under discussion.

CASE STUDY

After losing a discrimination case in the Employment Tribunal, a small retail chain decided to employ an Employment Law specialist to come into the organisation and run a series of training courses on discrimination legislation.

At the end of the first training course, the senior management were aghast. They had never realised that there was so much relevant legislation. Although they accepted that ignorance was no defence, they were daunted by the amount that their supervisors and managers now needed to learn. Discussions took place to determine the most effective ways to achieve this, and a number of measures, including training, a management handbook and access to a helpline, were put in place.

This is a very simple case – but it is so common! Many organisations do not realise the extent of discrimination legislation.

TASK

New cases of discrimination are frequently reported, and it is important that you remain up to date with new cases during your studies. Work out now what source you will use to find out about new cases (eg Personnel and Management magazines, employment law websites), and plan to access the source regularly.

The impact of all the discrimination legislation, and the areas covered by it, are explored in detail in Chapter 4.

THE IMPACT OF EUROPEAN LAW ON UK DISCRIMINATION LEGISLATION

All the anti-discrimination legislation in Britain is governed by European law. Because EU law has supremacy over national law, it will take precedence in the event of a conflict or inconsistency between the two. Furthermore, the principle of supremacy applies irrespective of the timing of the implementation of national law – ie it makes no difference whether the relevant UK legislation was implemented before or after the EU measure that regulates it.

It should be noted that Member States of the European Union have until 2 December 2006 to bring in legislation relating to age discrimination. The first discrimination legislation in the UK resulting from EU legislation was the Disability Discrimination Act 1995. This was further amended in October 2004, bringing it into line with the European Directive – two years earlier than was required. At the time of writing, further changes to the Disability Discrimination Act 1995 are planned. Under proposals contained in the Disability Discrimination Bill:

- People with mental illnesses will no longer need to show that their condition is 'clinically well-recognised' in order to fall within the scope of the Act.
- People diagnosed with HIV, multiple sclerosis and cancer will be deemed disabled from the point of diagnosis, irrespective of how the condition is affecting them at that point in time or the future prognosis. To date, some people with these conditions have been held not to be protected by the Act.
- Public authorities will be required to positively promote equality of opportunity for disabled people both within employment and in the exercise of their public functions.

ELIGIBILITY TO COMPLAIN OF DISCRIMINATION

In general, the anti-discrimination laws in Britain offer protection not only to an organisation's direct employees, but to a much broader range of people who work for the organisation (known as 'workers'). Employees are defined as individuals who have entered into or work under a contract of employment. However, workers are those who either work under a contract of employment, or work under any other contract where that individual agrees to personally perform work or services for another party (Employment Rights Act 1996, Section 230).

The one exception is the Fixed-Term Employees (Prevention of Less Favourable Treatment) Regulations 2002, which apply only to employees (ie those engaged directly by the organisation on a contract of employment).

Job applicants are also covered by the Sex Discrimination Act 1975, the Race Relations Act 1976, the Disability Discrimination Act 1995, the Employment Equality (Sexual Orientation) Regulations 2003 and the Employment Equality (Religion or Belief) Regulations 2003.

Workers and job applicants are protected against discrimination on the grounds listed above irrespective of their age, the number of hours they work or their length of service.

As already noted, the definition of 'employment' for the purposes of defining who is protected is 'those who either work under a contract of employment, or work under any other contract where that individual agrees to personally perform work or services for another party'. Protection therefore extends to cover:

- part-time workers
- temporary staff and those engaged on fixed-term contracts

- workers engaged via a contract with an employment agency, including those whose contract with the agency is set up through their own personal services company
- employees of other organisations who may visit the employer's premises – for example, to repair equipment or deliver goods
- self-employed people who perform work personally
- apprentices.

Essentially any worker who is engaged to perform work for an employer on a personal basis (ie the individual performs the work personally rather than organising others to do the work or delegating the work) is protected against discriminatory treatment on grounds of sex, race, disability, sexual orientation and religion or belief (and, in the future, age).

Protection against discrimination on the prohibited grounds is afforded to job applicants at every stage of the recruitment process, including during any interview, and in the arrangements made for selection (see Chapters 6 and 7). For existing workers, protection is available in relation to:

- the terms and conditions of the job, and any other benefits, facilities and services that a worker can access in connection with their employment (see Chapter 8)
- opportunities for promotion, transfer and training (see Chapter 9)
- arrangements made for termination of employment, including dismissal, and (in some cases) post-employment discrimination, provided the treatment meted out to the individual has a connection with their employment (see Chapter 10)
- discrimination in the form of 'any other detriment', which has been interpreted simply as meaning any treatment that puts an individual at a disadvantage.

In complaining of discrimination, the complainant needs to show that the treatment they have suffered was to their detriment. They do not need to establish that there was any economic or physical loss in order to establish that they have suffered a detriment, as is shown in the following case:

Shamoon v *Chief Constable of Royal Ulster Constabulary (2003)*

In this case Shamoon was a female Chief Inspector in the RUC. Following a complaint from one of her officers about his appraisal, the task of carrying out staff appraisals was removed from her duties. She took a claim of sex discrimination because two other male Chief Inspectors continued to carry out appraisals. The Employment Tribunal determined that she had not suffered any detriment as a result of the decision to remove the appraisal duties, because there was no economic or physical loss resulting from this. However, the House of Lords ruled that a complainant does not have to show that they have suffered economic or physical loss in order to establish that they have suffered a detriment. The Lords held further that, so long as the complainant's view that their treatment was to their detriment is reasonable, this will be sufficient to give rise to a detriment.

Throughout the book there will appear boxes like this one which take a central debate of the topic being discussed. Some of these will be particular to the subject. Some will refer back to the central debates mentioned here. They are intended to allow you to decide for yourself what your view is. You might want to use them as a starting point for a seminar discussion to see what other people think. They could certainly be the basis of further investigation to look at other people's writing.

Overseas workers are usually excluded from the scope of discrimination legislation if they work wholly outside Great Britain. 'Great Britain' excludes Northern Ireland (the latter is included within the term 'United Kingdom'), although similar anti-discrimination legislation is in force there. The Channel Islands and the Isle of Man are also excluded. However, people who work offshore in the oil and gas industry within British waters are covered, as are employees who work on board ships, hovercraft or aircraft registered in Great Britain (unless they work on a ship that operates wholly outside British waters).

The general principle is that, so long as a worker does some of their work in Britain, they will be eligible to complain in a British tribunal of any treatment that amounts to unlawful discrimination. Thus, protection would cover (for example):

- British workers who are based in Britain but spend a great deal of their time working overseas
- British employees temporarily assigned overseas but who make regular or occasional trips back to Britain for work-related purposes
- overseas employees temporarily posted to Britain
- those working in Britain for foreign-registered corporations under contracts that are governed by law other than English or Scots law
- those based overseas who make regular or occasional business trips to Britain.

A worker's eligibility to bring a complaint of discrimination to a British employment tribunal will be unaffected by the fact that the worker is engaged on a foreign contract. Equally, the worker's nationality is irrelevant to the question of eligibility to bring a claim.

CASE STUDY

An employee of UK-white ethnic origin was sent to work overseas in an African country as General Manager. The assignment was for two years. About halfway through the placement, the senior management in the UK became aware that there were difficulties within the operating company. The employee from the UK was one of very few employees of white ethnic origin, and was not being accepted well by the local management.

A senior manager visited the operating company and found that the seconded manager had made no effort to understand the local culture, and had introduced a number of working practices that the local management viewed as being unacceptable. As a result of this, working relationships were very poor.

It was decided to return the seconded manager to the UK immediately, as there were no prospects that the relationships would improve. On return the seconded manager claimed unfair racial discrimination – that he had been treated unfairly because of his ethnic origin. The claim was never pursued, because a new position was found for him within the organisation and he felt it more appropriate to put his energies into that role, rather than fighting the case.

It would be interesting to consider what the outcome might have been if he had pursued the case. Would he have been allowed to bring the case? Had he been discriminated against?

Under the Employment Equality (Religion or Belief) Regulations 2003, the Employment Equality (Sexual Orientation) Regulations 2003 and the Race Relations Act 1976 (for the purposes of discrimination on grounds of race or ethnic or national origins only), an employee who works wholly outside Great Britain is protected against discrimination if their work is done for the purposes of a business run at an establishment in Great Britain and if the employee is, or was, ordinarily resident in Great Britain either when they were recruited or at some time during their employment. British employees who are assigned to other countries and who do not, in the course of their work, return to the UK will therefore be protected by these statutes.

TASK

Find out how your organisation, or an organisation with which you are familiar, has adapted current procedures and policies to address the requirements of the recent legislation relating to sexual orientation and religion/belief.

EMPLOYERS' AND EMPLOYEES' LIABILITY FOR DISCRIMINATION IN THE WORKPLACE

Discrimination legislation very clearly places responsibility on employers for any discriminatory actions on the part of their workers – this is known as vicarious liability. For example, the Sex Discrimination Act 1975 states:

> " Anything done by a person in the course of his employment shall be treated for the purposes of this Act as done by his employer as well as by him, whether or not it was done with the employers knowledge or approval. "

Similar provisions occur in the Race Relations Act 1976, the Disability Discrimination Act 1995, the Employment Equality (Religion or Belief) Regulations 2003 and the Employment Equality (Sexual Orientation) Regulations 2003.

This means that whenever an individual says or does something discriminatory 'in the course of employment', the employer may be held liable in law for any detrimental effect that such conduct has on any other worker. Ignorance of the fact that discrimination was taking place will not provide the employer with a defence, nor will it be a defence for the employer to argue that there was no intention to discriminate.

Jones v Tower Boot Company Ltd (1997)

Jones was a 16-year-old man of mixed-race origin. When he started work at Tower Boot Company, he was subjected to a campaign of verbal and physical assaults from two colleagues. This included him being burnt by a screwdriver and having metal bolts thrown at his head. After one month he resigned and brought a claim of race discrimination. Tower Boot Company argued that the colleagues had been acting outside their work duties, and hence the employer was not liable for the discrimination. However, the Court of Appeal ruled that the employer was vicariously liable for the discriminatory acts as they had happened within the course of employment.

It is also important to note that, if the employer *is* aware that discriminatory acts are taking place, then the employer is expected to stop those acts. If the employer does not take any action to stop any discriminatory acts and is aware that they are happening, then the employer will become directly liable for the discrimination, rather than vicariously liable.

Chessington World of Adventures v Reed (1997)

Reed was a biological male who started the process of gender re-assignment four years after joining the organisation. A small minority of male colleagues subjected Reed to a series of unpleasant acts and verbal abuse. Reed attempted suicide. On her return to work, she asked her employers to move her to a different area of the organisation, but the organisation did nothing to help her. She resigned. The Employment Appeal Tribunal (EAT) found that the organisation was directly liable for the discrimination, because they had been aware of what was happening and had done nothing to stop it.

The interpretation of the phrase 'in the course of employment' has evolved considerably over the years. Obviously, the employer will be liable for the words and actions of an employee that take place while the individual is engaged in the normal duties or activities of their job. Conversely, the employer will not generally be liable for an employee's discriminatory conduct that takes place outside work and in the employee's own time. The distinction may not, however, always be absolutely clear.

Chief Constable of the Lincolnshire Police v Stubbs (1998)

Stubbs complained that a male colleague had sexually harassed her. There were two occasions of harassment that she cited – one in a pub after work with a group of colleagues and another at the leaving party of a work colleague. The employer argued that the events did not happen during normal work duties, and hence they were not liable for what had occurred. The EAT held the Employment Tribunal view that the social occasions were sufficiently linked to the officer's employment for the employer to be liable.

Employers should be aware, therefore, that they could be held liable for any acts of discrimination (for example, harassment) perpetrated by one employee against another at any work-related event, whether the event takes place on work premises or at an external venue. Examples could include office parties, workplace social functions and residential training programmes.

In the case of Jones v Tower Boot Company Ltd, the Court of Appeal held that the phrase 'in the course of employment' should be given a broad interpretation in accordance with a lay person's normal understanding of the words. The decision in this case marked a departure from the previous application of the common-law principles of vicarious liability in cases of discriminatory harassment.

Although the principal claim for discrimination in the course of employment must be taken against the employer, it is also open to the complainant to name one or more individuals who were personally responsible for the discriminatory treatment. This type of claim occurs most often in cases of harassment, which is of course a very personal, and potentially offensive, form of discrimination. It is not possible, however, for an employee to bring a case to an employment tribunal against a co-worker alone, as the principal case must be brought against the employer.

Yeboah v Crofton (2002)

In this high profile case (that lasted 104 days in the Employment Tribunal), Yeboah made a series of allegations of race discrimination against his colleague Crofton. The Employment Tribunal, upheld by the Court of Appeal, found that there had been race discrimination against Yeboah by both the employer (London Borough of Hackney) and by Crofton. It ordered Crofton personally to pay £45,000 compensation to Yeboah because of the various incidents of very serious race discrimination. The Court of Appeal endorsed the Employment Tribunal's decision that the individual was personally liable because he had knowingly 'aided' unlawful discrimination against a colleague, and that this would be the case even in circumstances where the employer could escape liability for the conduct in question. This award was in addition to the compensation paid by the employer.

As a result of case law, it was established some years ago that an employer may be held liable for an act of discrimination inflicted on one of their workers by a third party. Third parties in this context could include any outside person such as a customer, a supplier or a member of the public. The precedent was set in the case of Burton and Rhule v De Vere Hotels.

Burton and Rhule v De Vere Hotels (1996)

Burton and Rhule were two black Afro-Caribbean occasional waitresses. On this occasion they were serving at a function at the hotel. The after-dinner speaker was a comedian who was expected to make sexually explicit jokes, but it was known that he would also be racially abusive. When the comedian started his speech, he directed a number of sexually and racially offensive comments at the waitresses. The atmosphere was such that other guests joined in these offensive comments.

The next day the waitresses complained to the manager of the hotel who apologised to them. However, they proceeded with a claim of race discrimination against the hotel – on the grounds that they had been racially harassed.

The EAT found that the employer was responsible for racial discrimination because they should have taken steps to monitor the speech being given by the after-dinner speaker and made arrangements to remove the waitresses if there were any concerns. The employer could have prevented the racial harassment occurring if they had done this.

However, the House of Lords ruled that it was not sufficient for the waitresses to state that the conduct to which they were exposed was racist. They also needed to show that they were exposed to this conduct because of their race, and that waitresses of another race would not have been exposed to anything that they found offensive (eg the sexist jokes).

TASK

Talk to someone you know who is in a position of management. Ask them about their understanding of vicarious liability. Debate and discuss the concept of work-related duties, and to what extent they think liability should extend to duties such as office socials and parties.

CASE STUDY

Following the atrocities of 11 September 2001, a problem occurred in a small manufacturing company in the North-West of England. During a tea break, some employees expressed sympathy for the views of those who carried out the terrorist attack. These employees were of a different ethnic origin from the rest of the workforce. Immediately there was a very heated discussion, which resulted in other employees refusing to work with those who had expressed their sympathies. This group of sympathisers were excluded from all work banter, their tools were hidden and they were generally ostracised.

Eventually they claimed to the management that they were being discriminated against on the grounds of their race. The other employees strongly denied this, saying that the treatment was because of their opinions, not their race. The management decided that it was none of their business and left the employees to sort it out themselves.

It was actually resolved when the sympathisers resigned from the company, having found work elsewhere. They never made any claim of discrimination, and hence the issue went away. However, it would be interesting to consider whether there would have been a chance that a claim of discrimination would have been successful – particularly bearing in mind the issue of vicarious liability.

DIRECT DISCRIMINATION

Discriminatory treatment on grounds of sex, race, disability, sexual orientation and religion can be direct or indirect. Direct discrimination occurs where a particular individual is treated less favourably than another worker on one of the prohibited grounds. The treatment must be less favourable – being different treatment does not necessarily mean that the treatment is less favourable.

Peake v Automotive Products (1977)

Automotive Products had a practice that their 400 women employees were allowed to leave work five minutes earlier than the 3,500 men employees on safety grounds. Peake, a male employee, brought a claim to the Employment Tribunal of unlawful sex discrimination. However, the Court of Appeal determined that there was no evidence that the treatment of the men was unfavourable.

If the treatment is seen as unfavourable, then the employee must be able to identify a comparator who is being treated differently. The comparator must be someone whose circumstances in employment are the same or not materially different although, clearly, they must be of the opposite gender, a different race, etc.

The law also allows a comparison to be made with a hypothetical comparator in similar circumstances (where there is no actual comparator). For a claim to be made, therefore, the worker need only show that they were treated less favourably than another worker of the opposite sex, different race or religion, or different sexual orientation was or would have been treated in the same or similar circumstances, and that sex, race, religion or sexual orientation (as the case may be) was the reason, or one of the reasons, for the treatment.

Coleman v Skyrail Oceanic Ltd (1981)

Coleman was a booking clerk working in a travel agency. She married a man from a competitor, and two days after the marriage she was dismissed. The two competitors had discussed the situation and decided that Coleman should be dismissed as it was likely that her husband was the main breadwinner. The Court of Appeal ruled that the assumption that the man was the breadwinner, and the woman was not, was direct sex discrimination. In this case, Coleman's comparator was a 'hypothetical male' in the same situation.

It should be noted, however, that in claims under the Equal Pay Act 1970, there has to be an actual comparator of the opposite sex for someone to found a claim – ie hypothetical comparisons are not permitted. Similarly, under the Part-Time Workers (Prevention of Less Favourable Treatment) Regulations 2000 and the Fixed-Term Employees (Prevention of Less Favourable Treatment) Regulations 2002, the complainant must compare their treatment with a real person – ie a person on a part-time contract must compare themselves with a full-time person engaged on the same type of contract, or someone on a fixed-term contract must compare themselves with someone on a permanent contract.

If an employee can show that there has been less favourable treatment, in comparison to another real or hypothetical employee, the next step is for the employee to show that the reason for the treatment related to the sex/race/disability, etc. This is known as the causation question.

> ### *Bradford Hospitals NHS Trust* v *Al-Shabib (2002)*
>
> Al-Shabib was a man of Iraqi origin. He joined the staff gym and broke one of the rules by allowing his wife and child to use it. He was reprimanded by the gym manager. An investigation followed (during which Al-Shabib was not interviewed) and it was decided to withdraw his gym membership. Al-Shabib believed that his treatment was a result of his race and hence brought a claim of direct race discrimination to the Employment Tribunal. The Employment Tribunal compared Al-Shabib's treatment to a hypothetical white male and concluded that he had been subjected to direct race discrimination. However, the EAT overturned this decision finding that there was no evidence that his treatment related to his race in any way.

Everyone is protected equally under the legislation – for example, men and women are equally protected under the Sex Discrimination Act 1975 – and everyone, whatever their sexual orientation, is covered under the provisions of the Employment Equality (Sexual Orientation) Regulations 2003.

The position is somewhat different, however, under the Disability Discrimination Act 1995, where the worker merely has to show that they were treated unfavourably for a reason that relates to their disability.

> ### *Clark* v *TDG Ltd (trading as Novacold) (1999)*
>
> Clark suffered a back injury and was absent from work, with an uncertain prognosis about his condition. After he had been absent for a year and a half, he was dismissed. The Court of Appeal held that, in cases of disability discrimination, the test of whether a disabled employee has suffered less favourable treatment should be based on the reason for their treatment and not on the fact of their disability. This means that there is no need to draw a direct comparison with an employee who is not disabled, as the only relevant issue is whether the disabled employee suffered unfavourable treatment for a reason related to their disability.

Further examples of direct discrimination include:

- declining to appoint a job applicant because they have revealed during the interview that they are gay
- refusing to promote a woman who is qualified for the job because the department head takes the view that a man would cope better with certain aspects of the work
- refusing to transfer a black employee to a customer-facing role based on the view (whether accurate or not) that the employer's customers would prefer to deal with a white person
- refusing to recruit a qualified job applicant because they have revealed that they would wish time off on particular days on account of their religion
- refusing to renew a fixed-term contract on the grounds that the employee has become pregnant (in circumstances where the contract would otherwise have been renewed)

- dismissing an employee from an ethnic minority group on the grounds that they do not fit in following tensions between employees that are linked to racial differences

- refusing to take a request from a male employee to switch to part-time working seriously, where a female colleague in similar circumstances has been allowed to work part time

- refusing to appoint a disabled job applicant, who is suitably qualified for the particular job, on the basis of an assumption that the applicant would be unable to perform the job, and without reviewing what adjustments the employer could reasonably make.

Further, more detailed information on direct discrimination on the various grounds is provided in Chapter 4.

INDIRECT DISCRIMINATION

The concept of indirect discrimination is somewhat complex. The Sex Discrimination Act 1975, the Employment Equality (Sexual Orientation) Regulations 2003 and the Employment Equality (Religion or Belief) Regulations 2003 all contain varying definitions of indirect discrimination, whilst the Race Relations Act 1976 provides two different definitions, depending on whether discriminatory treatment is on grounds of colour or nationality on the one hand, or on grounds of race, ethnic origins or national origins on the other.

The other laws do not include indirect discrimination within their scope. In all cases, the legislation allows an employer potentially to defend indirectly discriminatory treatment by showing either that it is justified in all the circumstances or that it is proportionate to the achievement of a legitimate aim. The definitions and distinctions between the various provisions are explained below.

Different definitions of indirect discrimination under different statutes

Colour and nationality

In respect of discrimination under the Race Relations Act 1976 on grounds of colour or nationality, the principles are that indirect discrimination will occur where:

- the employer applies a requirement or condition to everyone

- the requirement or condition is such that the proportion of persons of a particular racial group who can comply with it is considerably smaller than the proportion of persons not belonging to that racial group who can comply

- the application of the requirement or condition has caused an individual a detriment because they cannot comply with it. If, however, the condition is one with which the person can comply, then there will be no discrimination.

An employer will be able to justify an indirectly discriminatory requirement or condition if there is an objective, job-based reason for its application, even though it may have had a detrimental impact on an individual (or group of individuals). In other words, if there is an objective, job-based reason for the requirement or condition, it will not be unlawful.

Gender

Under the Sex Discrimination Act 1975, the criteria for indirect discrimination are based on the following:

- The employer applies a provision, criterion or practice to men and women equally. The phrase 'provision, criterion or practice' has a broader meaning than 'requirement or condition' and could, for example, cover any policy, procedure, rule or practice that the employer adopted, whether formally or informally.
- The provision, criterion or practice has a disproportionately adverse impact on women (or men) generally.
- An individual is put at a disadvantage by the provision, criterion or practice.

Once again, the outcome of any claim for indirect sex discrimination will depend on whether the employer can justify the requirement. The criteria for justification are similar to those in place for indirect discrimination on grounds of colour and nationality – ie the employer must show that there is an objective, job-based reason for the provision, criterion or practice that has nothing to do with gender. If the provision is necessary or relevant to the effective performance of the employee's job, it will be justifiable.

Race, and ethnic or national origins

Following implementation of the Race Relations Act 1976 (Amendment) Regulations 2003, the principles for race, ethnic origins and national origins are that indirect discrimination will occur where:

- The employer applies a provision, criterion or practice to everyone.
- The provision, criterion or practice puts, or would put, people of a particular race or ethnic or national origins at a disadvantage when compared with others. (This wording suggests that the person alleging indirect discrimination would have to show only that the provision, criterion or practice was likely to have an adverse impact on the racial group to which they belong, rather than providing detailed statistical evidence to back up their claim.)
- The provision, criterion or practice must actually have disadvantaged the person alleging discrimination. There is no requirement, however, for the individual to show that they could not actually comply with the particular provision in practice.

It is open to the employer to put up a defence against any claim for indirect discrimination on grounds of race, ethnic or national origins, but the test is not one of justification, as is applicable to claims based on discrimination on grounds of gender, colour or nationality. Instead, the onus on the employer is to show that the application of the particular provision, criterion or practice was a proportionate means of achieving a legitimate aim. Breaking this down, there must first be a 'legitimate aim' – ie a proper objective that the organisation wishes to achieve. Second, the means devised to achieve the aim (ie the provision, criterion or practice) must be relevant to its achievement and proportionate – ie not excessive. So if, for example, an employer imposes rules that are not relevant to the achievement of a legitimate aim, or introduces provisions that are excessively rigorous or restrictive in relation to the achievement of an aim, and if the rules or provisions also place people from a particular racial group at a disadvantage, the employer would be unlikely to be able to justify their actions in the event of a claim for indirect race discrimination.

Panesar v The Nestle Co Ltd (1979) IRLR 60

This case demonstrates that there can be justification for indirect discrimination. Panesar was a Sikh and applied for a job at a Nestle factory where food products were made. Nestle did not allow employees to have beards on the grounds of hygiene; however, Panesar refused to shave his off. On these grounds he was refused a job interview. Panesar took a claim of indirect race discrimination on the basis that fewer Sikhs than non-Sikhs could comply with the requirement. It was ruled that the treatment was indirectly discriminatory, but it was justifiable because of the importance of hygiene in food processing.

Religion or belief and sexual orientation

The wording in the newer areas of anti-discrimination legislation (religion or belief and sexual orientation) is similar to that used for indirect discrimination on grounds of race or ethnic or national origins as described earlier. Thus, indirect discrimination will occur where:

- The employer applies a provision, criterion or practice to everyone.
- The provision, criterion or practice puts, or would put, people of a particular religion or belief (or sexual orientation) at a disadvantage when compared with others.
- The provision, criterion or practice has disadvantaged the person alleging discrimination.

An employer may defend themselves against a complaint of indirectly discriminatory treatment on the basis that the application of the particular provision, criterion or practice was a proportionate means of achieving a legitimate aim.

Case examples of indirect discrimination.

The following cases are examples of practices within organisations that have been claimed to be indirectly discriminatory:

Clarke v Eley (IMI) Kynoch Ltd (1982) IRLR 482

The employer announced a redundancy, and applied the selection criteria of dismissing part-time employees first and then applying 'last in, first out' to the full-time employees. As a result, 60 part-time women, 20 full-time men and 26 full-time women were made redundant. It was held that the selection process was indirectly discriminatory because more women worked part time, and hence the process had a significantly greater adverse impact on women.

Jones v University of Manchester (1993) IRLR 218

The University of Manchester advertised for a Careers Adviser who was required to be a graduate and between the ages of 27 and 35 years. Jones had started her degree at the age of 38 years and was 46 years old at the time that the advertisement appeared. In claiming indirect sex discrimination, she showed that female mature graduates tend to start their degrees at a later age than male mature graduates, and hence the age requirement for the job was indirectly discriminatory. The Court of Appeal held, however, that the correct comparison was between male and female graduates (not mature graduates) and hence there was no discrimination.

R v Secretary of State ex parte Equal Opportunities Commission (1995) 1 AC 1

At the time of this case, full-time employees had to have served for at least two consecutive years to gain statutory rights (eg for claiming unfair dismissal), whereas part-time employees had to serve for at least five consecutive years. The government was challenged over this by the Equal Opportunities Commission because a significantly larger proportion of women than men work part time, and hence this qualifying period was claimed to be indirectly discriminatory. The claim was upheld and the qualifying periods were changed to be identical (and are now one year for both full- and part-time employees).

Other examples of factors that may be indirectly discriminatory include:

- A decision that employees must be available to work during evenings or at weekends. This type of requirement could discriminate indirectly against women, since women are less likely than men to be able to comply with the hours' requirement owing to childcare commitments. This would be especially so if employees were asked to work overtime at short notice.

- Insisting that a particular female employee must be included within a shift roster and take her turn at night shift working. A woman who is a single parent might not be able to work nights because of childcare responsibilities. Because more women than men are single parents (about 90 per cent of single parents are women), the imposition of the shift pattern could amount to indirect sex discrimination unless the employer could show that it was justified on job-based grounds.

- A demand that candidates for a particular post must be of a minimum height. Such a requirement would clearly place women at a disadvantage when compared with men and, unless the height requirement could be justified objectively on job-based grounds, would be unlawful.

- A condition that applicants for a particular post must be willing to travel away from home on the employer's business for long spells. Because fewer women than men would be able to comply with this, owing to family commitments that might prevent them from being away for long periods of time, the condition would discriminate indirectly against women. It would be up to the employer to demonstrate that such travelling was necessary for the effective performance of the particular job.

- A criterion included as part of the recruitment process that applicants for a particular post must be able to speak, read or write fluent English. This criterion would discriminate indirectly against job applicants of foreign nationality whose first language was not

English, and it would be unlawful unless fluency in English was a genuine requirement of the job in question. Unless the job in question involved special demands, it could be difficult for an employer to demonstrate that the application of the criterion of fluency was proportionate. Requiring the post-holder to speak English at a standard that could be readily understood would be more likely to be upheld as lawful.

■ A rule that employees must not have beards. This would be indirectly discriminatory against (for example) Sikh men, whose religious beliefs mean that they do not shave. The rule would be unlawful unless it could be justified, as shown in the case quoted between Panesar and the Nestle Co Ltd.

■ A rigid policy that employees must wear a prescribed uniform if, for example, the uniform included a requirement to wear short-sleeved shirts. This would discriminate indirectly against, for example, some Muslim women who are required by their religion to have their arms covered at all times.

It should be noted that there are occasions when discrimination can be allowed for 'Genuine Occupational Requirements' or 'Genuine Occupational Qualifications'. This is dealt with in detail in Chapter 6.

TASK

Find a number of recent cases that have been reported relating to direct or indirect discrimination. Read the cases carefully and ensure that you understand why the claims have been judged to be discriminatory or not.

CASE STUDY

A pharmaceutical company required all its sales representatives to cover an area of the country which was about 100 miles in breadth. To keep costs down, the representatives were expected to arrange their appointments so that they had a number in one part of their area in a day – thus reducing travelling costs. If the appointments the next day were nearby, they were expected to stay in one of a chain of hotels that the company had negotiated reduced rates with.

One representative had recently returned from maternity leave and explained that she was not able to stay away overnight. She would continue to arrange her work so that travelling was kept to a minimum, but she would still return home at the end of every day. The management refused permission to allow her to do this.

She claimed indirect discrimination, stating that the rules regarding overnight stays made it more difficult for a woman to do the job than a man. The management argued with this, saying that a number of the male representatives also had young children and wanted to go home at nights to see them. The woman argued, in response, that she was the primary carer for the child and hence had to go home each night.

Eventually an agreement was reached to accommodate her needs. If she had taken a claim of indirect discrimination, would she have been successful? Or would the argument that the male representatives with young children also wanted to go home have been sufficient to refute indirect discrimination?

VICTIMISATION

As well as affording protection to employees and job applicants against direct and indirect discrimination, the laws prohibiting discrimination on grounds of sex, race, disability, sexual orientation and religion or belief all preclude an employer from victimising an employee on the grounds that the employee has:

- made a complaint to a court or tribunal alleging discriminatory treatment (including the initial act of lodging the complaint)
- given information or evidence in connection with someone else's complaint of discrimination
- alleged that the employer has committed an act that would contravene one of the discrimination statutes (this provision would include, for example, the making of an internal complaint about the employer's actions so long as the complainant is alleging that the employer has committed an act that contravenes discrimination law)
- done anything in relation to anti-discrimination legislation (this is a catch-all provision)
- intended to do any of the above.

This list is collectively known as the 'protected acts'. The victimisation provisions also apply to situations where the employer suspects that the employee has done one of the protected acts, or knows or suspects that they intend to do a protected act.

The purpose of the victimisation provisions in the legislation is to afford protection to people against retaliation on the part of their employer in the event that they raise a genuine complaint that the employer has done something in breach of discrimination legislation.

The victimisation provisions also cover the situation where an employee is penalised by their employer on account of complaining that someone else has discriminated against them. For example, if an employee were to bring proceedings in an ordinary civil court alleging sex or race discrimination against, say, a bank, building society or hotel, and if their employer disapproved of such action and responded by subjecting the employee to some detriment as a result, then a claim of victimisation could be brought against the employer.

Similarly, if an individual who has brought discrimination proceedings against a previous employer (irrespective of the outcome of such proceedings) is rejected in their application for new employment with a different employer (perhaps because the potential new employer takes the view that the individual might be a trouble-maker), the person could take victimisation proceedings against the new employer. The argument would be simply that the reason for the new employer's rejection of the individual was that they had previously made a complaint to a tribunal alleging discriminatory treatment.

Any type of detrimental treatment of an individual on the grounds that they have done one of the protected acts will be covered – for example, refusal to employ or promote, denial of a benefit, unpleasant or abusive personal remarks, dismissal, etc.

Causal link

In order to succeed in a complaint of victimisation, the employee alleging victimisation must be able to show that their treatment was caused by or motivated by their involvement in a complaint of discrimination. If there is no causal link between the employee's original complaint of discrimination (or involvement in someone else's complaint) and the less favourable treatment complained of, a claim for victimisation will not be able to succeed. Clearly, if an employer can show to a tribunal's satisfaction that they did not know that the employee had done a protected act, then the employee's case will fail. However, following the case of Nagarajan v London Regional Transport (1999) on p. 58, the principle was established that a claim for victimisation can succeed even where the employer's motive in treating the employee unfavourably was a subconscious one.

In Aziz v Trinity Street Taxis Ltd & ors (1988)

Aziz was a member of a group of taxi-drivers promoting the interests of all its members. He considered that he was suffering race discrimination and took a claim to the Employment Tribunal. During the tribunal proceedings, it came to light that Aziz had secretly tape-recorded a number of conversations. Because of these actions, a decision was made to expel Aziz from the group, and he brought a claim of victimisation. The Court of Appeal identified three elements that a complainant must prove if they are to succeed in a claim for victimisation (which Aziz did not succeed in doing). The complainant must:

- show that they have done one of the protected acts
- provide evidence that they have been treated less favourably than others in the relevant circumstances
- prove on the balance of probabilities that the less favourable treatment was by reason of their doing one of the protected acts.

Case examples of victimisation

The following are cases that illustrate victimisation in a range of situations:

Commissioners of Inland Revenue & anor v Morgan (2002)

In this case the EAT held that the employer had victimised a black barrister because she had recently brought a race discrimination claim against them in relation to unsatisfactory career progression. The treatment that gave rise to a finding of victimisation was the circulation of a memo informing colleagues that the employee had brought a race discrimination claim against the organisation and warning them that some of their personal details might have to be disclosed to the complainant and to the public in relation to the disposal of her race discrimination complaint. The circulation of the memo, the EAT held, had a detrimental effect on the attitude of the employee's colleagues towards her, and hence constituted victimisation.

Nagarajan v London Regional Transport (1999)

Nagarajan had previously brought various complaints of race discrimination against his employer. When at a later date he re-applied for employment, he was turned down, an action which he believed constituted victimisation. The House of Lords upheld the Employment Tribunal's decision that, in making the selection for the post, those responsible for the recruitment decision had been consciously or subconsciously influenced by the employee's earlier complaints. So long as the principal cause, or an important cause, of the unfavourable treatment was the fact that the complainant had done a protected act, the case could be upheld.

Tchoula v ICTS (UK) Ltd (2000)

Tchoula, a black security officer, made a number of claims of race discrimination to the Employment Tribunal three months before his dismissal. The month before his dismissal, he received a warning about falling asleep while on duty. The next month, his supervisor forced entry into the building where Tchoula was working and claimed Tchoula was seen getting up from a prone position. He was suspended on the allegation of falling asleep on duty, and was later dismissed. He succeeded in three claims for victimisation following his dismissal, which, the EAT judged, occurred because of the original race discrimination complaint. It judged that the forced entry into the building, the handling of the disciplinary hearing and the dismissal all related to the earlier claims that he had made.

McGuigan v T G Baynes & Sons (1998)

McGuigan, an employee who was on maternity leave, was considered for redundancy. She had previously voiced criticisms of her employer's attitude to women. For this reason, she was marked down two points in the employer's redundancy scoring exercise. The EAT held that this amounted to victimisation, even though the employee might have been made redundant in any event.

Chief Constable of West Yorkshire Police v Khan [2001] IRLR 830

Khan, a police officer who had applied to another police force for a job was refused a reference. The reason for this was that the officer had brought race discrimination proceedings against the Chief Constable that were still outstanding, and the Chief Constable feared that the provision of a reference could prejudice the defence of the claim. The House of Lords held ultimately that, although the refusal of the reference amounted to less favourable treatment, the reason for the treatment was not the bringing of the race discrimination complaint, but rather the Chief Constable's legitimate desire not to compromise the handling of the race discrimination proceedings. Thus the police officer's complaint of victimisation failed.

HARASSMENT AS DISCRIMINATION

Until recently, the concept of harassment was not mentioned anywhere in UK anti-discrimination legislation. Neither the Sex Discrimination Act 1975 nor the Race Relations Act 1976 (before it was amended) contained any provision that sexual or racial harassment would amount to unlawful discrimination. The Disability Discrimination Act 1995 fared no better.

Despite this former gap in the wording of the statutes, over the years courts and tribunals have consistently held that harassment on grounds of sex, race or disability in an employment context will constitute direct discrimination, as it will fall under the heading of 'any other detriment' (a phrase used in all three statutes mentioned earlier).

Finally, in 2003, race discrimination legislation was the first to be amended, at least in part, to incorporate a statutory definition of harassment. This was followed in October 2004 by specific protection against harassment on the grounds of disability being added to the Disability Discrimination Act. The Sex Discrimination Act 1975 has not yet been amended to incorporate any statutory definition of harassment, although this is planned for the future (October 2005).

The newer regulations governing discriminatory treatment on grounds of religion or belief and on grounds of sexual orientation do contain a definition of harassment consistent with the definition in the amended Race Relations Act 1976 applicable to race, ethnic or national origins. Thus harassment is described (for example) in the following terms:

> **" A person subjects another to harassment where, on the grounds of that others race or ethnic or national origins, he engages in unwanted conduct which has the purpose or effect of –**
>
> **(a) violating that others dignity, or**
>
> **(b) creating an intimidating, hostile, degrading, humiliating or offensive environment for that other.**
>
> **Conduct shall be regarded as having the effect specified in paragraphs (a) and (b) if, and only if, having regard to all the circumstances, including, in particular, the perception of that other, it should reasonably be considered as having that effect. "**

The subject of harassment is dealt with in detail in Chapter 11.

CLAIMS FOR DISCRIMINATION IN THE EMPLOYMENT TRIBUNALS

Claims for unlawful discrimination in employment are brought before employment tribunals, which sit in most major towns and cities throughout Britain. As discussed earlier, employees, workers, job applicants and in some cases ex-employees are eligible to bring a claim of unlawful discrimination to an employment tribunal.

Claims must be lodged with the tribunal service within three calendar months of the discriminatory treatment complained of (except for claims of equal pay, for which there is a six-month time limit). Tribunals have discretion to waive the three-month time limit for discrimination claims if, in their view, it is just and equitable to do so, taking into account the circumstances of the individual case.

If discrimination against an employee has persisted over a period of time rather than consisting of a single incident, the employee may bring an aggregated complaint to a tribunal, so long as the application is registered with the tribunal within three months of the most recent discriminatory incident. This is because the legislation allows for claims to be brought based on an 'act of discrimination extending over a period'. This provision could apply, for example, in a case where an employee was being regularly subjected to discriminatory harassment, but the incidents, when viewed individually, were relatively minor. The employee could argue that their employer's treatment of them constituted a course of conduct extending over a period of time and that the incidents, when viewed collectively, represented a detriment.

Hendricks v Commissioner of Police for the Metropolis (2003)

Hendricks was a black woman who had served in the police since 1987. She had been on sick leave from 15 March 1999 and received full pay until it was stopped on 1 April 2000. On 8 March 2000, Hendricks had brought a complaint that she had been subjected to sex and race discrimination throughout her 11 years' service. She cited more than 100 events of bullying, ostracism and harassment. The Court of Appeal interpreted the phrase 'act of discrimination extending over a period' broadly, and held that it could include any ongoing situation or continuing state of affairs in which female or ethnic minority officers were subjected to linked incidents of discrimination. Hence, Hendricks' claim was allowed. By contrast, if an employee were subjected to a succession of unconnected incidents, this would not represent an act extending over a period. Any claim for unlawful discrimination would therefore be limited to complaining about incidents that had occurred within the three months preceding the date the claim to tribunal was made.

Following the implementation of the dispute resolution measures contained in the Employment Act 2002 (Employment Act 2002 [Dispute Resolution] Regulations 2004), any employee wishing to take a complaint of unlawful discrimination to an employment tribunal must first submit a written grievance to their employer and allow a 28-day period for the employer to respond. At the same time, the three-month time limit for lodging a complaint may be extended by three months to allow internal procedures that have commenced to be completed.

COMPENSATION FOR UNLAWFUL DISCRIMINATION

Where a complainant succeeds in a case of unlawful discrimination at an employment tribunal, the usual outcome is that they are awarded compensation. Tribunals will calculate compensation under some or all of the following headings:

- loss of earnings to date
- future loss of earnings (where relevant)
- injury to feelings (not available under the Part-Time Workers [Prevention of Less Favourable Treatment] Regulations or the Fixed-Term Employees [Prevention of Less Favourable Treatment] Regulations)

- injury to health (not available under the Part-Time Workers [Prevention of Less Favourable Treatment] Regulations or the Fixed-Term Employees [Prevention of Less Favourable Treatment] Regulations)
- (in England and Wales only) aggravated damages.

There is no ceiling on the amount of compensation that can be awarded following a successful complaint of discrimination. Tribunals have the flexibility to award an amount they consider just and equitable in accordance with the particular circumstances of the individual case. According to the Employment Tribunals Service's annual report 2003/04 (www.ets.gov.uk), the median award for sex discrimination claims during 2003/4 was £5,425, for race discrimination claims £8,410, and for disability discrimination cases £5,652.

To date, the highest award for unlawful sex discrimination has been £1.37 million (Bower v Shroder Securities Ltd [2002]), for race discrimination £762,000 (Chaudhary v British Medical Association [2002]), and for disability discrimination £279,000 (Newsome v The Council of the City of Sunderland [2001]). The Chaudhary case is, however, subject to an appeal to the EAT.

Compensation for any financial loss that the complainant has experienced as a result of discriminatory treatment is calculated and awarded on a net basis.

Vento v Chief Constable of West Yorkshire Police (2002)

Vento was a probationary constable. Following the breakdown of her marriage, she claimed she was subjected to a series of bullying and harassment. At the end of her probationary period she was dismissed, and she brought a number of claims including one of sex discrimination. She won her claim, but the amount of damages awarded to her was contested. As a result of this, the Court of Appeal set down three recommended bands of compensation for injury to feelings:

1   a band of between £500 and £5,000 for 'less serious' cases – for example, an incident of discrimination that was a one-off occurrence

2   a band of between £5,000 and £15,000 for middle to serious cases

3   a band of between £15,000 and £25,000 for serious cases; this band would be applicable to the most severe types of case, such as those involving a lengthy and malicious campaign of serious discriminatory harassment against an individual; the sum of money awarded will depend on the tribunal's assessment of the level of genuine upset and distress that the complainant has suffered as a result of the discriminatory treatment inflicted on them.

Injury to feelings

For injury to feelings, tribunals have a wide discretion when deciding how much to award, and awards can vary greatly.

Injury to health

In cases where the employee has become ill as a result of discrimination or harassment at work, tribunals also have the authority (in appropriate cases) to award a separate sum of money in respect of injury to health (also referred to as 'personal injury' or 'psychiatric injury'). In the Lincolnshire Police v Stubbs case (cited earlier), the employment tribunal distinguished between injury to feelings and injury to health. They described the concept of injury to feelings as dealing with 'emotions such as anger, frustration, humiliation and loss of confidence', whereas injury to health was viewed as a 'type of personal injury which should attract a separate award'.

An award for injury to health could be made in a case where the complainant could demonstrate that their mental health had been damaged as a direct result of the discriminatory treatment they experienced – in other words, that the discrimination caused them to develop a mental illness. Medical evidence would, of course, be required to convince a tribunal that such compensation was appropriate, and such a claim would also depend on there being evidence that the employee's illness was caused by factors in the workplace (and not, for example, by external factors).

Aggravated damages

In very serious cases, an additional sum of money may be awarded to the complainant for aggravated damages. This could occur where the employer (in the tribunal's view) has acted in a 'high-handed, malicious, insulting or oppressive manner' towards the employee. Aggravated damages may also, for example, be awarded in a case where the employer has persistently refused to take any action to support an employee, who has complained internally of discrimination, or to resolve the problem.

Compensation following a successful equal pay claim

Although the issue of equal pay is dealt with in detail in Chapter 8, it is worth noting here that, if a claim for equal pay succeeds, the employee will be entitled to have their pay and/or contractual terms raised to a level equivalent to the level of their comparator's pay and conditions, with each term of the contract being considered individually. It is not open to the employer to solve the matter by reducing the pay package of the comparator.

There may also be compensation consisting of arrears of pay and/or damages for up to a maximum of six years in England and Wales and five years in Scotland. This will be based on the date that proceedings were lodged. However, in a case where there has been a deliberate concealment of relevant facts from the employee, up to 20 years' arrears of pay may be recovered.

In addition to financial compensation, the Employment Tribunal can issue:

- a declaration of the rights of the parties
- a recommendation that the employer should take certain actions to ensure that the situation does not recur; if the employer does not take these actions, without reasonable justification, compensation can be increased.

Leeds Rhino Rugby Club and others v Sterling (2002)

It is important that any recommendation must reduce an actual adverse effect, and not a hypothetical adverse effect. In this case, Sterling was employed by the rugby club on a series of three contracts, but was then not selected for the first team. The Employment Tribunal upheld his complaints of race discrimination and victimisation. The Tribunal presumed that Sterling would be less likely to be offered contracts by other clubs because he could be seen as a 'trouble-maker', and hence recommended that Leeds Rhino offer him a further contract. However, the EAT ruled that not being offered contracts by other clubs was a hypothetical adverse effect, and hence the recommendation was not allowed.

TASK

Access the Employment Tribunals' website (www.ets.gov.uk) and read about recent statistics relating to claims of discrimination. Find out whether any large awards have been made recently.

THE BURDEN OF PROOF IN DISCRIMINATION CASES

The general principles with respect to the burden of proof in a claim for unlawful discrimination are these:

- Tribunals do not require proof beyond reasonable doubt, but instead work to the 'balance of probabilities' test.

- Once the complainant has established facts that indicate less favourable treatment, the burden of proof shifts to the employer to show that the reason for the treatment had nothing to do with gender, race, etc. – ie that they did not discriminate.

- This means that, unless the employer can provide an alternative, credible explanation for their treatment of the complainant, the complainant will win the case. The position is, however, slightly different in cases of race discrimination founded on colour or nationality.

Even though there are currently different approaches to the burden of proof in different statutes, the difference in interpretation is not substantial. The different approaches can be summed up as follows:

- In cases of discrimination on grounds of gender, marital status, race, ethnic and national origins, disability, sexual orientation and religion, the burden of proof shifts to the employer once the claimant has shown facts that indicate less favourable treatment. If the employer cannot provide an alternative, non-discriminatory reason for their treatment of the claimant that the tribunal finds credible, the tribunal is bound to find in favour of the claimant.

- In cases of discrimination on grounds of colour or nationality, the burden of proof is technically on the claimant to prove – on the balance of probabilities – that they were treated unfavourably on the stated grounds. Because proof of discrimination is rarely available, tribunals may in practice (if they consider it appropriate to do so) draw an inference from all the facts of the case that the treatment of the claimant was racially discriminatory. Tribunals will normally do this in cases where they are satisfied the claimant has suffered a detriment and the employer's explanation of their actions is unsatisfactory. It is up to the tribunal to make the decision whether it is appropriate to draw an inference of discrimination, as they are not bound to do so.

■ In cases of equal pay, the claimant must show that they were being paid less (or afforded less favourable contractual terms) than a comparator of the opposite sex who was engaged in like work, work rated as equivalent or work of equal value. Once this is established, the burden of proof is on the employer to show that there was a material factor that justified paying the claimant a lower rate of pay. If they cannot do this, the claimant will win the case.

■ In cases of disability discrimination, it is for the claimant to show that their condition meets the statutory definition of disability contained in the Disability Discrimination Act 1995, and to provide some basic evidence that any unfavourable treatment they experienced was on disability-related grounds. If the complainant succeeds in doing this, the burden of proof will then be on the employer to demonstrate to the tribunal's satisfaction that they did not discriminate, or that their treatment of the complainant (if discriminatory) was justified on grounds that were material and substantial, or that they had fulfilled their duty to make 'reasonable adjustments' as required under the Act..

■ In cases of discrimination against an employee on grounds of their fixed-term or part-time status, the employee must first show that they suffered less favourable treatment than a valid comparator. The burden of proof will then be on the employer to justify any less favourable treatment – ie to show to the tribunal's satisfaction either that the fixed-term or part-time employee was not in fact treated less favourably than the comparator, if they were less favourably treated, or that there was a valid reason that justified their treatment.

CASE STUDY

An employee of black ethnic origin complained to the management of the organisation within which he worked that he was being subjected to racial discrimination. He complained that, when the machines in the factory were being cleaned at the end of the day, he was always given the dirtiest and most unpleasant job.

This particular job involved cleaning inside a machine which had been grinding metal all day. There were lots of small pieces of metal that were extremely sharp and – due to the oil used in the machine – it was also a very dirty job.

When the supervisor was asked about this, he expressed great surprise that he was being accused of discrimination. He stated that this particular employee had always carried out the job so effectively that he automatically asked him to do it. He also commented that no-one else had been trained to do the job.

In this case there was no intention to discriminate – but the supervisor had not taken time to think about how his actions could be interpreted by the employee involved.

KEY POINTS FROM THIS CHAPTER

■ Legislation in Britain protects workers against discrimination on grounds of gender, trans-gender status, marital status, sexual orientation, colour, race, nationality, ethnic or national origins, religion or belief, disability, part-time status and fixed-term status.

■ Any worker who is engaged to perform work for an employer on a personal basis (ie the individual performs the work personally rather than organising others to do the work or delegating the work) is protected against discriminatory treatment on the prohibited grounds.

■ Employers may be held liable in law for discriminatory treatment perpetrated by one employee against another in the course of employment, irrespective of whether there was any intention to discriminate.

■ Discrimination may be direct (ie targeted at an individual) or indirect (ie where a provision criterion or practice applied by the employer has an adverse impact on the group to which the individual belongs, places them personally at a disadvantage and cannot be justified).

■ Victimisation provisions in the legislation afford protection to workers against retaliation on the part of their employer in the event that they raise a genuine complaint that the employer has done something in breach of discrimination legislation.

■ Employees and other workers are protected against harassment on a range of protected grounds either by dint of statute or because harassment has been deemed by courts and tribunals to constitute a detriment.

■ There is no ceiling on the amount of compensation that can be awarded following a successful complaint of discrimination, and tribunals have flexibility to award an amount that they consider just and equitable in accordance with the particular circumstances of the individual case.

■ In order to succeed in a claim of unlawful discrimination at tribunal, the claimant does not require proof beyond reasonable doubt, as tribunals work to the 'balance of probabilities' test.

EXAMPLES TO WORK THROUGH

1 An employee of Asian ethnic origin complains to you, the Personnel Manager, that a colleague is making a number of racist verbal taunts to him. You discuss this with the Line Manager who states that he is not aware of any taunts, and suggests that the claims are not true. What action should you take, and what are the implications of your decisions?

2 You have noticed that male employees are promoted more often in the organisation in comparison with female employees. What evidence should you gather in order to determine whether indirect sexual discrimination is taking place?

3 A key customer of the organisation has declared that he only wants to deal with a white male manager. Your Managing Director is adamant that the organisation cannot lose this customer. What should you do?

Grounds for Discrimination (1)

CHAPTER 4

OBJECTIVES OF THIS CHAPTER:

- to evaluate the grounds on which discrimination is prohibited
- to consider practical issues associated with discrimination issues
- to understand the key provisions relating to the right to request flexible working
- to look specifically at issues associated with discrimination on the grounds of sex, sexual orientation, race and religion/belief.

In the last chapter we looked at the structure of discrimination legislation and the various associated legal concepts. In this chapter we are going to look at more specific issues relating to the grounds on which discrimination is prohibited, and also at some of the practical issues that arise from this.

SUMMARY OF THE GROUNDS ON WHICH DISCRIMINATION IS PROHIBITED

Listed below are all the grounds on which discrimination is prohibited. In this chapter we will take each of these grounds in turn and examine the requirements in more detail:

- Sex discrimination is prohibited by the Sex Discrimination Act (SDA) 1975, and means unfavourable treatment on grounds of gender. The Act protects men and women equally.

- Trans-gender status or gender re-assignment (covered by the Sex Discrimination Act 1975) means the process by which an individual changes their gender (male to female or female to male) under medical supervision. Protection against discriminatory treatment is available as soon as it is known that a worker intends to go through the process of sex change.

- Sexual orientation discrimination is prohibited by the Employment Equality (Sexual Orientation) Regulations 2003. These Regulations protect workers (and job applicants) against discriminatory treatment on the grounds that they are, or are perceived to be, gay, lesbian, bisexual or heterosexual. Discrimination on account of another person's sexual orientation is also prohibited.

- Marital status is covered by the Sex Discrimination Act 1975, although only discrimination on grounds of married status is prohibited, and not discrimination on the grounds that a worker is single.

- Pregnancy and maternity discrimination is not dealt with in any of the UK's anti-discrimination statutes, but it has consistently been deemed unlawful by UK courts and tribunals and by the European Court of Justice (ECJ). Any unfavourable treatment of a woman on any grounds related to pregnancy, childbirth or maternity leave is unlawful.

- Discrimination against parents may occur if an employee who is the parent or carer of a child under the age of 6 is refused a request for flexible working under the Flexible Working (Procedural Requirements) Regulations 2002 and there is no proper business reason for the refusal.

- Part-time workers are protected against unfavourable treatment on grounds of their part-time status under the Part-Time Workers (Prevention of Less Favourable Treatment) Regulations 2000. The Regulations confer the right to equality of treatment for part-time workers as compared with equivalent full-time workers engaged on the same type of contract, unless less favourable treatment can be justified.

- Fixed-term employees are protected against unfavourable treatment on the grounds of their fixed-term status by the Fixed-Term Employees (Prevention of Less Favourable Treatment) Regulations 2002. The Regulations confer the right to equality of treatment to fixed-term employees as compared with equivalent permanent employees with the same length of service, unless less favourable treatment can be justified.

- Race discrimination (prohibited by the Race Relations Act [RRA] 1976) means unfavourable treatment on grounds of colour, race, nationality, ethnic origins or national origins. Everyone is protected equally whatever their race or racial origins. Discrimination on account of another person's race is also prohibited.

- Religion or belief is covered by the Employment Equality (Religion or Belief) Regulations 2003, which prohibit discrimination on grounds of a worker's actual or perceived religion, religious belief or similar philosophical belief. Discrimination on account of another person's religion or belief is also prohibited.

- Trade union membership (or the decision not to be a trade union member) is covered by Section 137(1) of the Trade Union and Labour Relations (Consolidation) Act 1992. This prohibits discrimination on the grounds of trade union membership.

- Disability discrimination (prohibited by the Disability Discrimination Act 1995) covers discrimination that is in any way related to a worker's disability. The Act also imposes a duty on employers to make reasonable adjustments to working practices and premises to accommodate the needs of job applicants and workers who are disabled.

- Age discrimination is not, at the time of writing, prohibited by UK law, but legislation banning age discrimination in employment is set to be implemented in October 2006. This legislation will cover workers and job applicants of all ages.

TASK

Find out if your organisation, or an organisation with which you are familiar, is aware of this full range of discrimination legislation and has policies and procedures to address it.

SEX DISCRIMINATION

Sex discrimination is prohibited in the UK under the Sex Discrimination Act 1975 and the Equal Pay Act 1970. These Acts together form a comprehensive package providing substantial protection to all workers and job applicants against all forms of gender discrimination. In general, the Equal Pay Act 1970 covers pay and all other terms of employees' contracts of employment, while the Sex Discrimination Act 1975 protects individuals from discrimination in:

- all stages of recruitment and selection (see Chapters 6 and 7)
- terms and conditions of employment (see Chapter 8)
- benefits, facilities and services offered to employees (see Chapter 8)
- opportunities for promotion, transfer and training (see Chapter 9)
- dismissal, including redundancy (see Chapter 10)
- post-employment discrimination (see Chapter 10)
- any other detriment.

The Sex Discrimination Act 1975 prohibits both direct and indirect discrimination, and also victimisation. Sexual harassment is also unlawful on account of consistent findings by courts and tribunals that it constitutes a form of detriment.

The Sex Discrimination Act 1975 affords protection equally to men and women. Although the Act was implemented primarily to redress the problem of discrimination against women, men have exactly the same rights and entitlements as women under the Act. The same principle applies to the Equal Pay Act 1970, although in practice far more women than men bring claims under both Acts.

Certain limited exemptions exist to the general principle that is unlawful to take an individual's gender into account when deciding whom to recruit, transfer or promote. These are explored fully in Chapter 6 under 'Genuine occupational requirements and qualifications', p. 114.

The Sex Discrimination Act 1975 covers not only unfavourable treatment on grounds of gender, but also discrimination on grounds of marital status.

It is important to note that treatment that appears to be unreasonable is not necessarily discriminatory. The unreasonable treatment could be indicative of an employer being unreasonable to all employees, or it could be for a reason that is not related to a discriminatory factor in any way. This is shown in the case on p. 69 relating to both sex and race discrimination.

Bahl v Law Society and others (2004)

Bahl, a black Asian woman was Vice President of the Law Society. There was a complaint made by the MSF Trade Union (now known as Amicus), on behalf of one of its members, which included allegations of bullying and intimidation. She was suspended and subsequently resigned claiming both race and sex discrimination. The Employment Tribunal upheld her claim, drawing an inference that the language used during the investigation in the accusations and her general treatment by those carrying out the investigation were a result of race and sex discrimination.

However, both the Employment Appeal Tribunal (EAT) and the Court of Appeal supported the appeal of the employer. They determined that it was not possible to conclude that direct discrimination had occurred – it could well have been that the treatment given to Bahl was the result of some antagonism felt towards her that was unrelated to race or sex discrimination.

The UK's laws on sex discrimination are governed by European law, which means that the Sex Discrimination Act 1975 and the Equal Pay Act 1970 must be consistent with, and fully implement, the relevant EU Directives, which are the Equal Treatment Directive (Council Directive 76/207) and the Equal Pay Directive (Council Directive 75/117). Article 141 of the Treaty of Rome also applies.

The ECJ, which sits in Luxembourg, is the supreme court for all EU member states, with responsibility for interpreting EU law and ensuring that it is observed throughout the Community. Cases of sex discrimination can, in certain circumstances, be appealed to the ECJ when the scope of the national courts/tribunals has been exhausted without a satisfactory remedy. Tribunals and appeal courts may also refer matters to the ECJ for guidance.

TASK

A significant number of claims of sex discrimination are brought to the Employment Tribunals every year. Find at least five recent cases and ensure that you understand what the allegations were, and the legal reasons for the decisions of the Employment Tribunal.

GENDER RE-ASSIGNMENT

In 1999, the Sex Discrimination Act 1975 was amended by the Sex Discrimination (Gender Re-assignment) Regulations 1999. As a result, legislation now expressly provides that it is discriminatory and unlawful to treat an employee or job applicant unfavourably on the grounds that they:

- intend to undergo gender re-assignment
- are in the process of undergoing gender re-assignment
- have undergone gender re-assignment.

'Gender re-assignment' is defined as:

" **A process that is undertaken under medical supervision for the purpose of re-assigning a persons sex by changing physiological or other characteristics of sex, and includes any part of such a process.** "

Thus, protection against unfavourable treatment starts as soon as an employee makes it known that they intend to go through the process of changing their sex. The legislation does not, however, offer protection to individuals who are transvestites – ie cross-dressers.

It is important for employers to be aware that an individual who indicates that they intend to go through the process of sex change is protected against all forms of discrimination, including harassment, and the employer is required to take appropriate measures to support the employee. This will include allowing a reasonable amount of time off work for the employee to undergo the necessary medical or surgical treatment. It would be unlawful to penalise an employee for taking time off work for this purpose if the employer would allow a similar amount of time off for reasons associated with sickness or injury.

There are limited exceptions to the principle that an individual's trans-gender status must not be taken into account when deciding whom to recruit or promote into a particular post. These are covered in Chapter 6 under 'Genuine occupational requirements and qualifications'.

In order to manage the practical matters that may arise when an employee announces that they intend to undergo a sex change, the employer should first and foremost talk to the employee confidentially and establish how they would prefer the matter to be handled in terms of communication with colleagues, customers, etc., and how certain practical matters are to be dealt with. The following matters will need to be addressed:

- the expected timescales for the employee's transition to the opposite sex and how much time off for medical or surgical treatment will be required

- at what point the sex change will be complete, thus necessitating changes to the employee's records to give recognition to their new gender identity

- whether the employee wishes to remain employed in their current post or to be considered for a transfer to another department or another part of the organisation

- at what point in time colleagues and others (eg customers) are to be informed of the employee's intentions and what precisely is to be communicated. People seeking to undergo gender re-assignment are required to undergo a 'real-life test' – ie to live exclusively as a member of the opposite sex – before any medical treatment or surgery is undertaken. Clearly management should ensure that communication about the employee's plans takes place at or before this stage

- who is to inform the employee's colleagues and others about the sex change – ie whether the employee would prefer to do this themselves or have the employer make the announcement on their behalf

- whether any briefing, coaching or training might be required for the employee's colleagues, in particular to help them understand that no harassment or other detrimental treatment of the employee must take place

- agree a procedure for the employee's adherence to any dress code, or the point in time when the employee will begin wearing the opposite sex's version of the staff uniform – allowing flexibility where necessary

- agree when the employee will commence using single-sex facilities (such as toilets) as a member of their new gender.

The question of which toilets an employee going through the process of sex change should use can be problematic. Useful guidance was provided by the Court of Appeal in Croft v Royal Mail Group plc:

Croft v Royal Mail Group plc (2003)

The Court of Appeal upheld the finding that an employer had not discriminated unlawfully against a male-to-female trans-sexual by refusing to allow her to use the female toilet facilities prior to gender re-assignment surgery. The employee, who had worked for Royal Mail for 10 years as a man, had begun taking female hormones as part of the process of gender re-assignment.

Having sought advice, the employer informed staff that the employee should be treated as a woman and emphasised the organisation's anti-harassment policy. They suggested to the employee that she should use a unisex disabled toilet on a temporary basis until the completion of gender re-assignment surgery. The employee was unhappy with this arrangement, however, and subsequently resigned and claimed sex discrimination and constructive dismissal.

The Court held that, because the employee was still a man in law at the time in question, she had no right to insist on using the female toilets until after the process of gender re-assignment was complete, and the employer's action in asking her to use the unisex disabled toilet for a period of time had been appropriate in the circumstances and lawful.

It will be very important, if an employer is to avoid liability for sex discrimination, to ensure that the organisation's equal opportunities and anti-harassment policies and procedures include trans-gender people. If and when a case arises, the employer should, as in the Croft case, seek to balance the rights of the individual not to suffer discrimination against the legitimate interests of other employees.

During the period of time that the employee is undergoing the 'real-life test', the employer should handle such practical matters with sensitivity. If it is possible to do so, for example, it would be preferable to permit the employee to use a designated unisex toilet (preferably not the disabled toilet) during this time, and to allow flexibility with regard to any dress code.

Two other important cases that reached the European Court of Human Rights resulted in the conclusion that, once an individual has completed the process of gender re-assignment, they have the right to be treated in every respect as legally belonging to their acquired sex.

Goodwin v UK (2002) and I v UK (2002)

In this case Goodwin made five specific points:

1 the failure of the UK government to award Goodwin a pension at the age of 60 years

2 the refusal of the UK government to issue Goodwin with a new national insurance number

---

3   the refusal of the UK government to allow Goodwin to marry her male partner

4   the requirement of the UK government that 'I' produce a birth certificate showing her original sex in order to start a nursing course

5   the requirement of the UK government that 'I' produce a birth certificate showing her original sex in order to obtain a student loan

The Court held that the UK's lack of recognition of trans-sexual people's new gender identity for legal purposes represents a breach of Article 8 of the European Convention on Human Rights (the right to respect for private life) and Article 12 (the right to marry). It is important to note that this decision only affects post-operative trans-gender people 'I' – ie those who have completed all the relevant medical and surgical processes.

At the time of writing, the Gender Recognition Act has been passed but not yet implemented. This will invoke changes to UK law to apply the Goodwin and 'I' decision. It will thus be essential for employers to treat trans-gender people in the same way as all other employees of their acquired gender in every respect once the process of the sex change is complete. This will affect occupational pension schemes and other fringe benefits.

CASE STUDY

At the start of the new school year, Mr Jones, one of the science teachers, has returned to school and announced that in future he wishes to be known as Miss Jones. During the summer holidays he has started the process of gender re-assignment.

The Headteacher accepts his request and meets with the children taught by Miss Jones to explain the situation to them. He also writes to the parents of all the children. Immediately there is a flood of protests, mostly from the parents of the children. They do not want their children taught by a transsexual – many parents commenting that their children are at an impressionable age, and should not be required to think about issues such as sex changes. The Headteacher takes legal advice and decides to insist that the children are taught by Miss Jones.

This action results in a number of parents withdrawing their children from lessons when they are being taught by Miss Jones. As a result of all this, Miss Jones is signed off sick with stress by her GP. Miss Jones never returns to teach at the school.

This is a very difficult situation, because the law requires the employer not to discriminate on the grounds of transsexuality, but the parents were making it impossible for her to teach. As with many of these cases, it was never really solved, but it would be interesting to consider what the solution might have been if Miss Jones had returned from sick leave.

SEXUAL ORIENTATION

Until recently, protection against discrimination on grounds of an individual's sexual orientation was not provided by UK law. Numerous attempts had been made to assert that the Sexual Discrimination Act 1975 should be interpreted so as to encompass discrimination on grounds of sexual orientation, but these arguments consistently failed both in the UK courts and at the ECJ. The word 'sex' in the Sex Discrimination Act 1975 clearly means 'gender', and not 'sexual orientation' or 'sexual preference'. The following case demonstrates the difficulty of applying the Sex Discrimination Act 1975 to issues of sexual orientation.

Grant v South West Trains Ltd (1998)

Grant was a clerical officer working for South West Trains. Under a scheme run by the company, employees and their spouses, or long-term partners with whom they had had a meaningful relationship for at least two years, were entitled to travel concessions. Grant applied for her long-term lesbian partner to receive travel concessions, but was refused. She took a claim of sex discrimination to the Employment Tribunal. However, it was found that there was no sex discrimination – because a male employee with a long-term homosexual partner would have been treated in exactly the same way.

The position was changed in December 2003 with the implementation of the Employment Equality (Sexual Orientation) Regulations 2003. The Sexual Orientation Regulations, which implement the EU Framework Directive for Equal Treatment, provide that unfavourable treatment on grounds of an individual's sexual orientation during recruitment, employment, at termination of employment and post-employment will be unlawful. The Regulations prohibit direct discrimination, indirect discrimination, victimisation and harassment, which is defined as a distinct form of discrimination (see Chapter 11). 'Sexual orientation' is defined in the Regulations as a sexual orientation towards:

- persons of the same sex (this covers gay men and lesbian women)
- persons of the opposite sex (this covers heterosexual men and women)
- persons of the same sex and of the opposite sex (this covers people who are bisexual).

The Sexual Orientation Regulations are in the spirit of true equality, as they protect everybody equally. They do not, however, protect people on account of an involvement in sexual practices, preferences or fetishes such as (for example) sado-masochism. Equally, an orientation towards children would not entitle a paedophile to protection under the Regulations.

In understanding the legislation, it is important to note that the EU Framework Directive for Equal Treatment refers specifically to the European Convention of the Protection of Human Rights and Fundamental Freedoms. In doing this, it makes particular reference to the Human Rights Act 1998. There are three articles within that Act that are of particular importance:

1   Article 8 that provides that everyone has the right to respect for his/her private and family life, his/her home and correspondence
2   Article 10 that provides that everyone has the right to freedom of expression
3   Article 14 that prohibits any direct or indirect discrimination *whatsoever.* This means that if there is an element of discrimination in any particular case it will be unlawful, even if it is not seen to be the substantial cause of the complaint.

People who have changed their sex (trans-gender people) are not covered by these Regulations, as trans-gender people are expressly protected by the Sex Discrimination Act 1975 (as mentioned earlier).

Protection is also available under the Regulations to employees treated unfavourably on account of a *perception* that they are gay, lesbian, bisexual or heterosexual, whether or not that is their actual sexual orientation. For example, harassment based on an incorrect assumption that a particular individual was gay could give rise to a legitimate claim for unlawful discrimination. Furthermore, if an employee is treated unfavourably in any way (for example, being taunted or teased) because they associate with someone of a particular sexual orientation (for example, if they have a gay brother or lesbian daughter), or because they refuse to carry out an instruction to discriminate against gay or lesbian people, that will constitute unlawful treatment.

One exception to the general principle that employees must not be subjected to any disadvantage in employment on grounds of their sexual orientation is in the provision of benefits to employees' partners. The Regulations contain a clause that expressly permits employers to offer benefits (eg pension and insurance benefits, or access to discounted goods or services) by reference to marital status, if they wish to do so. Thus, schemes that offer benefits only to employees' married (but not unmarried) partners are lawful, even though on the face of it this type of arrangement discriminates indirectly against gay and lesbian people, who of course cannot marry. Where, however, an employer elects to offer benefits to their employees' unmarried heterosexual partners, they must provide equivalent benefits to employees who have same-sex partners.

It should also be noted that, in March 2004, the government introduced the Civil Partnership Bill into Parliament. This Bill would allow lesbian and gay couples to gain formal legal recognition of their relationship if they chose to do so. Civil partners would gain a range of rights giving them parity with married couples. At the time of writing, consultation regarding the Bill is still continuing. Progress is reported on the Women and Equality Unit website (www.womenandequalityunit.gov.uk), which is co-ordinating the development of this piece of legislation.

The Sexual Orientation Regulations also contain two 'genuine occupational requirements', or GORs, that are relevant to decisions to recruit, transfer, promote or dismiss an employee on grounds of their sexual orientation in certain narrowly defined circumstances. The first GOR relates to the situation where a particular sexual orientation is a genuine and determining requirement for the post in question, while the second may apply where the employment is 'for the purposes of an organised religion' – for example, where an organisation such as a church is opposed to employing gay or lesbian people for reasons rooted in the doctrines of the particular religion. These issues are dealt with in Chapter 6 under 'Genuine occupational requirements and qualifications'.

In many cases, an employer may not know the sexual orientation of their employees, and arguably there is no reason why they should know, since the Regulations do not place an obligation on individuals to disclose their sexual orientation, even in a court or tribunal hearing. Evidence suggests, however, that gay and lesbian employees are particularly likely to be the victims of stereotyping, prejudice and harassment in the workplace (see also Chapter 1). Many will conceal their sexual orientation for fear of unfavourable treatment by colleagues or by the employer generally. Myths and stereotypes about gay and lesbian people abound, including the false assumptions that they are:

■ promiscuous
■ a risk to children

- HIV-positive
- 'effeminate' (gays) or 'butch' (lesbians).

These views are completely false, and any such negative attitudes or assumptions in the workplace should of course be guarded against by employers and speedily redressed if they manifest themselves in any way. Policies and procedures should clearly identify sexual orientation as a ground entitling employees to equality of treatment and freedom from all forms of harassment. Employers should in particular be alert to any instances of banter, taunts or jokes based on sexual orientation (see Chapter 11 for a full discussion of different forms of harassment) that could create an uncomfortable working environment for a particular employee (whatever their sexual orientation) and thus constitute unlawful harassment.

TASK

At the time of writing, there are no reported cases under legislation relating to sexual orientation. During your studies, check whether any cases have been reported, and ensure that you understand the reasoning behind any claims that have been brought, and the conclusions that have been reached.

MARITAL STATUS

The Sex Discrimination Act 1975, as well as outlawing discrimination on the grounds of gender and trans-sexual status (as amended), also covers discrimination against employees on grounds of marriage. Specifically, the Act states that married employees (of either sex) must not be treated less favourably than unmarried employees on grounds of their marital status.

Curiously, the Act does not afford similar protection to single people, and so it would appear on the face of it that discrimination against single employees on grounds of their being single would not be unlawful (although such treatment would not, of course, be in the spirit of equality and is not therefore to be recommended!).

One example of a case in which an employee was held to have suffered discrimination on grounds of marriage is Chief Constable of Bedfordshire Constabulary v Graham.

Chief Constable of Bedfordshire Constabulary v *Graham (2002)*

Graham was an Inspector in the Bedfordshire force, and married a Chief Superintendent in the same force. In May 1999 she was appointed as an Area Inspector in the division her husband was responsible for, but one month later the appointment was rescinded. She was told this was because her appointment was inappropriate because of her husband's role in the division. Her claims of indirect sex discrimination, and direct and indirect discrimination on the grounds of marital status, were all upheld.

This does not mean, however, that employers can never impose a rule that people related by marriage or living together as partners should not be employed in the same department or section. However, before applying such a policy or rule, the employer should analyse:

- whether any real risk or practical difficulty is likely to arise if people in close relationships work together
- whether a policy or rule banning people in close relationships from working in the same department or section can be justified on business-related grounds
- whether such a policy or rule, if it is thought to be necessary, needs to be applied throughout the organisation or only in certain areas, or in certain defined circumstances (for example, where an employee would be the manager or supervisor of their partner, son, daughter, etc.).

If it is established that a policy or rule of this type would be necessary and appropriate in relation to a genuine business need, then the employer may be able to apply the policy without being in breach of anti-discrimination legislation. It is advisable, however, that to ensure avoidance of marital discrimination any policy or rule on this matter should be applied to both married and unmarried partners, and also to other close personal relatives such as siblings, parents and sons/daughters.

PREGNANCY AND MATERNITY

The Employment Rights Act 1996 contains provisions that make it unlawful to dismiss a woman on any grounds related to pregnancy, childbirth or maternity, or to subject her to a detriment on any of these grounds. In order to bring a claim for unfair dismissal on account of a dismissal on pregnancy-related grounds, the employee is not required to have any minimum period of qualifying service.

The Sex Discrimination Act 1975 does not deal with discrimination on grounds of pregnancy or maternity leave. Nevertheless, courts and tribunals have over the years interpreted discrimination on pregnancy/maternity grounds as sex discrimination, on the basis that such treatment is 'gender-specific'. One of the earliest cases of its kind was Dekker v Stichting Vormingscentrum voor Jonge Volwassen.

Dekker v Stichting Vormingscentrum voor Jonge Volwassen (1990)

Dekker applied for a job as a training instructor, and was recommended as being the best person for the job. However, she was three months pregnant and the employer refused to give her the job on these grounds. Part of the argument of the employer was that the organisation's insurers met the costs of paying for long-term absence, but they would not pay when the absence was foreseeable within six months of the insurance being taken out. In this situation, therefore, the insurer was not going to pay.

However, the ECJ held that a refusal to appoint a pregnant woman amounted to direct sex discrimination. It held that any discrimination based on pregnancy or on the consequences of pregnancy (eg the employee's inevitable absence from work on maternity leave) will be direct sex discrimination. This is because only women can become pregnant, and hence the refusal to employ was an action directed specifically at one sex. Even though there were no men who had also applied for the job, the act was discriminatory because it was an act that would only be taken against women.

A further case supported this decision:

Webb v *EMO Air Cargo (UK) Ltd (1994)*

Webb had been recruited specifically to cover the maternity leave of another employee, and then found out that she was also pregnant. As a result she was dismissed – because she was required by the organisation to cover the leave of the other employee, and she was no longer able to do this. The ECJ held that the dismissal of a woman for reasons connected with pregnancy will always amount to direct sex discrimination simply because only women (and not men) can be pregnant. It was also held in this case that the fact that an employee's presence at work at a particular time is essential to the employer's business is not a defence. A woman has an absolute right not to suffer pregnancy discrimination, and this right cannot be dependent upon the particular circumstances of the employer at the time.

The basic principle is that any unfavourable treatment of a female job applicant, existing employee or ex-employee, on the grounds that she is (or was) pregnant or took maternity leave will constitute direct sex discrimination. This principle has the advantage of being absolutely clear, unlike some areas of employment law! Employers who subject an employee who is pregnant or who has taken maternity leave to any form of detriment on grounds that are related in any way to pregnancy, childbirth or maternity leave will be liable for sex discrimination. It is important to bear in mind that, where unfavourable treatment of a pregnant woman is caused by the consequences of her pregnancy (rather than the pregnancy itself), this will also constitute unlawful sex discrimination.

Consequences of pregnancy might, for example, include pregnancy-related illness leading to absence from work, or tiredness at work leading to inferior job performance. It is essential that a pregnant employee is not penalised for reasons of this nature.

It may be helpful for employers to devise guidance notes for managers to highlight their responsibilities towards employees who are pregnant, and also a general guide for pregnant employees to outline their rights and the employer's policy and procedures in respect of pregnancy and maternity leave.

Examples of unfavourable treatment that could constitute sex discrimination during pregnancy or maternity leave (unless there is a different and valid reason for the employer's action) would include:

- excluding a woman from training just because she is pregnant
- denying a woman a promotion because she is about to go on maternity leave (or is currently on maternity leave) and will not be available immediately to take up the position
- moving a pregnant employee to another job to avoid her coming into contact with customers or clients
- carrying out disciplinary proceedings against a pregnant employee when she is unable, owing to an illness resulting from pregnancy, to attend a disciplinary hearing
- denying a woman a full and fair appraisal on grounds of her absence on maternity leave, especially if appraisal is linked to pay and/or promotion opportunities

- failing to consult an employee over proposed redundancies on the grounds that she is absent on maternity leave

- dismissing a pregnant employee on account of time off work for a pregnancy-related illness

- denying the woman the right to occupational sick pay if she is absent from work with a pregnancy-related condition where other employees would have been granted this benefit.

CASE STUDY

An IT company has a fast-moving product range, with an average of 50 new products being introduced each year, and around the same number falling obsolete. Twice a year there is a conference for all the sales representatives when they are informed of new products that are being introduced, and told which products are to be phased out. This conference is the major piece of communication for the sales force.

A female employee announced that she was pregnant, and planned to take six months' leave. She was told that, because of her impending maternity leave, she was not required to attend the next conference. It was explained that she did not need to know the information as when she returned from her maternity leave the range of products would have changed again. Her manager asked her to stay back at the office and carry out a range of administrative tasks.

The employee claimed that this action was sex discrimination. Although some of the information would not be relevant to her immediately, she would need to know about the products on her return. Her manager argued that she would need a full induction on her return, as she could not possibly remember all the product changes when she was not actually working with the products. After a heated discussion, she was allowed to attend the conference. What would have been the implications if this had been refused?

The following case illustrates an example of potentially unfair treatment to a woman who is absent on maternity leave:

Visa International Service Association v Paul (2004)

Paul worked for the organisation as an administrator, although she had expressed an interest in moving into dispute resolution. Prior to her maternity leave she had attended a training course in dispute resolution, and was hoping to make the move in the future. During her maternity leave a vacancy in dispute resolution arose, but she was not informed about the vacancy. When she found out about it, the vacancy had already been filled, and she raised a grievance. Her employer told her that she had been told about the vacancy on a home visit (which she strongly denied) and that she did not have the necessary experience. She resigned and made a series of claims including unfair constructive dismissal and sex discrimination. She won her case. The Tribunal held that she had suffered a detriment due to being on maternity leave, which was sex discrimination, and this had amounted to unfair constructive dismissal.

Risk assessments in relation to pregnancy

Employers should bear in mind the important requirement to conduct risk assessments in relation to pregnancy, and to take action to reduce or eliminate any risks to new or expectant mothers that are identified. It is equally important to note that the duty to conduct such risk assessments arises as soon as a woman of child-bearing age is employed, and not just after an employee has become pregnant. The relationship between carrying out a risk assessment and sex discrimination is illustrated in:

Hardman v Mallon (trading as Orchard Lodge Nursing Home) (2002)

Hardman was a care assistant working in the Nursing Home. When she became pregnant, she discussed with her employer the need for a risk assessment to be carried out, with particular reference to lifting heavy residents. It was not carried out, and then Hardman produced a certificate stating she should avoid heavy lifting. As a result of this, she was offered the job of a cleaner which she refused, because the job was less preferable to her. Hardman made a claim of sex discrimination to the Employment Tribunal. The Employment Tribunal found that there had been no sex discrimination, because a man would have been treated in the same way. However, the EAT overturned this decision because there is no requirement to make a comparison with a real or hypothetical male. Any detrimental treatment that relates to pregnancy is sex discrimination because only women will become pregnant.

TASK

Find out what policies and procedures your organisation, or an organisation with which you are familiar, has for supporting pregnant employees. Are there any aspects of these policies that appear to be discriminatory in any way?

DISCRIMINATION AGAINST PARENTS

Discrimination against parents may occur in certain circumstances if a valid request for flexible working is received and the employer either fails to follow the procedure prescribed for dealing with the request in the Flexible Working (Procedural Requirements) Regulations 2002, or refuses the request without having a valid business reason for doing so.

Under the Flexible Working (Eligibility, Complaints and Remedies) Regulations 2002, employees (but not other workers) who have a child under the age of 6 may submit a formal request for flexible working to their employer. The employer is not under an obligation to agree automatically to such a request, but must follow a prescribed procedure for considering the request seriously (see p. 80).

The Employment Act 2002 introduced protection against unfair dismissal for employees with less than one year's service who request flexible working.

The entitlement to request flexible working extends to any employee (male or female) who is the parent, adoptive parent, foster parent or guardian of a child, or the partner of any of these (including a same-sex partner), provided the employee has a minimum of six months' service. If an employee has a disabled child, a request may be submitted up until the child's 18th birthday. To be valid, the employee's request must be made for the purpose of caring for a child. Requests cannot be made more often than once a year.

Irrespective of the statutory right for employees who are the parents of young children to request flexible working, employers may prefer to extend such a policy to all employees, and not just those who are the parents or carers of children under the age of 6.

The right to request flexible working includes the right for employees to request changes to:

- the number of hours they work
- the times they work – ie days worked and start/finish times
- the place of work – ie the employee may submit a request to do some or all of their work from home.

Requests could, for example, include requests for part-time working, job-sharing, compressed hours, staggered hours, shift working (or removal from shift working), flexitime, tele-working, term-time working, annualised hours, etc.

An employee who wishes to use the statutory procedure for making a request for flexible working must do so in writing (otherwise the request will not be valid). The request should state:

- that it is a request for flexible working for the purpose of caring for a child
- whether the employee has previously submitted any request for flexible working and, if so, when
- the change(s) to working arrangements that the employee is seeking
- the date on which the employee proposes the change(s) should take effect
- the effect (if any) that the employee thinks the change(s) will have on the employer, and how any such effect might be dealt with.

Any request that does not fulfil these criteria will not, technically, be valid. However, if an application for flexible working does not contain all the required information, the employer should not simply reject it but, instead, should inform the employee of the omission(s) and ask them to resubmit the application with all the relevant information.

Irrespective of the legislative requirements governing employees and employers in respect to statutory requests for flexible working, there is nothing to stop an employer from applying a more informal approach to requests to changes in working hours and dealing with requests irrespective of the manner in which they are submitted.

An employer who is in receipt of a statutory request for flexible working is not obliged to agree to it automatically, but must follow a defined statutory procedure. If, however, the employer elects to agree to the employee's request at the outset, the only requirement will be to notify the employee in writing of the changes to their terms of employment and the date on which they are to take effect.

Under the statutory procedure, the employer must:

- hold a meeting with the employee who has made the request within 28 days in order to explore how the request might be made to work (and, if appropriate, seek compromises)
- allow the employee to be accompanied at the meeting by a colleague, if they wish
- provide a written reply to the request within 14 days of the meeting which must, if the request is rejected, explain the specific business grounds for the refusal and why these are relevant to the employee's case
- grant a right of appeal within 14 days if the request is refused, hear the appeal within another 14 days and communicate the outcome within yet another 14 days.

If an employee's request is granted, the change to their pattern of working will be regarded as a permanent change to the terms of their contract (unless expressly agreed otherwise). It follows that the employee will have no automatic right to revert to their previous pattern of working at a future date. Similarly, the employer will not be able to insist that the employee reverts to the previous working arrangements when the child reaches the age of 6.

Despite this rule, there is nothing to stop an employer and employee from agreeing to a trial period in respect of any new working arrangement. A trial period would give both parties a clear insight into the viability of the new arrangement and would allow the employer to see whether it was likely to cause any real problems for the organisation. At the end of the trial period, the employer could decide whether or not to agree to make the arrangement permanent. One advantage of this approach is that, if the request ultimately has to be refused, the employer will have some evidence to back up the assertion that the employee's request was not workable for one of the permitted reasons (see below).

If a trial period is agreed, it will be very important to document clearly that the new working pattern represents a temporary variation to the terms of the employee's contract, and that the employer reserves the right to require the employee to revert to their previous pattern of working at the end of the stated period if, in their view, the new working arrangements have not worked successfully. The start and end date of the trial period should be clearly stated, and the document should be signed by both parties. If a request for flexible working is refused, there must be a specific business reason for the refusal. Valid reasons are contained within the legislation and are as follows:

- burden of additional costs
- detrimental effect on ability to meet customer demand
- detrimental impact on quality or on performance
- inability to reorganise work among existing staff, or recruit additional staff
- insufficiency of work during the periods the employee wishes to work
- planned structural changes
- inability to receive additional staff
- any other grounds the Secretary of State may specify by regulations.

This represents an exhaustive list, and employers are not entitled to invent their own reasons for refusing an employee's request for flexible working, whatever their motives.

According to a major piece of research by CIPD and Lovells (2003) in the first six months from the date of the regulations coming into force, over a quarter of organisations saw an increase in the number of requests for flexible working. 62 per cent of employers have agreed to these requests, either fully or in a modified form of what was originally requested. 72 per cent of employers stated that they were prepared to consider requests from all employees, even if they were not legally entitled to make such a request.

Of those who made the request for flexible working, 44 per cent were clerical workers, 21 per cent were managers, 20 per cent were technical staff and 27 per cent were classed as professionals. The most commonly requested forms of flexibility are part-time work and coming in late/leaving early.

The law is very clear on who is entitled to request flexible working, and the way in which such requests should be considered. However, this is an area of law that can actually have negative impacts on teamworking and diversity within the workforce. The CIPD and Lovells (2003) report refers to some concerns expressed about employees who are not eligible to request flexible working, particularly if they have reasons for wanting flexible working that are not connected with childcare. Some employees might perceive that they are having to work harder, or work the unpopular hours, in order to cover for other colleagues. The Secretary of State for Trade and Industry has hinted that the government might consider extending the rights to flexible working to employees who care for elderly or disabled relatives, although no firm proposals have been made. Clearly any such extension of the right to request flexible working needs to be carefully considered, particularly considering whether such an extension would be manageable within organisations.

TASK

Find out if your organisation, or an organisation with which you are familiar, has developed a policy to deal with requests for flexible working. If it has, read the policy and consider whether it meets the requirements of the legislation. If it has not, try to draft a policy that could be used.

RACE

The Race Relations Act 1976 prohibits discrimination on grounds of:

- colour
- race
- nationality
- ethnic origins
- national origins.

The Race Relations Act 1976 affords equal protection to everyone, whatever their race or racial origins. Although the Act was originally designed to outlaw detrimental treatment of people from ethnic minority groups, it applies equally to all. Thus a white, British employee is protected against race discrimination in the same way as (for example) a black employee of Nigerian nationality.

Like the Sex Discrimination Act 1975, the Race Relations Act 1976 protects individuals from discrimination in:

- all stages of recruitment and selection (see Chapters 6 and 7)
- terms and conditions of employment (see Chapter 8)
- benefits, facilities and services offered to employees (see Chapter 8)
- opportunities for promotion, transfer and training (see Chapter 9)
- dismissal, including redundancy (see Chapter 10)
- post-employment discrimination (see Chapter 10)
- any other detriment.

Certain limited exemptions exist to the general principle that is unlawful to take an individual's race into account when deciding whom to recruit, transfer or promote (or, in certain cases, dismiss). These are explored fully in Chapter 6 under 'Genuine occupational requirements and qualifications'.

The distinction between 'nationality' and 'national origins' can sometimes be blurred. 'Nationality' includes citizenship, and is a legal concept that a person can change after birth. A person may even choose to have dual nationality. A person's 'national origins', on the other hand, subsist at birth and depend largely on the person's ancestry. For example, a British citizen may have Polish national origins if their parents (or even grandparents) emigrated from Poland to Britain. Another guideline comes from the House of Lords, which ruled many years ago, before the Race Relations Act was enacted (in Ealing London Borough Council v Race Relations Board [1972]) that national origins meant 'nation' in the broad sense of race and not in the legal sense of citizenship.

In a more recent case, the definition of national origin was defined more clearly:

BBC Scotland v Souster [2001]

Souster was a presenter of the programme, *Rugby Special*, for BBC Scotland. He had been employed on a succession of contracts. In November 1997, it was decided not to renew his contract, and the role of presenter was given to a Scottish woman. Souster claimed that he had been discriminated against because his national origin was English and not Scottish, and BBC Scotland wanted a presenter of Scottish national origin. It was held that for the purposes of the Race Relations Act 1976, the Scots and the English are separate racial groups by reference to their national origins. The Scottish Court of Session upheld the principle that the English, Scots, Welsh and Northern Irish are all British in nationality because they are citizens of the United Kingdom, but ruled that national origins is a separate concept from that of nationality, involving such issues as history and geographical separation. Since Scotland and England were once separate nations, it was clear to the Court that the Scots and the English are distinct groups in terms of national origins. This decision means in effect that it is just as unlawful to refuse (for example) to appoint someone because they are Scottish (or English, as the case may be) as it would be to refuse to appoint someone because they are black.

'Ethnic origins' is not defined in the Race Relations Act 1976 but has been interpreted by courts and tribunals as meaning 'a group with certain defined characteristics'. This was demonstrated in the case of:

Mandla & anor v Lee & ors (1983)

Mandla and his son were Sikhs. The son was refused a place at an independent school in Birmingham because he insisted on wearing his turban. The headteacher determined that this contravened the rules on school uniform. The Court of Appeal determined that Sikhs were not a group defined by their ethnic origin, and hence dismissed the appeal against the headteacher's decision. However, the House of Lords held that for a group to be of separate ethnic origins, it has to have the following characteristics:

- a long-shared history, distinguishable from other groups, the memory of which it keeps alive

- a cultural tradition of its own, including family and social customs and manners, often but not necessarily associated with the group's religious observance.

Over and above these essential characteristics, there might be other characteristics which, although not essential, may be relevant to the question of whether a particular group is of separate ethnic origins when compared with the surrounding community. These further characteristics are:

- a common geographical origin or descent from a small number of common ancestors

- a common language (which need not be peculiar to the group)

- a common literature peculiar to the group

- a common religion different from that of other neighbouring groups or from the general community surrounding it

- being a minority or oppressed group, or being a dominant group within a larger community.

It concluded that Sikhs did have these characteristics and hence Sikh is an ethnic origin.

It has been established that, for the purposes of the Race Relations Act 1976, Sikhs, Jews and Gypsies (ie genuine Romany people) are groups of separate ethnic origins. Sikhs and Jews are also protected against discrimination under the Employment Equality (Religion or Belief) Regulations 2003.

In contrast, Muslims are not, in law, deemed to be a group with separate ethnic origins (although Muslims are of course protected by the Religion or Belief Regulations).

As well as affording protection to employees against discriminatory treatment on grounds of their race, the Race Relations Act 1976 also affords protection to individuals treated unfavourably on grounds related to another person's race.

Showboat Entertainment Centre Ltd v Owens (1984)

Owens was a white, male manager of an amusement arcade. He was dismissed for refusing to obey the instruction to refuse admission to young blacks. The EAT expressly held that, to succeed in a claim for race discrimination, the complainant only had to show that the detrimental treatment they had suffered was based broadly on racial grounds, and such grounds could apply to either their own racial characteristics or to the racial characteristics of another person. On this basis, Owens had been subjected to unlawful racial discrimination.

This approach is confirmed in the case of Weathersfield Ltd t/a Van & Truck Rentals v Sargent:

Weathersfield Ltd t/a Van & Truck Rentals v Sargent (1999)

Sargent was recruited by the organisation to work as a receptionist in the car and van rental business. During her induction on the first day, she was told that the company had a policy of avoiding rentals to blacks and Asians. She was told that she would normally be able to tell over the telephone if an enquiry was from a person of such a race and, if so, she was to tell the caller that no vehicles were available. She was so upset and shocked by this instruction that she resigned. The Court of Appeal held that giving an employee instructions to carry out a racially discriminatory policy or practice will amount to discrimination on racial grounds irrespective of the racial group of the person given the instruction. The Court also commented that this type of instruction will place the person in an 'outrageous and embarrassing position'. As a result of this case, employers should be aware that any company policy or procedure that in any way requires employees to carry out racially discriminatory practices may result in claims of direct race discrimination from an employee who is expected to comply with the policy or procedure against their will. It is also likely that such instructions would give an employee with one year's service (or more) grounds to resign and claim constructive dismissal.

The RRA 1976 contains a provision that specifically makes it unlawful to segregate persons on racial grounds. Thus, any practice of keeping employees of a particular racial group apart from those of another racial group will amount to unlawful race discrimination, no matter what the motive behind it might be.

The Race Relations Amendment Act 2000, which was brought into force in April 2001, imposes a duty on all public authorities to eliminate race discrimination and positively promote racial equality in the exercise of their public functions. Although most of the Act does not relate specifically to employment, the Act and the accompanying RRA 1976 (Statutory Duties) Order 2001 impose on public-sector employers a duty to prepare and publish a 'race equality scheme' – ie a document setting out the organisation's processes for fulfilling their general and specific duties under the Act and the Order.

The Act also imposes certain duties on public-sector employers to have systems in place to monitor the ethnic balance of staff, job applicants and applicants for training and promotion.

Furthermore, where a public authority employer has 150 or more full-time staff (or the equivalent number, taking into account any part-timers), there is a duty to monitor the number of staff (in terms of ethnic background) who receive training, benefit or suffer detriment as a result of performance assessment, raise formal grievances, are the subject of disciplinary action, and leave employment.

Although the duty to monitor means simply collecting information, under the general duty to promote racial equality, public authorities would then be under a duty to use this information to investigate and resolve any possible unfairness of treatment or discrimination on racial grounds.

The effect of EU law on the RRA 1976

The RRA 1976 prohibits direct and indirect discrimination, victimisation and harassment if the treatment of the individual is on grounds of colour, race, nationality, ethnic origins or national origins. However, the Act was amended in July 2003 by dint of the RRA (Amendment) Regulations 2003 to bring it into line with the EU Race Directive. Since then, the definition of indirect discrimination and the interpretation of what constitutes harassment differ slightly depending on the sub-heading under which a claim for discrimination is brought.

This rather unsatisfactory state of affairs has come about because of the way in which the UK government chose to implement the EU Race Directive. While the UK's RRA 1976 covered discrimination on grounds of colour, race, nationality, and ethnic and national origins, the EU Directive only required protection from discrimination on grounds of race, and ethnic and national origins. The UK government implemented the Directive by means of Regulations, rather than by primary legislation, with the result that only the measures contained in the Directive could be implemented (and not any wider or additional measures).

The position now is therefore as follows:

- Discrimination on grounds of race, ethnic origins and national origins is governed by EU law.
- Discrimination on grounds of colour or nationality is not governed by EU law.
- Depending upon which grounds a claim for discrimination is founded on, the definition of indirect discrimination, the circumstances in which indirect discrimination can be justified and the interpretation of what constitutes harassment will be different. The EU Race Directive imposed a new statutory definition of indirect discrimination, and also made harassment a distinct form of unlawful discrimination.

CASE STUDY

Teamwork had been poor in a fast-food restaurant for a while. The Manager asked the Supervisors why they thought this was, and they replied that the main reason was that the employees did not mix during their breaks. Indeed, the employees were from a number of different ethnic backgrounds and in their breaks they spoke to each other in their native languages. This prevented relationships being built.

The management decided, therefore, to ban the speaking of any language apart from English while on the company premises, and informed employees accordingly. The decision caused uproar – with employees of a non-UK ethnic origin claiming that the decision was race discrimination.

The manager was concerned about the negative reaction, and removed the ban. However, teamwork continued to be poor and there seemed to be no clear way to make any improvements. Were the manager's actions race discrimination?

RELIGION OR BELIEF

In December 2003, the Employment Equality (Religion or Belief) Regulations 2003 were brought into force in order to implement the EU Framework Directive for Equal Treatment. The Regulations provide that unfavourable treatment on grounds of an individual's religion or belief during recruitment, employment, at termination of employment and post-employment will be unlawful. The Regulations prohibit direct discrimination, indirect discrimination, victimisation and harassment, which is defined as a distinct form of discrimination.

The Regulations define 'religion or belief' as 'any religion, religious belief or similar philosophical belief'. This definition is wide enough to cover fringe or cult religions, and a range of other philosophical beliefs. For example, someone who was an animal rights activist might be able to argue successfully that their beliefs fell within the definition. Political belief is, however, not included within the scope of the definition, unless the belief in question is similar to a religious belief. The distinction between a religious belief and a political belief is not always clear, however, as there can be a cross-over between politics and religion. For instance, the Islamic Party of Britain, Communism, National Socialism (Nazism) and Pacifism could all be said to be belief systems that affect an individual's view of the world, with the result that members of any of these groups would be protected against discriminatory treatment.

At the time of writing, there has only been one case reported where a tribunal has had to rule on whether something amounts to a belief:

Williams v South Central Ltd (2004)

Williams wore an American flag patch on his uniform and claimed he was constantly abused at work because of this. He claimed that he was eventually dismissed because he stood up for his belief as an American citizen. The tribunal held that loyalty to a nation's flag, or loyalty to one's native country, is not classed as a belief under the Regulations.

What is inconveniently unclear from the wording of the Regulations is whether an employee who is discriminated against because they do not have any religious beliefs would be protected. Ultimately, this will remain unclear until an EAT or higher court makes a decision on this specific point.

The Guidance Notes of the Department of Trade and Industry (DTI) on the Regulations (which are not legally binding) state that courts and tribunals may consider a number of factors when deciding whether an individual's beliefs fall within the scope of the Regulations. As examples, they cite collective worship, a clear belief system and a profound belief affecting one's way of life or view of the world. However, there is no requirement for a religion or belief to have a minimum number of followers for it to qualify as a religion under the Regulations.

Protection is also available under the Regulations to employees who are treated unfavourably on account of a perception that they are of a particular religion or hold certain religious beliefs, whether or not that perception is accurate. For example, harassment of an employee based on an incorrect assumption that they were Muslim could give rise to a legitimate claim for unlawful discrimination. Furthermore, if an employee is treated unfavourably in any way (for example, being taunted or teased) because they associate with someone of a particular religion (for example, if their partner is Catholic), or because they refuse to carry out an instruction to discriminate against, say, Muslims, that will constitute unlawful treatment.

The Religion or Belief Regulations also contain two 'genuine occupational requirements' (GORs) that are relevant to decisions to recruit, transfer, promote or dismiss an employee on grounds of their religion or belief in certain narrowly defined circumstances. The first GOR relates to the situation where a particular religion or belief is a genuine and determining requirement for the post in question, while the second may apply where the employment is in an organisation with an ethos based on a particular religion or belief, such as a church or religious school. These issues are dealt with in Chapter 6 under 'Genuine occupational requirements and qualifications'.

Practical issues associated with employees' religious beliefs

This strand of discrimination law gives rise to particular difficulties, in that the majority of employers will have little knowledge of different religions and the beliefs and practices of their followers.

In order to promote equality of opportunity among employees of different religions, and avoid unlawful discrimination, employers should:

- review all their policies and procedures to ensure that none of their provisions could place employees of a particular religion or belief at a disadvantage
- consult employees and ask them what their needs are with respect to religion and belief or (where appropriate) set up an employee body to advise on religion and belief so that employees' needs can be identified and accommodated where possible
- review any dress codes, rules on dress and appearance or staff uniform requirements, and ensure that these allow for modes of dress that are linked to religious beliefs wherever possible
- review policies on time off and holidays to ensure these are sufficiently flexible to allow employees of different faiths to be granted time off on days or dates that are significant to them on grounds of their religion or belief
- check that anti-harassment policies and procedures cover harassment on grounds of religion or belief, and ensure that these provisions are drawn to the attention of all staff
- train managers on how to deal with workplace issues that may arise as a result of employees' religious beliefs.

Some employers will inevitably be faced with the challenge of how to resolve conflicting legal rights. An individual's religion or belief may lead to discrimination against other people on grounds of:

- gender
- sexual orientation
- race
- disability.

The issue of conflicting rights is not dealt with directly in the legislation, but what is certain is that, if a clash of rights should arise relating to an individual's religious beliefs, the employer would need to handle the matter very carefully and with great sensitivity. For example, if a male employee refused to follow instructions from a female supervisor because his religious beliefs involved a strong view that women are inferior, the employer would face the rather daunting task of having to try to reconcile the situation without discriminating unlawfully against either employee. Doing nothing would constitute sex discrimination against the female supervisor, as she would be able to claim that her employer's failure to support her occurred because she was a woman. To reprimand the religious employee for his refusal to follow his supervisor's instructions might give rise to a claim for religious discrimination.

Another example could be if an employee who, on account of religious beliefs, held strongly censorious views about homosexuality and persisted in imposing his views on a gay colleague to the extent that the colleague found the behaviour offensive. Again, if the employer did nothing to protect the gay employee, this could lead to a claim for sexual orientation harassment, whiles instructing the religious employee to desist from his behaviour might lead to a claim for religious discrimination (or even an argument that the individual's human rights had been breached under the right to freedom of thought, conscience and religion).

Employers may take some heart in the general principle that to apply a requirement to an employee to follow reasonable instructions, or to require them not to harass a colleague, would normally be viewed as appropriate where the purpose of the instruction was clearly to promote equality and prevent the employee from breaking the law. In the second example, the instruction to the religious employee would not, arguably, be on the grounds of their religion or belief, but rather on the grounds that all employees are required to adhere to the employer's equal opportunities policy and/or anti-harassment policy. Even if the employer's actions were deemed to be indirectly discriminatory on grounds of religion, the employer would be able to show that such actions were proportionate to the achievement of a legitimate aim, and thus not unlawful. It is well established in both domestic and EU law that employees have the right to work in an environment in which equality and dignity are respected, and this right is unlikely to be overridden by the religious interests of individual employees.

A useful source of information about Britain's main religions is available in ACAS's *Guidance on Religion or Belief and the Workplace (Appendix 2)*, available on the ACAS website: www.acas.org.uk. Other useful sources are:

http//www.bbc.co.uk/religion
http://www.bbc.co.uk/worldservice/people/features/world_religions/index.shtml.

TASK

At the time of writing, there have been no notable cases brought under legislation relating to religion/belief. During your studies, be aware of any cases that are reported and try to understand the allegations and the reasoning behind the judgement that was made.

In Northern Ireland there is specific legislation relating to discrimination on the grounds of religious belief. The Fair Employment (Northern Ireland) Act 1976 made direct discrimination on the grounds of religious belief or political opinion unlawful in employment. The Fair Employment (Northern Ireland) Act 1989 extended that legislation to outlaw indirect discrimination, and provided for the use of affirmative action to secure fair participation in employment. The provisions of the Employment Equality (Religion and Belief) Regulations 2003 also apply in Northern Ireland.

KEY POINTS FROM THIS CHAPTER

- Sex discrimination against both men and women is prohibited by the SDA 1975, which bans gender discrimination in recruitment, employment and termination of employment, and by the Equal Pay Act 1970, which covers pay and all other terms of employees' contracts of employment.

- The SDA 1975 (as amended) provides that it is discriminatory and unlawful to treat an employee or job applicant unfavourably on the grounds that they intend to undergo, are in the process of undergoing, or have undergone, a sex change.

- The Employment Equality (Sexual Orientation) Regulations 2003 protect gay and lesbian people, bisexual people and heterosexuals against any form of detrimental treatment on grounds of their actual or perceived sexual orientation.

- The SDA 1975 states that married employees (of either sex) must not be treated less favourably than unmarried employees on grounds of their marital status.

- Any unfavourable treatment of a female job applicant, existing employee or ex-employee on the grounds that she is (or was) pregnant or took maternity leave will constitute direct sex discrimination.

- Discrimination against parents may occur if a valid request for flexible working is received and the employer either fails to follow the procedure prescribed for dealing with the request or refuses the request without having a valid business reason for doing so.

- The RRA 1976 prohibits discrimination in recruitment, employment and termination of employment on grounds of colour, race, nationality, ethnic origins and national origins.

- The Employment Equality (Religion or Belief) Regulations 2003 provide that unfavourable treatment on grounds of an individual's actual or perceived religion or belief during recruitment or employment, at termination of employment and post-employment will be unlawful.

EXAMPLES TO WORK THROUGH

1   Mary has informed her manager that she is pregnant. She has requested to move on to part-time hours immediately, and also to move away from the warehouse where she

currently works because of the fumes from delivery vehicles. Her line manager does not believe that the fumes are any real danger to the pregnancy, and does not want to reduce Mary's hours. What would you advise?

2   One of your employees has recently converted to Buddhism. He is very passionate about his new beliefs, and is constantly trying to persuade colleagues to come with him to meetings. The colleagues are complaining about this – and have asked for him to be moved to another section. He does not want to move. What would you advise?

3   In the packing department there are 20 employees. Twelve of these employees are women, 8 of whom are mothers of pre-school children. All eight mothers have requested to reduce their hours of work. Within the requirements of the legislation there is no reason to refuse the requests, but you have received representations from the other employees saying that allowing these eight employees flexibility is unfair. How would you proceed?

Grounds for Discrimination (2)

CHAPTER 5

OBJECTIVES OF THIS CHAPTER:

- to further evaluate the grounds on which discrimination is prohibited
- to consider practical issues associated with discrimination issues
- to understand the key issues relating to part-time and fixed-term contracts
- to consider the issues associated with disability discrimination
- to examine the issues associated with forthcoming legislation relating to age discrimination.

DISCRIMINATION AGAINST PART-TIMERS

A part-time worker is someone who works fewer hours per week or month than the organisation's standard full-time hours. Interestingly, there is no legal definition of full-time working or full-time hours, and each employer is therefore entitled to make their own decision as to the number of hours per week that they regard as full-time hours.

Part-time employees have the same statutory employment rights as full-time employees, irrespective of the number of hours they work. Thus, for example, an employee who worked two days a week would have the same entitlement as a full-time employee (on a pro-rata basis) to statutory paid annual leave under the Working Time Regulations 1998, and the same entitlement to take maternity or paternity leave under the Employment Rights Act 1996. Where, in order to qualify for a particular statutory right, an employee must have a defined minimum length of service, the same length of service is required of a part-timer. Thus, the part-timer who works two days per week would need to have gained six months' continuous service in order to qualify for additional maternity leave, as is the case for a full-time employee.

When the Part-Time Workers (Prevention of Less Favourable Treatment) Regulations 2000 were implemented in July 2000, part-timers gained the right to equality of treatment in relation to contractual terms and also non-contractual benefits. The Regulations provide that employers must not treat their part-time workers less favourably than comparable full-timers just because they work part-time, unless there is an objective reason justifying different treatment in the particular case. It is important to note that the Part-Time Workers Regulations apply to all workers, and not just to employees engaged directly by the organisation.

The 'comparator' in the context of part-time working is a full-time worker engaged by the same employer and performing the same or broadly similar work on the same type of contract. Comparisons may not be made on a hypothetical basis, unlike comparisons for the purposes of sex, sexual orientation, race or religious discrimination legislation. It is important to note, however, that no distinction is made in this context between work on a permanent contract and work on a fixed-term contract – ie a part-time employee working on a fixed-term contract could compare their treatment with either a full-time employee working on a permanent contract, or a full-time employee engaged on a fixed-term contract. If, however, the part-timer was working for the employer via a contract with an employment agency, the person would be unable to compare their treatment with a full-time employee engaged directly by the employer.

One further criterion: if there is a full-time person working at the same establishment, they must be the comparator (but the comparator can be someone working at a different establishment if there is no full-time comparator at the same establishment).

The Part-Time Workers (Prevention of Less Favourable Treatment) Regulations 2000 cover:

- rates of pay (ie a part-time employee must not be paid at an hourly rate that is less than the rate payable to a full-time employee performing the same or similar work just because the person works part-time)
- premium overtime rates (but these need only be paid once the part-timer has exceeded the employer's standard full-time hours)
- contractual holiday entitlement, including entitlement to paid public holidays
- contractual sick pay (ie equal access to occupational sick pay and equivalent rates of sick pay)
- contractual maternity, paternity, adoption and parental leave schemes (equal access to and benefits under any contractual scheme that offers benefits in excess of the statutory minimum)
- access to and benefits from an occupational pension scheme (unless different treatment can be justified on objective grounds)
- access to career breaks unless the exclusion of part-timers can be objectively justified on grounds other than their part-time status
- part-time workers are entitled under the Part-Time Workers Regulations to request a written statement giving the reason(s) for any treatment that they believe is in breach of their rights under the Regulations. If such a request is received, the employer must provide the employee with a written statement within 21 days, giving particulars of the reason(s) for the treatment.

There is no right contained in the Part-Time Workers Regulations for an employee to be permitted to work part-time. However, as noted in the Chapter 4, parents of children aged 6 years or under, or of a disabled child aged under 18 years, may request flexible working.

Under the Part-Time Workers Regulations 2000, where a switch from full-time to part-time working is agreed, the employee will have the right to terms and conditions under the new part-time contract that are no less favourable (on a pro-rata basis) than those that were applicable as part of the previous full-time contract. This means, for example, that it is not open to an employer to agree to an employee's request to move to part-time working on condition that the employee accepts a lower rate of pay.

If the switch to part-time working is accompanied by a requirement that is particularly difficult for one gender to comply with, then there is a possibility that the requirement will be indirect sex discrimination. This is demonstrated in the following case:

Chief Constable of Avon & Somerset Constabulary v *Chew (2001)*

In this case a female police officer succeeded in a claim for indirect sex discrimination when her employer insisted that she should work shift rosters in order to be entitled to work part-time. The employee, who had two pre-school-age children, had recently separated from her husband and wished to work part-time on day shifts only.

The Employment Appeal Tribunal (EAT) reviewed the well-established principle that a requirement to work shifts or unsocial hours will have a disproportionately adverse impact on women as compared with men. The issue was not whether the police force could justify shift working in a general sense, but rather whether it was justifiable for them to apply the requirement to work shifts to the police officer in question under all the relevant circumstances. The evidence suggested that, at the relevant time, other posts involving regular day shift working were available. The EAT thus held that the police force's insistence that the police officer must work the shift patterns in order to be granted part-time working was not justifiable.

CASE STUDY

A bank decided to run a series of training seminars on new products and services that had been developed over the recent year. The seminars would run from 8.30am-9.30am every Thursday. On these days the bank would not open until 9.30am, and a notice was put in the window informing customers that staff training would be taking place.

A few months later, one employee was found to be still selling products to customers that were due to be phased out in the next three months. The employee was asked to attend a disciplinary meeting to discuss this – because the customers had had to be compensated by the bank for the incorrect selling that had taken place.

At the meeting, the employee was asked why she had not been promoting the new products as explained in the training seminars. She did not know what was being talked about. It transpired that no-one had realised that she had missed all the training seminars because she worked part-time and did not start work until 10.30am each day. The disciplinary action was withdrawn and the appropriate training was arranged.

In this case, there was no deliberate discrimination occurring, but it is interesting to note how easily it can occur if the range of employees in the workforce is not considered fully.

DISCRIMINATION AGAINST FIXED-TERM EMPLOYEES

On 1 October 2002, the Government implemented the Fixed-Term Employees (Prevention of Less Favourable Treatment) Regulations 2002. As well as giving general protection to those on fixed-term contracts, the Regulations attempt to stop employers using fixed-term contracts to ensure that employees never accrue any statutory rights. This is demonstrated in the following case:

Booth v United States of America (1999)

Booth and two others worked at a USAF airbase in the UK. They were employed on a series of fixed-term contracts, each one ending in a short break of employment before a further contract was issued. After each break in employment, the employees returned to exactly the same job using the same tools and equipment. However, the breaks in employment meant that they never accrued sufficient continuity of service to claim statutory rights (eg one year's continuous service in order to take a claim of unfair dismissal). The EAT ruled that they were unable to show evidence of continuity of service, because of the breaks in service. The actions, at the time, were lawful even though they seemed unfair.

In terms of the principle of non-discrimination, the Fixed-Term Employees Regulations largely mirror the Part-Time Workers Regulations, but with one key difference. As is clear from the titles of the two sets of Regulations, the Part-Time Workers Regulations protect all workers (and not only employees) against discriminatory treatment, while the Fixed-Term Employees Regulations apply only to employees – ie those engaged directly by the employer on a contract of employment. The Fixed-Term Employees Regulations do not extend to cover temporary staff engaged via a contract with an employment agency.

A fixed-term contract is defined in the Regulations as a contract that is set up to:

- last for a specified period – ie the contract has a predetermined termination date, or
- continue until a particular task or project is complete, or
- continue until the occurrence (or non-occurrence) of a specified event – for example, the non-renewal of funding upon which the post is dependent.

Thus, a wide range of different employment 'arrangements' will fall within the definition of fixed-term work, including, for example, summer seasonal work, employment to cover absence on maternity, adoption, paternity or parental leave, extra cover for peak periods, and contracts to carry out a specific task such as setting up a new database or even running a series of training courses.

Under the Fixed-Term Employees Regulations, employees engaged on fixed-term contracts must not be treated less favourably than comparable permanent employees, unless there is an objective reason for the different treatment of fixed-term staff, or there is some other reason that provides objective justification for less favourable treatment of the individual. Protection against discrimination covers all terms and conditions of employment, including pay and pension benefits, and also general treatment at work. Thus, non-contractual benefits such as access to promotion, training and appraisal are covered.

In order to found a claim, a fixed-term employee has to compare their treatment with that of a permanent employee who is performing the same or similar work and is working or based at the same establishment. In the event that there is no equivalent permanent employee at the same establishment, then the fixed-term employee can draw a comparison with a permanent employee performing similar work at another of the employer's workplaces. Comparisons may not be made on a hypothetical basis, unlike comparisons for the purposes of sex, sexual orientation, race or religious discrimination legislation.

The comparison to be made is, however, not a term-by-term balancing act (as is required in a claim for equal pay under the Equal Pay Act 1970), but rather a 'whole package' comparison. Thus, an employer may justify treating a fixed-term employee less favourably in relation to one specific benefit, provided that the package as a whole is no less favourable than that of a permanent employee engaged to perform similar work. For example, an employer may legitimately decide not to allocate a company car to an employee engaged for a three-month fixed term, even though a permanent employee performing the same work is allocated a car, so long as the lack of a car is offset by, for example, a higher rate of pay.

Fixed-term employees, like their permanent equivalents, are entitled under the Working Time Regulations 1998 to a minimum of four weeks' paid leave each year. If, however, a fixed-term employee works for less than a year, then the annual entitlement should be pro-rated accordingly. It is permissible, where an employee (permanent or fixed-term) leaves their employment part-way through a holiday year, for the employer to pay them for any holiday leave that they have accrued but not taken. Thus, where a fixed-term contract is set up to last, for example, six months (creating a statutory holiday entitlement of two weeks), the employee could be required to work through the six months without taking any holiday leave and then be paid for the two weeks upon termination of the contract (assuming the contract is not extended or renewed).

Under the Fixed-Term Employees Regulations, employers are obliged to inform fixed-term employees of any suitable permanent vacancies that arise within the organisation. The Regulations further stipulate that fixed-term employees must be given the same opportunity to apply for promotion, transfer and training as comparable permanent employees with the same length of service.

As well as implementing the non-discrimination principle in relation to employees engaged on fixed-term contracts, the Fixed-Term Employees Regulations introduced a restriction on the renewal of fixed-term contracts in the form of a cut-off date after four years' continuity of service.

This means that, once a fixed-term employee has gained four or more years' continuous service and has had their contract renewed at least once, they are automatically entitled to have their contract converted to permanent status, unless the employer can justify continuing the employment on a fixed-term basis. Two examples demonstrate how this works in practice:

1 Employee A is engaged on a fixed-term contract for three years. The contract is then extended for another two years (without a break). At the four-year point, employee A will be entitled to have the contract converted to a permanent contract, because there has already been a renewal.
2 Employee B is engaged on a fixed-term contract for a period of five years. At the four-year point, nothing will happen because there has been no renewal of the contract. However, if the contract is renewed or extended upon completion of the five years, the new contract will have to be a permanent contract.

As can be seen from the second of the two examples above, the four-year provision does not affect the initial length of a fixed-term contract, which can be any length that is agreed between the employer and the employee.

An important point to note in relation to the four-year restriction is that it was not made retrospective. Specifically, any service on a fixed-term contract before 10 July 2002 (the date by which the Fixed-Term Employees Regulations should have been implemented) will not count towards the four-year cut-off. In effect therefore, this provision will not take effect until 10 July 2006.

Prior to the implementation of the Fixed-Term Employees Regulations, it was permissible for an employer who engaged someone on a fixed-term contract for two years or more to include a waiver clause in the contract for the purpose of excluding the employee's entitlement to statutory redundancy pay on termination. This provision was abolished by the Regulations, but not retrospectively. Thus, any properly agreed waiver clause entered into prior to the date the Regulations were implemented (1 October 2002) will remain valid until the date the fixed-term contract expires. The waiver clause will not, however, be able to be included in any extension or renewal to the contract.

Fixed-term employees are entitled under the Fixed-Term Employees Regulations to request a written statement giving the reason(s) for any treatment that they believe is in breach of their rights under the Regulations. If such a request is received, the employer must provide the employee with a written statement within 21 days, giving particulars of the reason(s) for the treatment.

The expiry of a fixed-term contract without renewal is, rather curiously, regarded as a dismissal in UK law. This is despite the fact that the employer and employee will have agreed at the outset that the contract will terminate on a particular date or on a particular occasion. The dismissal will be by reason of redundancy, or possibly on grounds of 'some other substantial reason' (SOSR) (as defined by Section 98 of the Employment Rights Act 1996).

It is important to remember that, where an individual is employed on a series of separate, but continuous, fixed-term contracts, they will gain the same service-related employment rights as someone engaged on a normal open-ended contract. Such rights will include the right to claim unfair dismissal after one year's continuous service, and the right to be paid statutory redundancy pay after two years' continuous service.

Normally, the dismissal because of the expiry of a fixed-term contract will be fair in law, but in certain circumstances an employment tribunal may take the opposite view – for example, if:

■ the employer recruits a replacement for the fixed-term employee shortly after the expiry of the contract (suggesting that the reason for the fixed-term employee's dismissal was not in fact the expiry of the contract, but in reality some other reason) – and matters could be even worse if the replacement employee were of the opposite sex or a different race

■ there was another job into which the fixed-term employee could have been transferred on the expiry of their contract, but the employer did not discuss this opportunity with the fixed-term employee to establish whether such a transfer would have been of interest to them

■ the employer in some other way acted unreasonably in terminating the fixed-term employee's contract.

To ensure fairness in termination, therefore, the employer should first review (in consultation with the fixed-term employee) whether the employee can be offered alternative work (whether permanent or fixed-term). If no alternative work is available, the employer should still be certain that the real reason for the proposed dismissal of the fixed-term employee is (for example) that the term has expired, the work is complete or the person whom the fixed-term employee replaced has returned to work.

TRADE UNION MEMBERSHIP

In accordance with the Trade Union and Labour Relations (Consolidation) Act 1992 employers must not refuse employment to an applicant because:

- they are or are not a member of a trade union
- they refuse to accept a requirement that they become a member of a trade union
- they cease to become a member of a trade union
- they refuse to make payments to the trade union if they fail to join.

As a result of this legislation, the old style 'closed shop' – where all employees had to join a trade union in certain organisations or departments – is no longer lawful. According to the legislation, refusing employment on trade union grounds covers the following:

- refusing to consider a job application or enquiry
- asking the applicant to withdraw an application
- refusing to offer employment
- making an offer of employment that includes terms that no reasonable employee would agree to, thereby making it difficult or impossible for the person to accept the employment offer
- withdrawing an offer of employment that has been made, or causing the applicant to withdraw acceptance or to refuse the offer
- including a requirement that goes against the four points listed at the start of this section.

The following case gives an example of unlawfully refusing employment on the grounds of trade union membership:

> ### Harrison v Kent County Council (1995)
>
> Harrison worked for Kent County Council as a social worker. He was a trade union member with a reputation for being a strong and forthright negotiator. For family reasons, he resigned from the Council but later reapplied for his job. The Council refused his application for re-employment because of his 'confrontational and anti-management approach'. The Employment Tribunal held that this was a fair refusal because it related to Harrison's actions rather than his trade union membership. However, the EAT overturned that decision, stating that the actions and the membership could not be separated, and hence this was a refusal on the grounds of trade union membership and was unlawful.

The Trade Union and Labour Relations (Consolidation) Act 1992 further provides that employees must not suffer any detriment by an act of the employer if the act relates to:

- preventing or deterring them from becoming a member of an independent trade union or penalising them for doing so
- preventing or deterring them from taking part in the activities of an independent trade union, or penalising them for doing so
- compelling them to become a member of a trade union.

The Act also states that dismissal of an employee will be unfair if it relates to any of the following reasons:

- The employee was, or proposed to become, a member of an independent trade union.
- The employee had taken part, or proposed to take part, in the activities of an independent trade union.
- The employee was not a member of a trade union, and had refused to become a member.

The following two cases illustrate these points:

British Airways Engine Overhaul Ltd v Francis (1981)

Francis, a trade union shop steward, made a statement to the press criticising her trade union for taking too long to process a complaint relating to equal pay from her members. She made the comment in her lunch break. She received a formal warning from her employer when the article was published, because it did not allow unauthorised statements to the press. Although the criticism was about the trade union, the employer argued that it came about after an informal meeting of the members, and was too remote from her union duties to be classed as trade union activity. However, the Tribunal found that the statement was linked to trade union activity and hence the warning was unfair because it was a detriment related to such activity.

Port of London Authority v Payne and others (1992)

The Port of London Authority announced a redundancy as well as derecognising the TGWU trade union. Following the selection for redundancy, 17 shop stewards were identified as redundant. They claimed that they had been selected because of their trade union activities, particularly their involvement in a campaign by the TGWU to restore negotiating rights, and hence their dismissal was unfair. The Tribunal and the EAT supported this claim, and found that the shop stewards had been unfairly dismissed.

The legislation, and the cases quoted, clearly show that any detrimental actions, including dismissal, against a trade union member that is related to their trade union membership is unlawful discrimination.

DISABILITY

Disability discrimination became unlawful as a result of the Disability Discrimination Act (DDA) 1995. Initially it did not apply to organisations with fewer than 20 (later reduced to 15) employees. However, that exemption was removed by the Disability Discrimination Act 1995 (Amendment) Regulations 2003 that became law in the UK on 1 October 2004.

The key provisions of the DDA 1995 are that employers:

- should not, for a reason that relates to an individual's disability, treat that person less favourably than they treat or would treat others to whom the reason does not or would not apply
- should make reasonable adjustments to working arrangements, working practices and premises in order to accommodate the individual needs of disabled workers.

The DDA 1995 defines a disabled person as one who:

> **" has a physical or mental impairment which has a substantial and long-term adverse effect on his ability to carry out normal day-to-day activities. "**

This definition is very broad, and employers should note the following points:

- The Act covers both physical and mental impairments.
- 'Long-term' is defined as 12 months or more – ie an individual who has been disabled for at least 12 months, or whose condition is reasonably expected to last 12 months or more, is protected by the Act. Thus, someone who becomes disabled suddenly (for example, as a result of an accident) would fall within the ambit of the Act immediately. It should also be noted that any individual with a terminal illness is covered by this definition, despite the anticipated remaining length of life.
- 'Normal day-to-day activities' means 'life' activities and not the duties of the individual's job. Thus, the question as to whether an employee's impairment amounts to a disability will depend on the extent to which it affects the sorts of activities that most people carry out fairly regularly and frequently as part of their day-to-day lives. For example, lifting heavy weights is not a normal activity for most people in their everyday lives, and so the fact that a particular individual cannot lift heavy weights as part of their job does not qualify them as a disabled person in law. A 'normal' day-to-day activity might be to lift and carry a bag of shopping, or lift and carry a small pile of books or files. Equally, highly specialised activities such as playing a musical instrument to a professional standard or running three miles to the office would not be classed as normal day-to-day activities.

Quinlan v B&Q plc (1998)

This case illustrates this last point. As a result of open heart surgery, Quinlan was unable to lift heavy loads. In his job as a general assistant in the garden centre, he needed to lift heavy loads, and he was dismissed because he was no longer able to carry out his duties. The EAT and the Employment Tribunal both concluded that he was not suffering from a disability because he was still able to carry smaller loads, even if he was not able to carry the loads required in his job.

This ruling contrasts with the ruling in the next case. Here an employee was able (as in the Quinlan case) to carry out most normal day-to-day activities, but was unable to carry out normal duties at work. Despite this, however, he succeeded in establishing that he was a disabled person in law.

Cruickshank v Vaw Motorcast Ltd (2001)

Cruickshank developed work-related asthma and, as a result, was moved to the job of a fork-lift truck driver. His symptoms disappeared while he was doing this job. However, as a result of a reorganisation, he needed to use his fork-lift truck near an area of the business that emitted fumes that triggered his asthma. His asthma was only triggered at work, and not by anything at home. There were no other suitable opportunities for Cruickshank and hence he was dismissed. The EAT found that, although his normal day-to-day activities were not affected by the asthma, his normal work activities were, and hence the illness was to be classed as a disability.

- The cause of a person's impairment is not relevant to the determination of whether or not it will be classed as a disability under the Act. Thus, for example, someone who has developed lung cancer as a result of heavy smoking will be able to claim protection under the Act on account of the lung cancer.

- If a disabled person's condition is controlled by medication or other forms of support such that they are able to carry out normal day-to-day activities, they may nevertheless be regarded as disabled in law if they would be impaired without the medication or support. For example, if an employee with epilepsy is symptom-free as a result of prescribed drugs, but would, without the drugs, be substantially impaired, they are regarded as disabled in law. Similarly, if an employee with a hearing impairment can hear near-normally by using a digital hearing aid, but would be substantially deaf without the aid, they are protected by the Act. (The only exception to this general principle is poor eyesight – if a person's eyesight is correctable by the wearing of spectacles or contact lenses, they are not considered to be disabled under the Act.)

- Employers should beware of assuming that an employee is not disabled on account of the employee's appearance or visible behaviour, and should bear in mind that an individual may have developed coping strategies that make their disability less obvious to others.

CASE STUDY

A woman applied for a job as a teacher. On her application form she stated that she had some level of vision impairment. It was decided not to interview her for the role because the teaching post was with very young children and it was felt that there was a safety need to be able to see them at all times, in case they were doing anything that caused them personal risk or danger.

The school felt that their decision was well justified and that there were no reasonable adjustments that they could make to allow them to employ the teacher. However, they made the decision without meeting the applicant and discussing the situation with her. Had they done so, they would have found that her vision was correctable with the spectacles that she wore, and that she had only mentioned it in response to a question on the application form. It did not cause her any impediment in her work. The school had not taken time to investigate any coping strategies that might be in place to enable her to work effectively.

An employer cannot be held to have discriminated on the grounds of disability if they were unaware that a disability existed, as held in the following case:

O'Neill v Sym and Co (1998)

O'Neill started work as an accounts clerk. Three months after she started work, she was dismissed for sickness absence. At her interview, she told the organisation that she had previously suffered from viral pneumonia but had recovered. During her employment, she was diagnosed as suffering from myalgic encephalomyelitis (ME) but did not tell her employers. As her employers were not aware of her diagnosis, her claim of disability discrimination failed.

An impairment will only be taken to amount to a disability if it has a substantial and long-term adverse affect on one or more of the following: mobility; manual dexterity; physical co-ordination; continence; the ability to lift, carry or otherwise move everyday objects; speech, hearing or eyesight; memory or ability to concentrate, learn or understand; or perception of the risk of physical danger. A person with a severe disfigurement is also classed as disabled under the Act. Each of these is explained below:

Mobility

This covers a person's ability to walk, move about generally, change position, reach up and down, turn around, etc. Normal day-to-day activities that involve mobility include walking, climbing or descending stairs, getting in and out of a car, reaching up to a high shelf and bending down to pick an object up from the floor.

Manual dexterity

This means the ability to use the hands and flex the fingers normally, and to co-ordinate the use of both hands to perform a single task. Activities that involve this ability include picking up a cup of coffee, using a pen to write, applying make-up and shaving.

Physical co-ordination

This category covers a person's ability to balance and co-ordinate the movements of different parts of the body. Examples of the effects of such an impairment are an inability to co-ordinate the movements of hands and feet when driving a car, difficulty in pouring hot water from a kettle into a cup without spillage, and an inability to carry out more than one task at the same time without serious difficulty.

Continence
This heading covers a person's ability to control the functioning of their bladder and bowels normally.

Ability to lift, carry or otherwise move everyday objects
This category covers a wide range of activities involving lifting and moving objects around. An employee may be disabled under this heading if they are unable to pick up with one hand ordinary objects such as a carrier bag containing grocery shopping, hold ordinary objects firmly without hand-shake, or carry a tray with a moderate load of filled coffee cups steadily.

Speech, hearing or eyesight
An impairment could be classed as a disability if it adversely affects the person's ability to articulate ordinary words, hear what is being said at a meeting in a moderately noisy environment (without a hearing aid), or read a newspaper at a normal distance even when wearing prescribed spectacles or contact lenses.

Memory or ability to concentrate, learn or understand
This category potentially includes a wide range of physical and mental conditions and illnesses that might give rise to inherent difficulties in concentration, comprehension or learning. Examples of difficulties in normal day-to-day activities are an inability to understand or follow simple instructions owing to learning difficulties, an inability to concentrate on routine tasks for more than a very short period of time, and behavioural problems caused by mental illness or brain damage.

This impairment was the subject of the following case:

Hewitt v Motorola (2004)

Hewitt suffered from an autism spectrum disorder and/or Asperger's Syndrome. He brought a claim that Motorola had failed to make reasonable adjustments, following an assessment of his performance. He claimed that his illness had particular adverse effect on his memory or ability to concentrate, learn or understand. He said this was primarily because he found social relationships difficult, particularly the concentration he had to give to the 'coded messages' that we rely on so much in social relationships. The EAT ruled that Hewitt did have difficulty in 'understanding'. This was not a lack of understanding of instructions, but a lack of understanding of normal social interaction. On this basis, his illness fell within the definition of a disability.

Perception of the risk of physical danger
This covers both the over- and under-estimation of risks to the safety, health or well-being of self or others. Someone with such an impairment might not understand the importance of following safety instructions when carrying out tasks (thereby inadvertently putting others at risk), not fully understand the risks involved in reckless behaviour such as horse-play, or neglect physiological needs such as eating or keeping warm.

Severe disfigurement

Severe disfigurements include large visible scars or birthmarks, severe burn marks, visible skin diseases, limb deformities and so on.

The range of conditions that can come within the scope of the DDA 1995 is very wide indeed. The following may all be covered, provided their effects on the individual's normal, day-to-day activities are long-term and substantial:

- the full range of physical illnesses
- progressive illnesses, such as cancer and multiple sclerosis as soon as they are diagnosed and have some effect on the person, even if the effect is not, in the beginning, substantial (however, a medical diagnosis of a progressive condition which as yet causes no symptoms will not qualify the person as disabled under the Act)
- AIDS and symptomatic HIV
- conditions that occur intermittently (for example, rheumatoid arthritis) provided that, when the condition does occur, it has a substantial adverse effect on the individual; in this case, the person is protected by the Act at all times, including periods when the condition is in remission
- conditions that fluctuate so that at times the effects are substantial and at other times they are not, in which case the person retains protection under the Act throughout
- clinically recognised mental illnesses such as schizophrenia and bipolar disorder (also known as manic depression)
- conditions such as severe dyslexia, ME and some stress-related illnesses, so long as the effects are substantial and long-term; although stress alone is not regarded as a disability under the Act, stress can lead to an illness (for example, depression or post-traumatic stress disorder) that could amount to a disability
- learning disabilities or difficulties.

It is important to note also that, if an employee had an illness in the past which at the time amounted to a disability (or would have counted as a disability if it had occurred before the Act was implemented), then they retain permanent protection against discrimination for a reason related to that disability.

Excluded conditions

Certain conditions are excluded from the scope of the DDA 1995. These are:

- addiction to nicotine, alcohol or drugs (other than prescribed drugs)
- hay fever
- tattoos that have not been removed
- any type of body-piercing
- certain mental conditions, including a tendency to set fires, steal or abuse other persons (physically or sexually), exhibitionism and voyeurism
- a genetic predisposition towards a particular illness.

However, employers should bear in mind that, although these conditions are excluded from the DDA 1995, if they are symptoms of another condition, then that other condition may amount to a disability. For example, an employee with a clinically recognised mental illness may exhibit a tendency to abuse other persons as a symptom of their illness. Such a person would be disabled within the meaning of the Act on account of their mental illness.

A further point to bear in mind is that, although addictions to alcohol and drugs are excluded from the scope of protection under the Act, an individual with such an addiction may become disabled as a consequence of it. For example, an alcoholic may develop liver disease as a consequence of persistent, heavy drinking, and thus become disabled. The cause of a person's disability is irrelevant to the question as to whether or not they qualify for protection under the DDA 1995.

It is not essential for an illness to have a clear diagnosis in order for an employee to be classified as disabled, as shown in the following case:

Howden v Capital Copiers (Edinburgh) Ltd (1997)

Howden suffered from sharp, gripping pains that necessitated him needing to lie down, and which generally had an adverse effect on his well-being. Despite three operations and a series of admissions to hospital, no diagnosis or cause for the pain was given. The Employment Tribunal held that this could be classed as a disability as it was clearly having a detrimental impact on his physical well-being and was long-term, substantial and affecting day-to-day activities.

Direct discrimination

The amended Act defines direct discrimination in relation to disability in the following way:

> **A person directly discriminates against a disabled person if, on the ground of the disabled persons disability, he treats the disabled person less favourably than he treats or would treat a person not having that particular disability whose relevant circumstances, including his abilities, are the same as, or not materially different from, those of the disabled person.**

For example, an employee who is facially disfigured applies to work as a waitress. The employee is rejected by the employer because it is feared that customers might be put off dining in the restaurant as a result of the disfigurement. The job is offered to a non-disabled person who has very similar experience and qualifications to the disabled applicant. This person would not have been rejected in the same way, and hence we have an example of direct discrimination.

The Act prohibits direct discrimination during all stages of recruitment, throughout employment, at termination of employment and post-employment. In the original legislation (DDA 1995), employers were able to discriminate on grounds related to a worker's disability if the particular treatment of the worker could be justified. However, the amended Regulations removed this option.

Discrimination may be on grounds of a job applicant's or employee's disability, but it may also be on grounds of the effects of the person's impairment. Effects can, for example, include reduced job performance, an inability to perform certain tasks, or absence from work (if the disability consists of an illness or results from an accident).

If an employee is able to show that they have experienced unfavourable treatment and that the treatment may have been related to disability (or harassment, which we will explore in Chapter 11), then the burden of proof moves to the employer who is required to prove that no discrimination has taken place. If the employer is unable to establish, to the tribunal's satisfaction, that there was another non-discriminatory reason for their treatment of the employee, the employee will win the case.

The legislation also provides for a questionnaire procedure whereby the employee who is potentially going to make a complaint can seek evidence that there has been discrimination. A statutory questionnaire is sent to the employer who then has eight weeks to respond to the questions. It is not a legal requirement to respond to the questionnaire, but adverse inferences can be drawn at an employment tribunal if it is not completed.

TASK

Go to the Disability Rights Commission (DRC), read their information on the questionnaire procedure and look at the example of the questionnaire that they provide. The website address is www.drc-gb.org.

The duty to make reasonable adjustments replaces the indirect discrimination provisions that occur within the other statutes. The employer is under a duty, whenever they know (or ought reasonably to know) that an employee is disabled, to take the initiative and identify any measures that will assist or support the disabled employee in the workplace. This will involve identifying changes to any working arrangements, working practices or physical features of premises that cause the disabled employee a substantial disadvantage on account of their disability. Measures should be sought that will have the effect of removing or reducing the employee's difficulties.

The definition of reasonable adjustments is extended by the amended Act (2004). Prior to the amendments, the requirement was to make reasonable adjustments to any 'arrangements' that place a disabled person at a disadvantage. The amended Act extends this to cover any 'provision, criterion or practice' that places a disabled person at a disadvantage.

The employer is, however, required to do only what is 'reasonable' in all the circumstances. What is reasonable will, in turn, depend on a range of factors such as the cost (if any) of the proposed adjustment, the size and resources of the business, the degree of disruption that any adjustment might cause, the likely effect on colleagues or customers and any other legitimate interests of the employer (such as safety).

The DRC 'Code of Practice for the elimination of discrimination in the field of employment against disabled persons' provides useful guidance to employers on a wide range of matters relevant to disabled workers. In relation to reasonable adjustments, the Code states that an employer should do all they 'could reasonably be expected to do to find out whether' an employee is disabled and thus disadvantaged by the employer's working arrangements or premises. For example, if an employee has had a substantial period of sickness absence (whether in one block or as several separate periods of absence), the employer should make enquiries of the employee to establish whether their condition might amount to a disability and whether there are any adjustments that can be made.

Examples of possible adjustments are:

- making physical adjustments to the workplace
- allocating some of the duties of the job to another employee
- moving the disabled person to another job
- altering the hours of work
- moving the employee to a different place of work
- allowing time off during working hours for treatment or rehabilitation
- allowing training for the employee
- acquiring or modifying equipment
- altering instructions or reference materials
- altering procedures for testing or assessment
- providing a reader or interpreter
- providing supervision

It is important that an employer takes the issue of reasonable adjustments seriously, and gives full thought to any adjustments that can be made. This is demonstrated by the following case:

Mid-Staffordshire General Hospitals NHS Trust v Cambridge (2003)

Cambridge worked as Team Leader in Reception Services in the NHS Trust. As a result of dust from a wall being demolished at work, she suffered from tracheitis and bowing of the vocal cords. She was absent from work for a time, and a doctor then recommended that she return on light duties and with reduced hours. The assessment of the time it would take her to make a full recovery was eventually established as 12 months. Cambridge tried to return, in accordance with an action plan drawn up by her line manager, but found it difficult. The NHS Trust decided that it would proceed to dismiss her unless she was able to return to work full-time within a reasonable period of time. She was eventually dismissed and it was upheld not only that she had been unfairly dismissed, but also that the Trust had failed to fully consider and make reasonable adjustments, and hence had treated her less favourably on account of her disability.

The EAT judged that the employer had breached the duty to make reasonable adjustments because they had failed to conduct a full assessment of the employee's position, which would have allowed them to decide properly what adjustments it would be reasonable for them to make.

The practical effect of this judgement is that, in order to meet the duty to make reasonable adjustments, the employer is under a duty to obtain a proper assessment of the employee's condition and prognosis, the effects of the condition on the employee's ability to perform their duties, the effects of the physical features of the workplace on the employee's ability to do the job, and the steps that the employer could potentially take to reduce or remove the disadvantages that the employee is experiencing.

AGE

At present there is no age discrimination legislation in the UK. As a result of the EU Framework Directive (Council Directive 2000/78), however, the UK (and other EU member states) will be obliged to implement age discrimination legislation by October 2006. The Framework Directive obliges all member states to introduce legislation banning direct and indirect age discrimination, victimisation and harassment. The Directive does, however, allow different treatment on grounds of age in certain circumstances.

The Government has already consulted widely on the matter of age discrimination and it is likely that the legislation, when it is enacted, will:

- apply to all employers irrespective of size or industry sector
- apply to job applicants and existing workers of all ages
- use the same definitions of direct discrimination, indirect discrimination, victimisation and harassment as already exist in the other strands of anti-discrimination legislation
- allow justification for age discrimination in certain circumstances
- ban age as a criterion in recruitment, selection and promotion unless it is objectively justified (for example, where a job requires a lengthy period of training)
- abolish compulsory retirement ages, or alternatively allow a default retirement age of 70, if this can be justified
- prohibit pay policies based on age (although pay based on length of service or experience will be potentially justifiable)
- remove the upper age limit for employees to bring unfair dismissal complaints and redundancy pay claims to tribunal (currently 65 years)
- alter the formula for calculating statutory redundancy pay (and the basic award for unfair dismissal) so that it no longer favours older employees or excludes service under the age of 18.

Until the implementation of age discrimination legislation, the only relevant guide to age in the context of employment is the Department of Work and Pensions' 'Code of Practice on age diversity in employment', published initially in mid-1999. The Code recommends that employers should not use age as a criterion in recruitment, employment or redundancy decisions. The Code (like other Codes of Practice) is not legally binding on employers, but it is important to note that its provisions may be taken into account (where appropriate) by an employment tribunal. This means in effect that a failure to follow the Code's recommendations could go against an employer at tribunal.

It is also important to consider that applying an upper age limit on recruitment decisions may in certain circumstances discriminate indirectly against women, as women are more likely than men to take career breaks for childcare reasons and hence might not have accrued the necessary qualifications and experience until they had passed the stated age limit.

Given the rapidly changing demographic mix of people in the UK, employers who have in the past discriminated against people on grounds of age will lose out unless they change their attitudes and policies. It is estimated that, by the year 2020, more than half the UK population will be over the age of 50, and that there will be two million fewer working people under the age of 50 than at present (Equal Opportunities Review, No. 115). People over the age of 50 represent a valuable source of experience and talent, and those organisations that fail to show enthusiasm towards the employment and retention of this group of workers are likely to face very severe skills shortages.

In preparation for the forthcoming age discrimination legislation, and to promote diversity, employers should:

- audit all their policies, procedures and practices now to ensure they are age-neutral, and to identify and eliminate any age-based criteria or features
- review pay systems and criteria for bonuses, etc. to eliminate any age-based or age-related features
- review any service-based criteria (for example, extra holiday entitlement granted to employees after a specified number of years' service) to ensure that such criteria are justifiable; adopting a policy or practice of requiring employees to achieve a minimum length of service in order to qualify for a benefit will in future be indirectly discriminatory against younger people and will therefore have to be based on a legitimate aim and be proportionate to the achievement of that aim
- check to ensure that equal opportunities and harassment policies include age within their scope
- abolish age limits in recruitment, unless there are exceptional circumstances justifying an age criterion in a particular case
- ensure that no age restrictions or indications of age appear in job advertisements (for example, such wording as 'young, energetic person required')
- amend application forms so as to remove any requirements for job applicants to provide their age or date of birth
- review graduate recruitment schemes to ensure they do not apply any age criteria, and to establish whether they can be justified as a method of filling entry-level vacancies
- ensure that employees are given access to promotion opportunities irrespective of age, and that promotion decisions are based on employees' skills and proven potential to do the job, irrespective of age
- amend any training and development policies to ensure that they afford equal opportunities to workers of all ages
- refrain from using age as a criterion in a redundancy selection exercise
- review retirement policies and prepare for the possibility that compulsory retirement ages will be abolished.

CASE STUDY

A fast-food chain was frustrated by the high turnover of staff, and the high levels of absence. Having looked at the data in detail, it was found that the older staff were absent less often, and were more likely to stay with the employer. The fast-food chain decided, therefore, to run a recruitment campaign directed specifically at the older age range.

An applicant for the job was only 20 years old and was told that she would not be considered for the role because the campaign was directed specifically at older applicants. The organisation saw this as a positive step – because it was promoting a positive attitude towards age in the workplace.

However, the fast-food chain had not considered that discrimination on the grounds of age can occur at the young end of the scale as well as the old. Although they were positively offering job opportunities to older applicants, they were discriminating on the grounds of age because they were excluding younger applicants.

TASK

As already stated, at the time of writing, legislation relating to age discrimination has yet to be introduced. During your studies keep up to date with the development of the legislation. Consultation documents, and the results of consultation, are usually well reported in the personnel press. Alternatively, the Department of Trade and Industry website, www.dti.gov.uk, is a useful source of information.

KEY POINTS FROM THIS CHAPTER

- Part-time workers are protected against all forms of discriminatory treatment on grounds of their part-time status, unless the treatment can be justified in the particular circumstances.
- Under the Fixed-Term Employees (Prevention of Less Favourable Treatment) Regulations 2002, employees engaged on fixed-term contracts must not be treated less favourably than comparable permanent employees, unless there is an objective reason for the different treatment.
- Once a fixed-term employee has gained four or more years' continuous service, they are automatically entitled to have their contract converted to permanent status, unless the employer can justify continuing the employment on a fixed-term basis.
- Employees engaged on fixed-term contracts – ie contracts that are set up to last for a specified period, continue until a particular task or project is complete, or continue until the occurrence (or non-occurrence) of a specified event – must not, without justification, be treated less favourably than comparable permanent employees.
- It is unlawful to discriminate against an employee on the grounds that they are, or are not, a member of a trade union.

- The DDA 1995 requires employers not to treat disabled workers or job applicants unfavourably for any reason related to disability, and to make reasonable adjustments to accommodate the needs of individuals who are disabled.

- The definition of 'disability' in the DDA 1995 is very wide and includes both physical and mental impairments, learning difficulties, and a wide range of illnesses and other conditions, including intermittently recurring conditions and conditions controlled by medication or support.

- Although there is no age discrimination legislation in the UK at present, the UK will be obliged to implement age discrimination legislation by October 2006 as a result of the EU Framework Directive which obliges all member states to introduce legislation banning direct and indirect age discrimination, victimisation and harassment.

EXAMPLES TO WORK THROUGH

1   Mark is the only cleaner employed by your organisation. He works from 5-8pm Monday to Friday. He is claiming that he is unfairly treated because full-time employees have access to a subsidised canteen while at work. However, he does not get any access to any subsidised food while he is at work. How would you address this problem?

2   Your organisation is going through a redundancy programme. Criteria for selection have been drawn up that include length of service, attitude to colleagues, flexibility and relevant experience. The line manager has selected James for redundancy using these criteria. James is a trade union representative, and the line manager has given him a very low score for attitude to colleagues and flexibility because he 'is always stirring up trouble and irritating everyone'. Does this amount to discrimination on the grounds of trade union membership?

3   Following an accident at work, Mary has very limited use of her right hand, and is no longer able to carry out her duties as a fork-lift truck driver. She wants to return to work. What should you do?

Recruitment, Discrimination and Diversity

INTRODUCTION TO RECRUITMENT

In the first five chapters of this book, we have looked at the psychological, practical and legal factors relating to diversity, equality and discrimination. In the next five chapters, we are going to apply that learning to particular issues that occur in people management. In this chapter we start with the issue of recruitment.

Effective recruitment requires an objective, systematic and planned approach if unlawful discrimination is to be avoided. Both short-listing and selection should be on the basis of candidates' relevant experience, skills, qualifications, knowledge and talent, and should be based on factual evidence. Our examination of legislation has shown that it is unlawful to use factors such as gender, marital status, race, religion and sexual orientation to make decisions in the recruitment process (except where a genuine occupational requirement exists – see section 'Genuine occupational requirements and qualifications' on p. 114).

In applying this legislation, there is also a need to think about the team that is being created through the process of recruitment. For example, we have studied research that shows that no diversity in a team results in poor creativity and decision making, whereas too much diversity can also hinder creativity and decision making. However, this does not mean that we can refuse to recruit any more people of a particular gender, race, etc. in order to achieve the best levels of creativity and decision making – because that would be unlawful discrimination. What it does mean is that people need to be educated and trained in order to work together most effectively.

It is advisable for all organisations to devise and implement recruitment procedures and guidelines for all staff involved in the process of recruitment, and to ensure that these incorporate the principles of the organisation's equal opportunities policy. It is also imperative that all those involved in recruitment and selection should be properly educated and trained in recruitment procedures and the principles of equality.

The laws prohibiting discrimination on grounds of sex, race, disability, sexual orientation and religion expressly outlaw discrimination in the process of recruitment and selection. Specifically, it is unlawful to discriminate:

- in the arrangements made for deciding who should be offered employment
- in the terms on which employment is offered
- in refusing or deliberately omitting to offer employment.

The word 'arrangements' in the context of recruitment incorporates all aspects of the recruitment process, including the design of job advertisements, the procedures used for short-listing, interview arrangements, the questions asked at interviews, any psychometric testing used as part of the selection process and the final decision as to whom to appoint.

It is important to consider ways in which discrimination can be avoided in the recruitment process. Examples are:

- ensuring that criteria being used for assessment are as objective as possible, to avoid any unintentional discrimination occurring
- avoiding the use of age limits in recruitment (this has been promoted by the CIPD as best practice for a number of years – but from 1 October 2006 it will be unlawful to use age as a criterion in the recruitment process).

It is interesting to note how the use of an age limit could result in indirect sex discrimination. For example, if an organisation specified that they needed someone with at least 10 years' experience and aged under 35 years, there will be significantly fewer women who will have had the opportunity to gain the 10 years' experience while under the age of 35 years because more women than men take career breaks for childcare reasons. Applying such criteria could, therefore, be indirect sex discrimination.

- avoiding the use of language that implies a bias (such as 'storeman' rather than 'stores assistant')
- having a well-thought-out person specification that is free of any bias – because that is the definition that has been written describing the best person for the job
- only gathering information about nationality and ethnic group for monitoring purposes (although it will also be necessary to check whether the candidate eventually selected has the right to work in the UK and, if they are of foreign nationality, whether a work permit is required); it is best to have this information supplied on a separate form, or a tear-off form – which is not shown to those who make the decisions on whom to invite for an interview
- ensuring that any selection techniques, such as psychometric assessment, are free of any cultural bias – and do not require language skills that are not needed in the job; the issue of psychometric assessment will be considered in more detail in Chapter 7
- using a structured interviewing process that does not include any intrusive personal questions
- having a clear aim of recruiting the person who best fits the person specification
- keeping clear records that show the reasons for the recruitment decisions.

CASE STUDY

A woman applied for a job of store operator. Before the actual interview, she was given a tour around the stores, and noticed that all the employees were male.

Her interview was conducted by the Store Manager. Throughout the interview he referred to the post of 'Storeman'. She had relevant experience, and was able to answer all the questions fully – but her application was turned down.

She then contacted the General Manager of the organisation to complain that she had been discriminated against, because the language of the interviewer had made it clear that the intention was to recruit a man. This was strongly denied, and it was argued that the old term had always been 'Storeman', and this was simply a slip of the tongue.

She refused to accept this and said she would be making a claim to the Employment Tribunal. In response to this, the organisation offered her a trial period in the job which she accepted.

GENUINE OCCUPATIONAL REQUIREMENTS AND QUALIFICATIONS

There are limited exceptions to the general principles that it is unlawful to use gender, race, religion or sexual orientation as criteria in the selection process. In certain limited circumstances that are specified in the relevant legislation, an employer may discriminate by expressly setting out to recruit either a woman or a man, a person from a specific racial or religious group, or a person of a particular sexual orientation based on the requirements of the job itself. Essentially this is lawful where being of a particular gender, race, religion or sexual orientation is a genuine occupational requirement (GOR) or genuine occupational qualification (GOQ) for the specific post.

Any potentially applicable GOQ or GOR should be identified at the beginning of the recruitment process. It is important, however, to avoid assuming that one of the exemptions will apply, without giving the matter thorough consideration. Jobs can change over time and, just because a particular GOQ applied to the job in the past, this does not automatically mean that it is still legitimate to apply it.

In general, in order for a GOR or GOQ to apply, it must genuinely be necessary, in order to ensure effective performance of the job in question, for the post-holder to be either a man or a woman (as the case may be), a person from a defined racial group, someone who belongs to a specific religion, or someone of a particular sexual orientation. It is not necessary for all the duties of the job to fall within the scope of the stated GOR or GOQ, so long as it can be shown that some aspects of the job create a genuine need for the job to be performed by a person from the specified group.

TASK

Read through job advertisements in newspapers and magazines. Try to find examples of advertisements that are targeted at a specific group of people because of a GOQ or GOR. Read them carefully to understand why this approach is justifiable (if it is!). It might be most fruitful to look at public sector advertisements because they tend to have more jobs that require GOQs or GORs.

However, it should be noted that, if sufficient numbers of employees of the 'necessary' group are already employed in the same position as the job into which a new employee is to be hired, and if the existing employees could in practice carry out the particular duties to which the GOR or GOQ applies, then it will not be lawful to apply the GOR to the new post. This is demonstrated in the following case:

Etam plc v Rowan (1989)

In this case, the employer set out to recruit a shop assistant to work in the ladies' fashion department of one of its shops. The job involved assisting female customers who could be in a state of undress in the changing rooms. Taking this into account, the employer rejected a man who applied for the job. When the man claimed sex discrimination, the Employment Appeal Tribunal (EAT) held that the decency/privacy requirement (see p. 116) could not apply to the job because the employer already had an adequate number of female shop assistants who could deal with female customers in the changing rooms.

Where a GOR or GOQ applies, it does not act to compel an employer to limit a job to one gender or racial group (for example), but merely makes it an option for the employer to apply the GOR or GOQ if they believe it is appropriate and necessary to do so.

It is important to note that in the sex discrimination legislation, GOQs apply only during recruitment (and, in some instances, during training) including the process of determining who should be promoted or transferred to a different post. It is not open to an employer to cite a GOQ in respect of the terms of employment offered to the successful applicant, access to company benefits or perks, or the process of termination of employment.

By contrast, the Race Relations Act 1976 (as amended by the Race Relations Act [Amendment] Regulations 2003), the Employment Equality (Religion or Belief) Regulations 2003 and the Employment Equality (Sexual Orientation) Regulations 2003 also allow a GOR to be applied in dismissal. This could be lawful (ie not discriminatory) where, for example, an employee changed their religion to one that made them unsuitable in relation to the performance of the job for which they had been employed.

The number and scope of GORs and GOQs that may be used by employers is very limited, and the list in each of the relevant laws is exhaustive. Thus, it is not open to an employer to invent their own reasons for insisting on recruiting a man, for example, no matter how strongly the employer's management may feel about the matter. Reasons that do not accord quite specifically with one of the defined GOQs or GORs will not be valid.

Gender – GOQs

The Sex Discrimination Act 1975 contains a list of GOQs that allow employers to seek to recruit either a man or a woman in limited circumstances. The GOQs are as follows:

Authenticity or physiology

A gender GOQ may apply where the essential nature of the job calls for either a man or a woman for reasons of authenticity in entertainment, acting or modelling, or for reasons of physiology (for example, in modelling jobs). It is important to note, however, that this GOQ does not incorporate a requirement for strength or stamina. It is therefore not open to employers to restrict employment to men (thus excluding all women who may apply for the job) for reasons of strength or stamina.

Decency or privacy

It is lawful to restrict employment to only one of the sexes where it is necessary for a job to be filled by either a man or a woman for reasons of decency or privacy. It is important to note that this GOQ will apply only if it can be shown that it is necessary for the post to be filled by either a man or a woman. A preference for either a man or a woman will not suffice. Thus, for example, a health authority would not be permitted to insist on recruiting a female gynaecologist for a hospital job just because a number of female patients at the hospital had expressed a preference or desire to be treated by a woman.

The decency/privacy GOQ may arise for one of three reasons:

1   because the job involves physical contact with either men or women
2   where the job has to be performed in a place where individuals are likely to be in a state of undress or using sanitary facilities
3   where the job involves the person working or living in a private home.

In all three cases, it must be shown that men or women might reasonably object to the job being carried out by a person of the opposite sex. Thus, jobs such as security officer (where the job duties involve conducting physical searches of men or women), lavatory cleaner and nursing assistant in a private home could be covered. The following case illustrates this point:

Sisley v Britannia Security Systems (1983)

The organisation operated a security station which was staffed by two female operators. They worked shifts up to 12 hours in length, and were allowed to sleep during the shifts for up to five hours. Within the control station, they had an area where they changed into their uniform, and a collapsible bed that they used. When they slept, they stripped to their underwear so that their uniforms would not become creased.

Sisley applied for a post as security officer and was rejected on the grounds that he was a man and there was a GOQ for a woman on the grounds of decency and privacy – because the employees had to 'live' on the premises, there were no separate sleeping and sanitary arrangements for different sexes, and because the employees stripped to their underwear while sleeping. Sisley claimed sex discrimination. The EAT held that the GOQ was allowed on the grounds of decency and privacy, and hence dismissed the claim of sex discrimination.

Live-in jobs with single-sex accommodation

If the nature of the job is such that the employee has to live in premises provided by the employer, and there are no separate sleeping quarters or toilet/washroom facilities for men and women, and where it is not reasonable for the employer to provide separate facilities, it will be lawful to seek to recruit only a man or a woman. An example of this GOQ could be a job on an oil-rig that has communal sleeping and shower facilities and where the people already employed there are exclusively or predominantly men.

Single-sex establishments

It may be permissible to insist on recruiting either a man or a woman where the job is in a single-sex establishment for people requiring special care, such as a hospital, prison, children's home or home for older people. One key point to note is that the residents in the single-sex establishment must be people who require special care. Thus the job of school teacher in a single-sex infants' school would not fall within the remit of this GOQ unless it could be shown that the infants had special needs – for example, if the school specifically catered for children with disabilities, and that involved care of an intimate nature. By contrast, the job of care assistant in a residential home for geriatric women might potentially be covered by the single-sex establishment GOQ, depending on all the circumstances.

The provision of personal services

This GOQ may apply where the job involves the provision of personal services promoting welfare or education, and these services can best be provided by a member of one sex. It is easy to imagine, for example, that a woman might respond more favourably to a female rape counsellor than to a man doing the same job. However, the services to be provided must be personal services for the GOQ to apply. Thus a managerial post in social work that does not involve personal contact with individual clients would not be covered.

Jobs outside the UK

It will be permissible to insist on recruiting a man where the job to be filled involves working in a country other than the UK, and the laws or customs of that country are such that the duties cannot be performed effectively by a woman. The most likely example of this would be a job in a country where women are forbidden to drive in circumstances where the ability to drive was a necessary component of the job.

Jobs for married couples

This GOQ allows an employer to seek to employ a husband and wife team (rather than two single people) where the job is 'one of two to be held by a married couple'.

Gender re-assignment

As the law stands at present, there are two situations in which it may be lawful to refuse employment to a trans-gender person. Specifically, an individual who has announced an intention to undergo a sex change, is part-way through the process of gender re-assignment, or has completed a sex change, may be refused employment in a job that involves:

- working and/or living in a private home in circumstances where objection might reasonably be taken to a trans-sexual
- conducting intimate physical searches.

Even in circumstances where the job involves conducting personal physical searches, however, the employer should consider whether the applicant could be employed and exempted from the requirement to conduct such searches. This is shown in the following case:

> **A v Chief Constable of West Yorkshire Police (2002)**
>
> In this case, a male-to-female trans-sexual who had applied to join the police was rejected on the grounds that she would be unable to carry out personal searches of people in custody. In considering the applicant's claim for sex discrimination, the Court ruled that the police force's assertion that the GOQ applied could not be upheld. This was because it would have been possible to exempt the applicant from the need to conduct searches, particularly in view of the fact that she had made it clear that she had no objection to her trans-sexuality being disclosed to colleagues if necessary.

As noted in Chapter 4, the UK government has confirmed that it will introduce legislation (the Gender Recognition Act) to give trans-gender people the legal right to be regarded as belonging to their acquired sex in every way. When the Act is implemented, the GOQ described here will no longer be applicable to people who have completed the trans-gender process.

Race – GOQs

Like the Sex Discrimination Act 1975, the Race Relations Act 1976 contains some GOQs that allow employers to restrict employment in certain posts to people of a particular colour or nationality. The GOQs are as follows:

Authenticity

The authenticity GOQ applies where the essential nature of the job calls for someone of a particular racial group for reasons of authenticity in entertainment or modelling. This GOQ expressly includes front-of-house jobs in public restaurants, cafés or bars. For example, the owners of a Chinese restaurant would be permitted to seek to recruit Chinese waiting staff in order to create an authentic atmosphere. This principle cannot, however, be lawfully applied to behind-the-scenes jobs such as that of kitchen porter, or to jobs in private clubs or staff canteens.

The provision of personal services

It is permissible to seek to recruit someone from a defined colour or nationality where the job involves the provision of personal services promoting welfare to people of that racial group, and there is evidence that these services can best be provided in this way. The services to be provided must be personal services if the GOQ is to be relied on. It might, for example, be legitimate to seek to recruit someone of Bangladeshi ethnic origin into the post of social worker, if the people in the community in which the post-holder is to be working are predominantly Bangladeshi and it is reasonably believed that they would respond more favourably to someone from their own country than to a person from a different ethnic origin doing the same job. However, it must be clear that the services are personal, as shown in the following case:

London Borough of Lambeth v Commission for Racial Equality (1990)

The London Borough of Lambeth was keen to encourage more applications for housing benefit from members of ethnic minorities. Hence, they advertised for two positions in the housing department stating that they would be filled by members of the 'black community'. However, the Commission for Racial Equality (CRE) argued that the GOQ of personal services did not apply in this situation because the jobs were primarily managerial, and hence the successful applicants would not be significantly involved in providing any specific personal services. They also noted that the definition of the section of the population that the job holders would be dealing with was vague. The Court of Appeal supported the view of the CRE. The jobs were too distant from the actual provision of personal services, and hence the GOQ did not apply.

Race – GOR

Over and above the permitted GOQs that apply to the concepts of colour and nationality, the Race Relations Act 1976 contains a general provision that, if it is genuinely necessary for the holder of a particular post to be of a particular race, ethnic origin or national origin, the prospective employer may lawfully discriminate in favour of someone from that race, ethnic or national origin, provided also that the race-related requirement is proportionate in the particular case. This genuine occupational requirement (GOR) was added to the Race Relations Act in July 2003 following the implementation of the Race Relations (Amendment) Regulations 2003.

The following case gives an example of how a GOR might be applied:

Board of Governors of St Matthias Church of England School v Crizzle (1993)

Crizzle was Deputy Headteacher at the school. She was of Asian origin and a non-communicant Catholic. The school was a voluntary-aided Church of England school. The Headteacher resigned; Crizzle applied for the job and was rejected. The advertisement for the job specified that the successful applicant should be suitably qualified, with inner city experience, and a committed communicant Christian. Crizzle claimed unlawful race discrimination.

The tribunal held that there had been unlawful race discrimination. They determined that there had not been direct discrimination because the decision had been made on the grounds of religion (there was no legislation relating to religious discrimination in force at the time) and not on the grounds of race. However, they found that there had been indirect race discrimination because a significantly smaller proportion of people of Asian origin would be able to comply with the criterion of being a committed communicant Christian in comparison with people from other ethnic groups. They also found that the criterion of being a committed communicant Christian was not justifiable because the primary purpose of the school was education and not the promotion of the Christian faith.

However, the EAT over-ruled this decision. They found that the criterion of being a committed communicant Christian was justifiable because the school was entitled to determine that their primary purpose went beyond education and also included the promotion of a particular approach to religious worship.

Religion – GORs

The Employment Equality (Religion or Belief) Regulations 2003 contain two provisions that allow employers to discriminate in favour of those who belong to a specific religion when recruiting, when considering individuals for promotion or transfer, or (in the event that an individual changes their religion) in dismissal.

Genuine and determining occupational requirement – general GOR

If it can be shown that being of a particular religion or belief is a genuine and determining occupational requirement for the post in question, then it is permissible to recruit someone from a specific religion. Thus recruitment into the job of minister in the Church of Scotland may be restricted to applicants who uphold the religious principles of the Church of Scotland. The job of cleaner in the church would not, however, fall within this GOR, since there would no logical need for the cleaner to uphold a particular faith in order to be able to perform cleaning duties effectively. This exception is therefore narrow and applies only where there is a very clear connection between the work to be done and the characteristics required to perform it. The GOR will only be valid where it is necessary for particular job duties to be carried out by someone of a specific religion and not merely because someone of that religion would be preferred.

Ethos – specific GOR

The second provision relates to organisations that have an ethos based on a particular religion or belief, such as churches or religious schools. In this case, the GOR based on religion or belief may be applied to any post so long as it can be shown to be a genuine requirement. The difference between this GOR and the general GOR described in the preceding paragraph is the word 'determining'. In other words, where the employer is an ethos-based organisation, being of a particular religion or belief need not be a decisive requirement for the post in question, although it must still be a genuine requirement that is broadly relevant to the organisation. Under the religious ethos GOR, a Catholic school (for example) may be able to justify requiring all its teachers to be Catholic on the grounds that teaching the principles of the Catholic faith to pupils is part of every teacher's responsibility. Even this GOR, however, would be unlikely to justify insisting that the school cleaners must be Catholic. Although the ethos-based organisation GOR is broader than the general GOR, this does not mean that it can be applied universally within the organisation.

In both cases, the employer must be able to demonstrate that it is proportionate to apply the religion or belief requirement in the particular case.

Sexual orientation – GORs

The Employment Equality (Sexual Orientation) Regulations 2003 also contain a general GOR and a specific GOR:

Genuine and determining occupational requirement – general GOR

The general GOR can be applied where being of a particular sexual orientation can be shown to be a genuine and determining occupational requirement for the post in question, and the employer can demonstrate that it is proportionate to apply the requirement in the particular case. This is parallel to the general GOR in the Employment Equality (Religion or Belief) Regulations 2003. A possible example could be a job whose main function was the provision of counselling to young people who are gay or lesbian.

Purposes of an organised religion – specific GOR

The second GOR in relation to sexual orientation is available where the employment is 'for the purposes of an organised religion'. However, the sexual orientation GOR can only be relied on if it is being applied either to comply with the doctrines of the particular religion or to avoid conflicting with the strongly held religious convictions of a significant number of the religion's followers.

The range of jobs that can be said to be 'for the purposes of an organised religion' is very narrow and is likely to include only such jobs as ministers of religion involving work for a church, synagogue or mosque where the religion in question disapproves of homosexuality or where many of the religion's followers find it unacceptable. This GOR will not therefore apply to all jobs in an organisation that has an ethos based on a particular religion. This is because the wording in the statute makes it clear that, in order for the sexual orientation GOR to apply, the job itself must exist for the purposes of an organised religion rather than just be a job in an ethos-based organisation. For example, it could be argued that the job of nurse in a religious hospice is not 'for the purposes of an organised religion' but rather that the job exists for the purpose of health care.

TASK

Find out if any jobs in your organisation, or an organisation with which you are familiar, have any GOQs or GORs. Read the relevant job descriptions and person specifications and try to understand why a GOQ/GOR is relevant.

CASE STUDY

A local church advertised for a youth worker, and it was clearly stated in the advertisement that the successful applicant must be a committed Christian. A youth worker who claimed to be an atheist saw the advertisement and decided to apply because he would like to work in this particular area of the country.

His application was refused on the grounds that he would not be able to carry out the main function of the job – which was teaching young people about the Christian faith. He responded that he was still able to give the teaching, even if he did not believe it himself. However, he then found out that a further requirement of the job was to be a regular attendant at Sunday services in the church, and at that stage withdrew his application.

If he had been prepared to teach the Christian faith, even if he did not believe it himself, should he have been excluded from the applications?

POSITIVE ACTION AND DISCRIMINATION

Positive discrimination (sometimes termed 'reverse discrimination') in employment is not permitted by UK law (unless one of the GORs or GOQs applies). In other words, it is not lawful to recruit a black candidate in preference to a white candidate, or a woman in preference to a man, if the white candidate or the man is better suited to the job in terms of qualifications, experience and skills (as noted later, there is an exception to this principle if the positive discrimination is on the basis of disability). This principle stands firm even if the motivation for appointing a particular person is based on a genuine desire to promote diversity, to increase the numbers of people from a disadvantaged group in employment, or to create a more balanced workforce. At the point of selection for the job, the principle of equality must always prevail, and gender, race, religion and sexual orientation must never be taken into account as a criterion for selection.

One example of an employer who misinterpreted the law in this area is shown in the following case:

Roadburg v Lothian Regional Council (1976)

In this case, two men and one woman were short-listed for the post of voluntary services officer. The Council wished to maintain a balance between the sexes in the team of officers, and therefore decided initially to appoint one of the men. The female applicant was offered a different job elsewhere in the Council. Subsequently, neither post was filled as a result of financial cuts. The woman nevertheless succeeded in a claim for direct sex discrimination on the grounds that the arrangements for filling the first post had been discriminatory.

In line with the principle that positive discrimination is unlawful, setting a quota – for example, for the recruitment of people from a minority racial group – would not be permissible because a quota would probably lead to positive discrimination. Conversely, establishing targets is allowable. The difference is that a target is something to aspire to and will encourage positive measures to be taken within the ambit of the law, while a quota would be a figure that would have to be achieved at all costs, irrespective of the merit of the individuals who applied for employment.

Within the above general framework, certain forms of positive action (sometimes known as affirmative action) are permitted by the legislation, provided they take the form of *encouragement* to members of an under-represented or disadvantaged group to take up opportunities for employment or training. In effect, positive action will widen the pool for selection, promotion or development, and increase the chances that people from a minority group can be legitimately employed or promoted.

However, where positive action is being planned or carried out in recruitment, this will not entitle the employer automatically to exclude people from consideration who do not belong to the under-represented group. At the point where any decision is being made as to whom to short-list or appoint, the principle of equality must prevail, and the gender, race, religion or sexual orientation of the applicants under consideration must play no part.

It will also be vital to make sure that the steps taken to encourage members of the minority group to come forward for employment do not overstep the mark of what is permissible in law.

Positive action in relation to gender and race may be undertaken only when either men or women, or people from a particular racial group, are under-represented. There will be an under-representation of a particular group if the number of people employed from that group in a particular type of work has, at any time during the previous 12 months, been disproportionately low when compared with the group's proportion in the workforce as a whole, or with the population from which the employer normally recruits.

Under a provision of the Race Relations (Amendment) Act 2000, public authorities in Britain have a statutory duty to promote race equality. Authorities have had to comply with the general requirements of the Act since April 2001, and with the specific duties since May 2002. The statutory duty only applies to race, although the Sex Equality (Duties of Public Authorities) Bill was introduced into the House of Commons in Autumn 2004 with the aim of placing a positive duty on public sector employers to promote gender equality and prevent discrimination. In addition, the Disability Discrimination Bill contains a provision that (when enacted – the date is not currently known) will compel public authorities to positively promote equality of opportunity for people with disabilities both within employment and in the exercise of their public functions.

The equivalent provisions related to religion and sexual orientation permit employers to take steps to encourage people of a particular religion (or sexual orientation) to take advantage of employment opportunities, provided such action is carried out to prevent or compensate for disadvantages linked to religion (or sexual orientation) suffered by those of that religion (or sexual orientation). Positive action is therefore a lawful means of attempting to redress an existing imbalance.

Despite the limitations, positive action may be a useful tool for employers who wish to promote diversity within their workforce. Employers may, however, wish to consider the possible negative effects of positive action – namely, that applicants who are not from the under-represented group may feel that their prospects are diminished, and may be discouraged from applying for employment. There may even be resentment from within the organisation from those who perceive (perhaps mistakenly) that women or people from minority racial groups (for example) are being given priority in recruitment or are receiving extra-favourable treatment.

It is important to note that positive action is not compelled by law (apart from the provision relating to race equality in public authorities) but instead is an option that allows employers to choose to take certain steps to increase the number of people from under-represented or disadvantaged groups that they employ.

Examples of positive action, where it is permitted, are as follows:

- targeting the advertising of a vacant post – for example, placing advertisements in publications that are known to be popular with Asian or Chinese people, advertising in a different geographical area, or using a business journal read predominantly by women
- stating in a job advertisement that applications from women or from people from a minority racial or religious group will be particularly welcome – although, if this is done, there should also be a statement in the advertisement that the job is open to both sexes and all racial (or religious) groups
- publishing a booklet promoting employment opportunities that exist within the organisation and targeting it at female undergraduates

- setting up a careers fair or promotional event targeted at overseas nationals to encourage them to learn about the organisation and apply for employment

- developing links with community groups that work to promote the interests of people from minority or disadvantaged groups

- stating in a job advertisement that focused training will be provided for new recruits from the under-represented group – for example, to increase the opportunities for women to be equipped for into supervisory or management posts

- promoting flexible working practices (which, arguably, benefit everyone).

The Disability Discrimination Act (DDA) 1995, although similar in many ways to the other anti-discrimination legislation, has some features that are distinct and different from the other laws. One difference is that the Act is structured so that it technically allows a disabled candidate to be selected for a job in preference to non-disabled person simply because they are disabled. In other words, the Act does not contain any provision that prohibits discrimination against someone because they are not disabled, although such favouritism in recruitment is not, of course, compulsory. Furthermore, the duty to make reasonable adjustments under the Act could, arguably, be viewed as a form of positive discrimination.

TASK

Return to the job advertisements that you looked at in the first task in this chapter. Did you see any evidence of positive action in any of the advertisements? If you did, did you think that people from the group that is not being targeted might be discouraged from applying for the job in question?

AVOIDING INDIRECT DISCRIMINATION IN JOB FACTORS

In the early stages of the recruitment process, an employee specification should be written that describes the type of person the employer seeks to appoint in terms of qualifications, experience and skills, etc. Such criteria may, however (if the employer is not alert to the possible difficulties), be potentially indirectly discriminatory on grounds of sex, sexual orientation, race or religion. Specifically, the imposition of inappropriate or unnecessarily high standards or criteria may indirectly discriminate against people of one sex compared with the other, or against people from a particular minority racial group or religion. It is therefore very important that the requirements and standards specified for job candidates' qualifications, experience and skills, etc. should be objectively and sensibly matched to the needs of the job without allowing personal opinions to play any part.

Two examples of potentially discriminatory criteria are:

1 a requirement for the post-holder to work unsocial or very long hours, which would discriminate indirectly against women; unless the requirement could be justified on objective grounds related to the job or to the business, it would be unlawful

2 a condition that whomever is appointed must speak fluent English, which would discriminate indirectly against anyone brought up in a country whose first language is one other than English; unless the requirement was relevant to the job and proportionate, it could be judged unlawful.

In writing person specifications, therefore, care should be taken to:

- write the employee specification objectively and in accordance with the needs of the job, excluding any subjective views or personal opinions
- scrutinise the proposed criteria for the job in order to ensure they are genuinely relevant, rather than being based on convenience, personal preference or somebody's whim
- review, even if a requirement is relevant to the job, whether it is proportionate (ie not excessive) and whether the aim to be achieved could be attained in a different (non-discriminatory) way
- take care not to overstate the qualifications and level of experience required to perform the job
- pay special attention to any personal qualities ascribed to the prospective job-holder (eg 'outgoing personality'), as they may be the result of somebody's personal opinion and therefore unnecessary
- avoid using age limits
- avoid stipulating that a candidate must be physically fit, unless this is necessary for the job (since this requirement could place disabled candidates at a disadvantage)
- avoid making general statements that are prone to subjectivity – for example, requiring candidates to be 'outgoing', 'enthusiastic' or 'energetic'; since most people believe that they have these qualities anyway, they will not assist the recruitment process and may inadvertently discriminate.

It will be helpful, in preparing an employee specification, to identify which criteria are necessary for the job to be done effectively and which are merely desirable. Having made these distinctions, it is advisable to stick to them. In other words, if a criterion has been stated as 'desirable', it should not subsequently be the sole reason for the rejection of a particular candidate unless there are two or more candidates who match the 'necessary' criteria equally in every respect.

It is important that all candidates for the job are fully informed of all the duties of the job at an early stage in the recruitment process. Doing this will ensure that applicants have an opportunity to consider fully whether any aspect of the job conflicts with their religion or belief. It may be, for example, that an applicant who is a vegetarian (and who believes strongly that it is morally wrong to use animals for human consumption or gain) would not wish to work in a job where animals were used for experimentation purposes, or in a job that involved preparing or serving meat in a restaurant. There is no obligation on an employer to offer employment to someone who, as a result of their religion or belief, is unable or unwilling to undertake key parts of the job.

It is generally good practice to exclude questions about gender, marital status, number and ages of children, nationality, age and disability from the main part of an application form. Although some of this information will be needed in respect of the person who is appointed, it is hard to envisage how any of it could be relevant to the short-listing process. Arguably, the exclusion of such information from the application form ensures that all job applicants are treated fairly and equally, and any conscious or subconscious bias in the minds of those responsible for short-listing will be avoided.

As already noted, one way of obtaining the required personal information about applicants without compromising the objectivity of the recruitment process is to design the application form with a tear-off page. The tear-off page can contain any necessary personal questions about gender, marital status, nationality, age and disability, and can be removed by the employer's HR department before the application form is passed to the line manager responsible for the vacancy. In this way, the risk of discrimination is minimised while at the same time HR staff have information to hand that they may need during the recruitment process.

The personal details form should encourage applicants to disclose any disability that they may have, while also making a statement about the employer's commitment to a positive approach towards the employment of disabled people. It is also a sound idea to make the application form available in alternative formats – for example, in Braille or extra-large print, and also electronically.

Job application forms should not contain questions that require applicants to reveal their religion or belief, or their sexual orientation.

It may be advantageous in any event to scrutinise the application form thoroughly to ensure it asks only questions that are relevant to the job. The Employment Practices Data Protection Code (Part 1) (www.informationcommissioner.gov.uk) (which provides guidance on how to comply with the Data Protection Act 1998 in the context of recruitment) recommends that employers should:

- use different application forms for different jobs
- aim to seek information from job applicants that is proportionate to their business needs
- not request information about applicants' private lives
- remove or amend any questions on application forms that are not directly relevant or necessary to the selection decision.

The Data Protection Code is not legally binding on employers, but an employer who does not adhere to its principles may find, in the event of a legal claim against them, that the court or tribunal will use the Code as a measure of assessing the appropriateness of the employer's actions. In other words, any evidence of non-compliance is likely to operate to the employer's detriment.

TASK

Look at the application form(s) used by your organisation, or an organisation with which you are familiar. Can you think of any ways that they could be improved to avoid any likely occurrences of discrimination?

MONITORING RECRUITMENT

It is generally considered to be good practice for employers to monitor their recruitment processes in order to promote equality. Indeed, public authorities are under a positive duty to conduct racial monitoring of job applicants as a result of the implementation of the Race Relations Amendment Act 2000.

Where an employer is planning or reviewing how it should monitor job applicants, they may wish to consider monitoring not only candidates' racial origins, but also their gender, age and whether they have a disability, since a comprehensive exercise is likely to produce maximum benefit. It is important, however, to distinguish between information that is needed for the purpose of monitoring, and information required for recruitment and selection. It will be equally important to communicate to job applicants that any personal information provided will not be used as part of the process of short-listing or selection, and that the information will be used to assist the organisation to review and improve its equality and diversity practices.

The objectives of monitoring in recruitment would generally be to:

- establish whether the proportions of men and women and people of different racial groups who apply for employment are proportionate to the numbers in each of these groups within the general community
- identify whether a higher proportion of applicants of one sex or racial group than another is rejected for employment, and at what stage in the recruitment process they tend to be rejected
- review the age profile of those who apply for jobs, and establish whether or not the correlation between this and the age profile of those who are appointed is the same
- review how many disabled people apply for employment and, of those who do apply, what proportion are subsequently employed
- take action to establish the reasons for any evidence that suggests that a disproportionate number of women, men, members of minority racial groups, people in different age bands or disabled people do not apply for employment or are rejected for employment, and to devise means of remedying this situation.

The Data Protection Act 1998 contains restrictions on the type of information that employers are allowed to gather about job applicants (and existing employees). In particular, the Act prevents employers from collecting certain information that is classed as 'sensitive data' unless one of a list of conditions is met. 'Sensitive data' is defined under the Act as information about an individual's racial or ethnic origins, religious or philosophical beliefs, sexuality, physical or mental health, trade union membership and the commission of any criminal offence. Essentially, the employer should ensure that they have clear, express consent from all job applicants to authorise the holding of any such data, and that job applicants are informed about the purpose for which the information is being gathered.

The easiest way to achieve compliance with the law in this area is to place a clause in the application form stating that the employer wishes to process certain information (which should be defined – eg information on ethnic origins), the purpose for which the information will be processed, and how and by whom it will be processed. The job applicant's signature should be requested against the clause to indicate their consent to the information being gathered and processed under the Data Protection Act 1998.

CASE STUDY

An organisation recruiting a large number of graduate trainees each year added a question to its application form asking all applicants to declare their sexual orientation. The applicants were very uncomfortable with answering this question, wanting to know why it was being asked.

The organisation responded that it was being asked so that it could monitor the recruitment data to ensure that people of a particular sexual orientation were not being discriminated against. However, the applicants were still unhappy with the approach that was being taken. Was the approach acceptable?

TASK

Find out if your organisation, or an organisation with which you are familiar, monitors its applicants for jobs. If it does, look at the statistics and see what they tell you. If it does not, ask if you could monitor recruitment for a while and, again, see what the statistics tell you.

ENSURING SHORT-LISTING IS DONE AGAINST OBJECTIVE CRITERIA

The key aim in short-listing should be to draw up a manageable list of candidates for interview for a specified post, all of whom could potentially do the job in terms of the qualifications and experience outlined in their job application form or CV. Short-listing is best done methodically by comparing each application with a previously prepared employee specification. Such an approach should ensure objectivity and minimise the risk of bias on sex, racial grounds or age influencing the choice of candidates. Obviously, factors such as gender, race, etc. should play no part in the short-listing process.

The criteria for appointment should be decided in advance rather than attempting at a later time to justify the selection of a particular applicant by 'post-hoc rationalisation' as shown in the following case:

Bishop v The Cooper Group plc t/a Coopers Thames Ditton (1992)

In this case, two male applicants were successful in their applications for work as car technicians while a highly qualified female applicant was unlawfully rejected. The employment tribunal determined that the organisation justified the decision after it had been made – rather than determining criteria in advance of the decision and then applying them.

If a disabled candidate appears to have the requisite experience and qualifications for the post in question, but there is some concern in the mind of the person responsible for short-listing about the person's abilities, the best approach is to invite the candidate to interview and explore their abilities in relation to the post through an open and fair questioning process. Negative attitudes towards disabilities are common in recruitment and should be strongly resisted. Rejection for employment purely on the grounds of a person's disability would constitute disability discrimination, which would be unlawful. Some employers adopt a policy of automatically inviting for interview any disabled applicant who meets the essential criteria for the post, and this approach is to be recommended.

The key to ensuring equality and diversity in short-listing is to make sure that decisions are based on an assessment of the facts provided on each candidate's application form or CV as measured against the requirements stated on the employee specification. Allowing personal opinions or attitudes to influence decisions may lead to discriminatory practices that could be unlawful.

Care should also be taken to avoid assumptions about individual candidates and the type of work they would want to do, or be capable of doing.

Some classic examples of discriminatory assumptions, invalid generalisations and stereotypes are:

- women are not suitable for jobs that involve heavy or dirty work
- a young female applicant is unlikely to remain in employment for long because she's bound to decide to start a family
- a woman with young children will be unable to work long hours or travel away from home on business
- a woman with children cannot be fully committed to her job
- part-time employees do not take their job responsibilities seriously
- problems of authority and effectiveness will arise if a young person is appointed to a supervisory post
- an older person, if recruited, will not stay long with the organisation
- older people take a lot of time off work due to sickness
- disabled people take a lot of time off work due to sickness
- disabled people are trouble because they will need all sorts of special arrangements made for them
- problems might arise if a woman is recruited into a post where she will be working alone with a man much of the time
- a candidate from a particular racial or cultural background will not fit into the team
- a candidate of foreign nationality will need a work permit, and that will inevitably cause an inordinate amount of hassle for the organisation
- someone from a particular religion will cause disruption because they will demand frequent time off work to pray
- it wouldn't be a good idea to recruit a gay or lesbian individual because they might be harassed by their colleagues.

It would be inherently unfair and unprofessional to allow any of these spurious assumptions to affect the decision as to whom to short-list. Blanket assumptions of this nature carry with them the risk that a job applicant who is highly suitable for the job could be rejected. Furthermore, in some cases, non-selection for the short-list based on this type of false reasoning could lead to a successful complaint of unlawful discrimination at an employment tribunal.

TASK

Find out how your organisation, or an organisation with which you are familiar, carries out the process of short-listing. Do you think that the process seems to be free of bias, or can you identify any improvements that could be made?

KEY POINTS FROM THIS CHAPTER

- The laws prohibiting discrimination on grounds of sex, race, disability, sexual orientation and religion expressly outlaw discrimination throughout the process of recruitment and selection.

- There are limited exceptions to the general principle that it is unlawful to use gender, race, religion or sexual orientation as a criterion in the selection process; these are known as genuine occupational requirements or genuine occupational qualifications.

- Certain forms of positive action are permitted in UK law provided they take the form of encouragement to members of an under-represented or disadvantaged group to take up opportunities for employment or training.

- The specifications for jobs should be carefully examined to ensure that there are no factors contained that are indirectly discriminatory.

- The monitoring of applications to an organisation can help identify if there are groups that are under-represented.

- The Employment Practices Data Protection Code (Part 1) recommends that employers should use different application forms for different jobs, seek only information that is proportionate to their business needs and refrain from requesting information about applicants' private lives.

- The process used for short-listing should be free of any factors that are potentially discriminatory.

EXAMPLES TO WORK THROUGH

1 You work in a residential home for older people, which has both male and female residents. Currently, all but one of the care assistants is female. Some of the male residents are complaining that they are being assisted by a female when bathing and dressing. One of the care assistants has resigned and hence there is a vacancy. The Manager of the home wants to state in the advertisement that a male care assistant is required. What do you advise?

2 The ethnic origin and gender of the applicants to your organisation have been monitored over a six-month period, and it is clear that a number of ethnic minorities that are well represented in the local population are under-represented in the applications that have been made. How could you address this?

3 Write a person specification for the job you hold, or a job that you have held. Make sure that there is nothing in the specification that is potentially discriminatory.

Selection, Discrimination and Diversity

CHAPTER 7

OBJECTIVES OF THIS CHAPTER:

- to understand how discrimination can occur in the selection process
- to consider specific issues associated with selection interviewing
- to outline possible discrimination in other selection methods
- to evaluate specific issues associated with the selection of disabled and pregnant employees
- to consider the specific issues associated with discrimination and the selection of asylum seekers and those requiring work permits.

INTRODUCTION TO SELECTION

Most organisations use an interview, in some format, as a key part of the selection process. However, when we look at the statistics relating to the validity (the extent to which the process of selection is successful in identifying the person who is most successful in the job), we see that the interview is not the most valid form of selection:

Table 7.1 *Validity of selection techniques*

Validity range*	Methods	Rating
0.4 – 0.5+	Work sample tests	Good-excellent
	Ability tests	
0.3 – 0.39	Biodata	Acceptable
	Assessment Centres	
	Structured interviews	
Less than 0.3	Personality assessments	Poor
	Typical interviews	
	References	
	Graphology	
Chance (0)	Astrology	

Source: adapted by Price [2004] from Smith [1991]

(*A validity of 1 would suggest a perfect predictor.)

As so many organisations still rely on typical interviews, we will focus much of our attention in this chapter on that method. However, we will also look at how discrimination can occur in the other methods listed.

All those involved in selection need to be constantly aware of the need to be objective in the way they assess candidates. Selection should be on the basis of candidates' relevant experience, skills, qualifications, knowledge and talent, and should be based on factual evidence rather than personal opinions or assumptions. This chapter aims to provide guidance on the processes of interviewing and selection with a view to promoting equality and diversity.

TASK

Find out which approaches to selection are used in your organisation, or an organisation with which you are familiar. Find out why these particular approaches have been chosen.

FIRST IMPRESSIONS

As we have already noted, selection interviewing is not rated as one of the most valid predictors of performance in the job. One of the issues that can have a negative impact on the validity of the interview is the interviewer's first impression of a job applicant. In research by Webster (1964), it was noted that interviewers tend to make up their minds about a candidate in the first few minutes of the interview. The candidate's appearance was found to be the most significant factor, followed by information that is given on the application form. Apart from the obvious disadvantage of causing a potentially suitable applicant to be rejected, taking some of these factors into account could lead to a discriminatory decision. If, for example, the interviewer allows a negative reaction to a candidate's accent to influence the selection decision, this could be racially discriminatory if the person is of a different ethnic origin from that of the interviewer.

The so-called 'halo-effect' occurs when something about the candidate creates such a favourable impression on the interviewer in the early stages of the interview that it is as if the candidate has a halo around their head thereafter and can say nothing wrong. The result can be that everything the candidate says passes through a 'favourable filter', and any negative aspects of the candidate are overlooked or minimised. The opposite effect (known as the 'reverse halo' or 'horns effect') can occur if the interviewer's first impression of the candidate is unfavourable in some respect. It is important for interviewers to recognise the dangers inherent in first impressions, which are inevitably based on personal views and attitudes. If not recognised, these can create a barrier to equality and diversity because they can prevent a truly objective assessment of the candidate's suitability for the job from taking place.

Discrimination during recruitment interviewing is often perpetrated subconsciously as a result of the interviewer's personal views, attitudes, assumptions or acquired stereotyped views. This was demonstrated in the following case:

Nagarajan v *London Regional Transport (1999)*

Nagarajan was of Indian racial origin. He applied for the job of travel information assistant with LRT, and was turned down on the basis of low marks for his verbal communication skills. However, Nagarajan considered that the reasons for his rejection amounted to victimisation because he had previously brought race discrimination proceedings against LRT. The House of Lords supported the Employment Tribunal's finding that the interviewers had been influenced, subconsciously or consciously, by the earlier complaints, and hence there was race discrimination. In making its judgement the House of Lords stated:

....all human beings have pre-conceptions, beliefs, attitudes and prejudices on many subjects and it is part of our make-up. People do not always recognise their own prejudices ... An employer might genuinely believe that the reason why he rejected an applicant had nothing to do with the applicant's race, but it could nevertheless be the case, whether the employer realised it at the time or not, that race was a reason why he acted as he did.

An interviewer may assume, for example, that a woman (or a man) would be unsuitable for a particular type of work based on a deep-seated stereotyped view of what constitutes 'men's work' and 'women's work', or they may hold a generalised view that older people are not likely to be fit or flexible enough to perform a particular job effectively. Generalised assumptions of this nature based on gender, race or age should be recognised as personal (and often stereotypical) views that are not necessarily true of individuals, so that they can be put to one side while interviewing.

CASE STUDY

A sales organisation commissioned some research on why some sales representatives were consistently more successful than others. In the findings were two interesting conclusions:

1   The appearance of certain sales representatives was more appealing to customers.

2   Customers preferred sales representatives who were of a similar background to themselves.

When the organisation next needed to recruit a sales representative, it decided to use this information and instructed the interviewer to look for applicants similar to the 'desirable' sales representatives whom the customers had been asked to describe.

Was this approach potentially discriminatory? If an organisation is looking to be successful, can it use information such as this to help ensure the success?

SELECTION INTERVIEWING

As we have already seen, selection interviewing is a notoriously unreliable process. While a job applicant's qualifications, experience and knowledge can usually be assessed objectively, it can be challenging (to say the least) to assess accurately such factors as personal motivation, attitude and flexibility in approach. To achieve maximum effectiveness from the interview process, while also promoting equality and diversity, the interviewer should:

- focus on the job and the skills needed to perform it effectively

- deploy open questions (ie questions beginning with 'what', 'which', 'why', 'how', 'who', 'where' and 'when')

- be prepared to probe for more information where appropriate

- listen actively and with an open mind to everything the candidate has to say

- ask specific questions about the candidate's actual experiences – for example, "Tell me about a time when you experienced conflict with a colleague, and how you handled it"

- recognise subjective views, opinions, biases and prejudices, and learn to put them to one side when interviewing – lack of awareness of these can have a negative effect on the objectivity of the interview process

- do not assume, but assess

- aim to select the candidate whose experience, skills, qualifications and abilities most closely match a previously prepared employee specification.

In order to ensure equality during the interview process, it is important to ask only questions that relate to the needs of the job and not to stray over into personal or intrusive questions that may inadvertently discriminate against a particular group of people. Another danger is that certain questions may inadvertently indicate a biased view on the interviewer's part, or may be motivated by the interviewer's personal attitudes towards people of a particular ethnic background. A tribunal may draw adverse inferences from the fact that certain questions were asked if they were such that they could place (for example) women at a disadvantage.

Nevertheless, interviewers will naturally and quite rightly wish to establish whether the candidate being interviewed could, if recruited, fulfil all the requirements of the job under review. To achieve this, direct (and possibly challenging) questions will need to be asked, but it is important that these are framed in an appropriate and fair way. It is likely to be viewed as discriminatory, for example, if a female applicant is asked personal questions concerning marriage plans, childcare arrangements or her husband's employment. Tribunals tend to perceive such questions as having a discriminatory undertone and interpret them as an intention in the mind of the interviewer (whether conscious or unconscious) to discriminate.

There will be rare exceptions, where direct questions about family circumstances may be appropriate in order to establish whether applicants have fully thought through the implications of a job that has special demands, but such occasions will be uncommon. In any event, it is better to re-frame such questions to make them job-related rather than family-related. Such a situation is demonstrated in the following case:

Woodhead v Chief Constable of West Yorkshire Police (1990)

Woodhead applied to join the West Yorkshire Police. She underwent a three-day assessment process and was rejected at the end of it. As part of the assessment process, she had an interview, about half of which was devoted to asking questions about her domestic arrangements. As a result of this, she claimed sex discrimination. However, the Employment Tribunal and the Employment Appeal Tribunal (EAT) held that she had not been discriminated against. The assessment panel argued that they had asked similar questions of all candidates, regardless of their gender. The Employment Tribunal commented that the assessment panel had given a disproportionate time to questions about domestic arrangements, particularly in comparison to the time given to questions about academic qualifications and work experience. However, they also noted that she had failed all other aspects of the assessment procedure. It was found that it was not discriminatory to ask such questions, because the assessment panel had to be sure that all candidates had thought through the demanding and stressful nature of the job before proceeding with their applications.

The Code of Practice published by the Equal Opportunities Commission (www.eoc.org.uk) (its full title is the 'Code of Practice for the elimination of discrimination on grounds of sex and marriage and the promotion of equality of opportunity in employment') emphasises that questions should be based on the requirements of the job, and that relevant issues should be discussed objectively without any assumptions being made by the interviewer about whether a candidate's personal circumstances could affect their ability to meet the requirements of the job.

TASK

Read the Code of Practice referenced above (details are available at www.eoc.org.uk).

In posing questions about candidates' availability for work at particular times, care should be taken not to ask questions in such a way that requires the applicant to disclose their religion, or whether they will require time off work at particular times on account of their religion or belief. This could be perceived as unlawful discrimination under the Employment Equality (Religion or Belief) Regulations 2003, in the same way as questions to female candidates about time off to look after their children could be perceived as sex discrimination. It would be equally inappropriate to ask questions about the job applicant's religious affiliation, place of worship or which religious customs they observe.

It is also possible that a homosexual job applicant may feel disadvantaged if asked questions about their marital status or whether they have any children. As gay men and lesbian women are less likely than heterosexual people to be married or have children, they may perceive a requirement to disclose their single and/or childless status as a detriment.

It may be tempting, in order to avoid the problems identified in the preceding section, to decide simply to ask all candidates exactly the same questions. While ensuring consistency, this approach will be unnecessarily restrictive and will not allow a full or satisfactory exploration of all the issues relevant to each candidate. Certain questions may be relevant to only one applicant – for example, based on something the person has stated on their application form that needs to be clarified. In addition, the interviewer will wish to respond to some of the answers a candidate gives, and they should not be limited on following up a particular topic just because previous candidates have not been asked similar questions.

In any event, asking the same questions of all candidates will not be sufficient on its own to protect the employer from a claim for unlawful discrimination. This is because it is not only the questions themselves that may be discriminatory, but also the purpose for which they are asked, the context within which they are asked and the use to which the candidate's answers are put. The overall test of whether questions at interview were discriminatory will be (for example) whether a female applicant was treated less favourably on grounds of sex than a male applicant was or would have been treated, or whether someone from a minority ethnic group was treated less favourably than someone from a majority ethnic group was or would have been treated.

This is illustrated in the following case:

> ### Saunders v Richmond upon Thames London Borough Council (1977)
>
> Saunders applied for a job as a golf professional. Seven candidates were interviewed in the morning, and three were short-listed for further interviews in the afternoon of the same day. She was not one of those short-listed. She claimed that she had been subjected to sex discrimination because seven of the questions posed to her were based on the assumption that a woman would have more difficulty holding the post than a man. However, the Employment Tribunal and the EAT found that she had not been invited back for a second interview because of a misunderstanding about her availability in the afternoon. Further, they ruled that it is not discriminatory to simply ask such questions – the important issue is whether, as a result of the questions, she was treated less favourably than a man.

If the EAT had found in this case that the answers given to the questions had been the reason that Saunders had not been short-listed, then it is likely that the outcome of the case would have been very different. It should be noted that it is difficult to show that any answers to questions relating specifically to gender, race, etc. are not going to be used in a less favourable way – one could contend that, if they are being asked, then the answers must be being used in some way to make the selection decision.

Nevertheless, there are considerable advantages in starting the interview programme with a planned list of questions that are relevant to every candidate for the job under consideration. Provided the list of questions is not viewed as a means of restricting the interview, it will provide a useful and consistent framework for the interviewer and can help to ensure that no key issues are overlooked.

All the necessary and relevant information required to assess whether someone is suitable for the job in hand can be obtained by designing questions so that they relate to the requirements of the job rather than to the applicant's personal circumstances. The following checklist provides some ideas.

Checklist of questions to ask/avoid during recruitment interviewing

While it is legitimate to ask direct questions relating to a candidate's ability and willingness to meet the genuine needs of the particular job, care should be taken to avoid discriminatory questions, especially when interviewing women.

Table 7.2 *Checklist of questions to ask/avoid during recruitment interviewing*

Ask	Avoid
To what extent would you be available to work overtime at short notice?	Who would look after your children if your manager asked you to work overtime at short notice?
The job involves travelling away on business on average two or three days a month. How would you feel about that?	How would your husband feel about you being away from home two or three days every month?
How frequently have you worked at weekends during the past year?	How would weekend working affect your family life?
What would you like to be doing in five years' time?	Do you have any plans to start a family in the next five years?
How many days sickness absence have you had in the past two years?	How many days absence have you had in the past two years due to childcare problems?
How do you cope with pressure of work?	How does pressure of work affect your relationship with your children?
How would you feel about working extra hours during the company's busiest periods?	Would you require any special time off due to your religion or beliefs?
What steps would you take to build a successful relationship with a new manager?	How do you feel about working for a male (female/black/gay) manager?
How would you deal with someone at work whose views were strongly opposed to your own views?	How would you deal with a difficult male colleague if his views were strongly opposed to your own views?
What do you think makes a good supervisor/manager?	What difficulties do you think you might have supervising men/women/white staff/ black staff?
What do you think is the best approach to handling minor disciplinary matters?	How would you handle a disciplinary matter if the employee concerned was black?

CASE STUDY

A retail organisation had become increasingly frustrated with the number of employees going on maternity leave. A new set of recruits were being interviewed, and the interviewers were aware that they must not discriminate in the selection process.

However, the organisation did not want to recruit yet more women who would be on maternity leave within the year, so they decided to ask all the applicants – male and female – if they planned to start a family. Clearly the responses from the men were not of the same implication as the responses from the women.

One of the female applicants refused to answer the question. She argued that the reasons for asking it were discriminatory, even if it was being asked of all applicants. Was she right?

Racial, cultural and religious differences between people can lead interviewers astray in other respects. For example, in Britain and in many other Western countries, eye contact is viewed as an indication that the person is honest and sincere. In some countries, however, lowering the eyes so as to avoid eye contact is a mark of respect when dealing with someone in a position of seniority or authority. The interviewer should take care therefore not to view lack of eye contact as a negative factor if the interviewee is from a country outside Europe, America or Australasia. Another point is that people of certain religions may not wish to shake hands. When starting and finishing the interview, therefore, the interviewer should take their cue from the applicant rather than automatically expecting the interviewee to shake hands.

An example of unlawful race discrimination based on gut feeling and lack of eye contact occurred in the following case:

Staffordshire County Council v *Bennett (1994)*

A black Afro-Caribbean candidate with excellent qualifications was rejected for the job of temporary assistant in a school in favour of an unqualified white woman. One of the interviewers had formed a view that the black candidate's personality was 'wrong' for the job and that she would 'not get on' with other staff members. This view was based partly on the fact that she had not made good eye contact with the interviewers during the interview. In light of evidence that people of Afro-Caribbean origin often avoid eye contact with people in authority, as such eye contact is viewed as impolite, the tribunal concluded that the black applicant's 'face did not fit' because she had a different racial background from those who conducted the interview.

Another feature of selection interviewing that can inadvertently lead to race discrimination is if candidates are assessed on the basis of their physical presence – in other words, where the selection decision is influenced by the degree of confidence, assertiveness and fluency with which the candidate communicates during the interview. Physical presence is a factor that often sways interviewers, despite the fact that it is, in many jobs, not a key element on which effective performance depends. Interviewers should therefore assess the information given and the mode of presentation as separate factors, and resist the temptation to be swayed by personal presence if it is not relevant to the job.

This is particularly important from a race point of view because candidates from certain racial groups may, for a variety of reasons, be less adept at selling themselves. For example, an applicant may come from a racial group in which boasting of one's achievements is culturally unacceptable, whereas modesty is highly valued.

An interviewer who is unaware of such cultural issues may not be favourably predisposed towards an applicant who displays such modesty. Conversely, a candidate from a different part of the world may have been brought up in a culture in which it is viewed as admirable to sell one's achievements in an assertive manner, and this candidate's forthcoming and direct manner may create an irrelevantly favourable impression. Furthermore, if English is not the candidate's first language, this could adversely affect the interviewer's perception of the candidate's degree of confidence or ability to communicate.

TASK

If you are not involved in interviewing as part of your job, ask if you can sit in on a few interviews within your organisation. After each interview, talk to the interviewer about the questions that have been asked, and discuss how the interviewer tries to ensure that no discriminatory questions are raised.

OTHER METHODS OF SELECTION

As we saw in the table at the start of this section, there are other approaches to selection apart from the interview. In this section we are going to consider some of the issues associated with these other approaches.

Psychometric assessment

Psychometric assessment can include personality assessments and aptitude assessments. Personality assessments aim to assess a range of personality factors by asking candidates to give responses to questions. These are typically statements that are rated from 'very like me' to 'not at all like me', or involve a forced choice from a set of statements – with the candidate having to choose the statement that best describes them.

Aptitude assessments involve the assessment of aptitude, rather than ability, in areas such as verbal reasoning and numerical reasoning. This is typically carried out through an assessment involving a series of questions that the candidate completes. The assessment is time-bound and, if the candidate does not complete the assessment, they are not allowed any additional time.

Wood and Baron (1992) carried out an analysis of the potential adverse effect that psychometric assessment can have on ethnic minority groups. An adverse impact is said to occur when a particular group is disproportionately preferred over another group as a result of the assessments. A number of difficulties were identified:

- In the UK it is typical for assessments to be conducted in English. If this is not the candidate's first language, then it is quite possible that their speed of reasoning will be slower. As a result the assessment could indicate a low level of verbal reasoning.

Presuming that speed of reasoning is not crucial to the job, this could lead to psychometric assessment being indirectly discriminatory as a method of selection.

- In addition, the nature of the assessments might require answers to be expressed in a very specific way. If the candidate expresses their answers in a different way, they could be marked down.

- Assessments can also be written in such a way as to be specific to particular cultural experiences. This could include reference to the use of particular tools or equipment that are not common in another culture, or refer to events that are common in a limited number of cultures.

The specific issue of intelligence tests has been the subject of a wide range of research. Gould (1982) looked at work carried out by Yerkes in 1915. During World War I Yerkes persuaded the American military to give mental assessments to all army recruits – and as a result he was able to assess 1.75 million recruits. He gave three types of assessments. Literate recruits were given a written test called Army Alpha, illiterate recruits (or those who failed Army Alpha) were given a pictorial test and those who failed this were called for an individual spoken examination. Yerkes claimed that the assessments measured intelligence that was unaffected by culture and educational opportunities. However, there was clear evidence that the questions asked required cultural knowledge – the following questions that were asked demonstrate this:

- Washington is to Adams as first is to ……..
- Crisco is a: patent medicine, disinfectant, toothpaste, food product
- Christy Mathewson is famous as a: writer, artist, baseball player, comedian.

Although the scores from all groups were low, Gould reports that the highest scores were achieved by white Americans. He reports that it was possible to grade European immigrants by their country of origin, according to their scores on the assessments – with people of northern and western Europe scoring better than those from eastern and southern Europe. The score of black men was considerably lower than that of white men. It was also found that, the longer a person had resided in the USA, the better the scores that they achieved.

Clearly, the overall scores indicate some concerns over the construction of the assessments. However, what is particularly concerning is that the performance in these assessments related to the ethnic origin of the applicants.

A number of researchers have determined that there are differences between performance in some assessments and ethnic group. Stevenson et al (1986) report that Asian Americans frequently outscore white Americans on the maths section of the Scholastic Aptitude Test, and students in China and Japan outscore Americans on standardised achievement tests in maths and science.

Neisser et al (1996) suggest that the differences in scores actually reflect the differences in cultural attitudes towards education, rather than differences in intelligence. Asian children are typically more motivated to work hard at school. Chinese and Japanese students and mothers are more likely to attribute academic success to hard work, whereas American mothers are more likely to attribute academic success to natural ability.

Clearly, there are issues associated with the assessment of intelligence, and with the use of psychometric assessment. For recruiters, it is important to be sure that the assessments are measuring potential performance in the job, and that the scores are not being 'muddied' by other factors.

Today, developers of psychometric assessments are more aware of these issues and try to address them in the assessments they develop. However, it is an issue that must be considered when using psychometric assessments and considering whether they are indirectly discriminatory.

If a disabled employee has a condition that might indicate a particular struggle with the assessments required, then the following options could be considered:

- allowing extra time to complete the assessment (although the assessment publisher would need to be contacted to discuss the potential impact on validity of the results)
- allowing breaks in the assessment (again, the impact on validity would need to be discussed)
- using a different form of assessment
- allowing assistance such as a reader (again, the impact on validity must be considered).

TASK

Try to find some examples of psychometric assessments. If you are not able to access any within an organisation, search on the Internet for psychometric assessment providers – some of them give examples of their materials on their websites. Try to get a better understanding of how discrimination could occur through the use of such assessments. Also, try to identify how assessment publishers have attempted to eliminate this discrimination.

Other forms of selection

As you will see from Table 7.1 at the beginning of this chapter, other forms of assessment that are commonly used include ability tests, work sample tests and assessment centres. The guidance for the use of these is largely the same as for psychometric assessment. Are you measuring what is required in the job, or is the measurement being 'muddied' by an irrelevant factor such as sex or race?

Work sample tests can be particularly useful if they are truly samples of the work that is to be done. If a candidate shows that they are unable to do the work, then it is unlikely that they will be a suitable choice. However, if the candidate is disabled and shows difficulties with the work sample, then the employer must consider what adjustments could be made to the job to make it accessible to the disabled candidate.

CASE STUDY

A manufacturing organisation decided to use a work sample test in the selection process. The organisation made printed circuit boards, and the manufacturing process involved quite fiddly work – putting small components on to the board and soldering them into position.

One of the applicants for the job was disabled and had fine motor skills difficulties; he argued that he did not want to carry out the work sample test because it would discriminate against him. However, the organisation argued that the whole point of the test was to screen out people who could not do the work, and this was not just disabled people: it had also been found that people with very thick fingers struggled with the work! If someone could not do the test, they could not do the work.

Eventually another job opportunity occurred in the organisation and the disabled applicant successfully applied for this – but was the use of the work sample test discrimination against disabled applicants?

It is important that the standards or requirements that are being set are relevant to the job. This is illustrated in the following case:

Perera v Civil Service Commission (1983)

Perera had practised as a lawyer in Sri Lanka and, after a period practising law in the UK, applied for a job as a legal assistant within the Civil Service. At the interview, the panel considered factors such as work experience in the UK, fluency with the English language, whether the candidates intended to apply for British citizenship and their age. Perera did not make the short-list, and he claimed race discrimination. His ability to communicate, personal qualities and intellectual qualities had been assessed as fair, but his potential as poor. However, the Employment Tribunal, the EAT and the Court of Appeal all supported the Civil Service Commission's decision. They found that it was the overall personal qualities of Perera that had meant he was unsuccessful, and not his fluency with the English language.

TEAMWORK

In the first two chapters, we considered the benefits of diversity within a team. We found that a diverse team has benefits in the level of creativity and decision making it achieves. However, we also found that – if the diversity causes conflict in the team – then there can be negative consequences of diversity. Employers want to achieve the most effective teams, because they will be most productive – but at the same time they cannot discriminate against applicants because of conflicts they fear might arise if a person from a particular gender, race, disability, religion or sexual orientation is placed in a team.

Even if the motive for refusing someone a place in a team is based on good intentions, if the reason relates to one of the prohibited grounds, it is not allowed.

> **_Grieg v (1) Community Industry (2) Ahern (1979)_**
>
> Grieg applied for a job with the organisation that employed educationally or socially disadvantaged young people. She was accepted into a painting and decorating team, along with another woman. The other woman dropped out, and Grieg actually turned up a week late. She was refused a place in the painting and decorating team because she would have been the only female and the organisation determined that this would give an unacceptable imbalance in the team's composition. Although the motive of the organisation was good, it still amounted to direct sex discrimination.

This dilemma leads to the difficult issue of the assessment of whether a particular candidate will fit in to an existing team. A job applicant's general attitude and likely degree of team effectiveness is of course very difficult to assess at interview, as most candidates will strive to put forward their best side and will do their utmost to avoid disclosing any negative attitudes or weaknesses. Questions such as 'Do you like working with people?' are less than useless – after all, how many candidates are likely to answer 'No'?

Sometimes, an interviewer may develop a 'gut feeling' that a particular applicant would or would not fit in to the team, but it can be dangerous to make a decision based on this alone, as such a gut feeling often occurs as a result of the perceived degree of 'sameness' between the interviewer and the candidate. For example, if the interviewer is a white, 35-year-old male, who has been born, brought up and educated in England, then it would be natural for him to feel comfortable in the presence of a candidate with a similar background. If, however, one of the candidates is (for example) a black, 55-year-old female who has been born, brought up and educated in Kenya, there will be many differences (both visible and invisible) between the interviewer and the candidate.

The interviewer may feel less comfortable with this candidate than with the English applicant and, if he has not received awareness training in racial and cultural issues, may conclude that the Kenyan candidate will simply not fit in to the department, or to the organisation as a whole. The racial and cultural differences between the two people may be enough to create a degree of unease (which may be at a subconscious level) which, if allowed to affect the outcome of the interview, could lead to race discrimination. This is the most likely criterion of all to result in a failure to practise diversity in recruitment.

This issue is summed up in the following case:

> **_Baker v Cornwall County Council (1990)_**
>
> The employer gave the defence of their selection decisions as 'we wanted someone who would fit in'. One of the Court of Appeal judges stated that this is a danger signal that the choice was influenced not by the qualifications of the successful candidate, but by the sex or race of that candidate.

Instead of making assumptions about a candidate's likely degree of success in fitting in to a team, the interviewer should ask specific questions about the person's past working relationships, when they have been successful or unsuccessful, what made them successful or unsuccessful, what kind of person they find it difficult to work with, why this is so, and how they have dealt in practice with conflict or disagreement in a team. In this way, the interviewer can gain information about how the applicant tends to behave in real situations, rather than make assumptions about their attitudes or behaviour. Thus, any conclusion at the end of the interview that the candidate would not fit in to a team will be based on factual evidence and not gut feeling. Interviewers should always be prepared to challenge their own thought processes and question whether there are facts to back up any view they may have formed that a particular candidate will or will not fit in.

SELECTION INTERVIEWING AND DISABLED APPLICANTS

Where a job applicant on the short-list has stated that they have a disability, the employer will need to consider whether it is appropriate to make any different or special arrangements for the interview. As explained in Chapter 3, the Disability Discrimination Act 1995 places a duty on employers to make 'reasonable adjustments' to their arrangements and practices in order to accommodate the specific needs of a disabled job applicant (or employee). The principle behind this requirement, as it applies to recruitment, is to ensure that a disabled candidate does not suffer any disadvantage in terms of their likely success in being appointed to the job.

Where a job applicant has indicated that they have a disability, the person responsible for arranging interviews should ask the person to indicate what (if any) special arrangements might be helpful for them in relation to the interview. Special arrangements could, for example, involve moving the location of the interview to somewhere with easier access, rescheduling the timing of the interview to suit someone whose movements depend on the availability of a carer, or permitting a deaf applicant to bring a sign language interpreter with them to the interview. Employers should aim to be flexible in their approach.

The Disability Discrimination Act 1995 does not place any duty on disabled job applicants (or existing employees) to volunteer information about any disability they have (although, clearly, all job applicants are under an implied general duty to tell the truth if asked direct questions). In interviewing, therefore, it will be up to the employer to seek relevant information from a disabled job applicant about their abilities in relation to the job in question. It is clear from case law that the responsibility lies with the employer to ask the necessary questions to establish the applicant's suitability for the job, and to identify relevant adjustments. This is shown in the following case:

Cosgrove v Caesar & Howie (2001)

Cosgrove was a legal secretary who was dismissed after she had been absent from work for a year suffering from depression. It was not known when she would be well enough to return to work. Neither Cosgrove nor her doctor could identify any adjustments that could be made to help her work, and hence the employer concluded that dismissal was the only option. However, the EAT determined that the responsibility was on the employer (and not the disabled person) to take the initiative in reviewing what reasonable adjustments could be made to facilitate the person's employment.

Questions should, of course, be asked in a sensitive way and only for the purpose of gaining a proper understanding of the employee's condition and its likely effect on their ability to do the job for which they are applying. It will also be helpful if the interviewer makes it clear that the reason the questions are being asked is to allow the employer to treat the applicant fairly and consider what steps might be appropriate or necessary to accommodate their needs if they were appointed.

Disabled people frequently face negative and discriminatory attitudes in seeking employment. Naturally, many interviewers will have little or no knowledge about a particular impairment or condition, and will not be in a position to objectively assess the person's suitability for the job unless they discuss the relevant issues with the applicant directly. It is very important that interviewers avoid making any negative assumptions about a disabled candidate's abilities or forming premature judgements that there might be problems if someone with a particular disability was recruited. Negative assumptions, or a failure to explore the relevant issues in a reasonable way, could lead to the unfair rejection of a disabled candidate who was suitably qualified and capable of performing the job. This in turn could lead to a claim of disability discrimination being taken to an employment tribunal.

Instead of making assumptions or forming negative views, therefore, interviewers should discuss the requirements of the job fully with the disabled candidate and ask the candidate to comment both on their abilities in relation to the duties of the job, and on what adjustments, if any, would help them perform the job satisfactorily. It is important that interview questions are framed in such a way that they neither display nor imply a negative attitude to the person's disability. While it is wholly appropriate for those conducting interviews to seek to establish whether the applicant being interviewed could, if recruited, fulfil the requirements of the job to a satisfactory degree, a positive approach should be taken to the questioning process. A good maxim in this context is the familiar adage that one should look for solutions, not for problems.

In enquiring generally about a job applicant's state of health, care needs to be taken to avoid discrimination on account of an applicant's past disability. The Disability Discrimination Act 1995 protects job applicants from discrimination on account of a past impairment (no matter when it occurred) if, at the time, it would have been judged to be a disability under the Act.

It may be that a job applicant's disability is disclosed as a result of a pre-employment medical examination. In these circumstances, the employer should not unquestioningly accept any conclusion put forward by an occupational doctor, but instead consider making further enquiries of the job applicant in order to establish their suitability for the job. This is demonstrated in the following case:

London Borough of Hammersmith & Fulham v Farnsworth (2000)

In this case the EAT held that an employer had subjected a job applicant to unlawful disability discrimination when they withdrew a provisional offer of employment following their acceptance of a medical report indicating that the applicant's medical condition could affect her performance and attendance at work. The EAT judged that the employer, instead of rejecting the applicant on these grounds, should have sought her views about the report and in particular about the impact of her illness on her employment in recent years. If they had done so, they would have discovered that in recent years she had enjoyed relatively good health, and that her attendance at work had not been adversely affected by her condition.

In making the final decision as to whom to select for employment, the interviewer should weigh up the skills and abilities of any disabled applicant after taking into account the likely effect of any adjustments to working arrangements or premises that the employer could reasonably make. By adopting this approach, the employer will ensure that disabled and non-disabled candidates are considered on a level playing field. A disabled candidate who meets the essential criteria for the job must not be rejected on grounds related to their disability unless the employer has first given proper consideration to the question of reasonable adjustments. Even then, any decision to reject a job applicant on grounds related to their disability will need to be capable of justification on grounds that are material and substantial.

A range of financial assistance and support is available to employers who decide to recruit someone with a disability. This is done primarily through the Access to Work Scheme and a programme called Workstep (for details see www.jobcentreplus.com), which specifically takes into account the fact that an employee with a disability may not always be capable of undertaking the full range of duties appertaining to the job, or may have a lower output than other employees doing the same job. Both schemes are administered by the Employment Service.

If an existing employee becomes disabled, the employer still has a duty to make reasonable adjustments to help that employee continue in work. If it is clear that the employee cannot continue in their previous role, then suitable alternative employment should be considered. The following case suggests that it is not acceptable to subject the employee to competitive interviews in finding that alternative employment:

Archibald v Fife Council (2004)

Archibald worked as a road sweeper. Following surgery, she suffered a complication that left her almost unable to walk. Clearly she could not continue in her duties. She underwent retraining to enable her to take up a post working in an office. She was unsuccessful in all her applications for such work within the council. As all the office jobs in the council were of a higher grade than her previous job, she had to take part in competitive interviews for all the posts, due to council policy. She claimed that this was a breach of the Disability Discrimination Act 1995 because the council were not making 'reasonable adjustments' in requiring her to undergo competitive interviews. The House of Lords upheld her claims.

TASK

Find out what arrangements your organisation, or an organisation with which you are familiar, has made to assist applicants who are disabled. Do you think the arrangements have fully met the requirement of the legislation?

ENSURING FAIR TREATMENT OF AN APPLICANT WHO IS PREGNANT

As already discussed, it is unlawful to refuse employment to a job applicant on the grounds of gender. Normally, for a claim for sex discrimination to be well founded, it must be structured around the argument that the applicant was treated less favourably than another candidate of the opposite sex was or would have been treated in similar circumstances. The one exception to this general principle is in a case where discriminatory treatment is on the grounds that a woman is pregnant.

As we saw in Chapter 4 (with reference to the Dekker case), there is no need for the woman to compare her treatment with that of a man. In the Dekker case, the judges pointed out the rather obvious fact that only women, and not men, can be pregnant and there cannot logically be a valid male comparator. They deduced from this that any discrimination based on pregnancy or on the consequences of pregnancy (eg the employee's inevitable absence from work on maternity leave) will be 'gender-specific'.

It will also be discriminatory and unlawful to refuse employment to a pregnant job applicant for a reason that is based indirectly on the fact she is pregnant.

Mahlburg v Land Mecklenburg-Vorpommern (2000)

In this case from Germany, a health authority had declined to appoint a nurse who had worked in one of their hospitals on a fixed-term contract to a permanent post that involved working in operating theatres. The decision was based on the fact that the nurse, who was eight weeks' pregnant at the time, would have been unable to take up her duties immediately owing to a health and safety law that prevented pregnant women from working in operating theatres.

The European Court of Justice (ECJ) held ultimately that the refusal to appoint the nurse in these circumstances was direct sex discrimination, and the fact that she would have been unable to take up the duties of the job initially had no impact on the key principle that a refusal to employ a woman owing to reasons associated with pregnancy is unlawful.

What an employer is obliged to do, in circumstances like the ones that arose in the Mahlburg case, is to recruit the woman (assuming she is the most suitable candidate for the post) and then, in accordance with the relevant health and safety legislation, treat her in the same way as they would treat an existing employee who becomes pregnant. Normally, this will involve offering the applicant suitable alternative work until the commencement of her maternity leave.

A more recent case dealt with the question of whether the general principles established in relation to unfavourable treatment of a woman for reasons connected with pregnancy should still be enforced in relation to work on a fixed-term contract.

Tele Danmark A/S v Handels-og-Kontorfunktionaerernes Forbund i Danmark on behalf of Brandt-Nielsen (a Danish case) (2001)

In this case, the applicant had applied for and been successful in being appointed to a job on a six-month fixed-term contract. A few weeks into the contract, she informed her employer that she was pregnant and that her baby was due some two months before the date the job was due to come to an end. She was consequently dismissed on the grounds that she had failed to inform the employer of her pregnancy when she was recruited (the evidence was that she had known, at the time of her recruitment interview, that she was pregnant).

Facing a claim for sex discrimination, the employer contended that the reason for their treatment of the employee was not her pregnancy as such, but rather the fact that she would be unable to fulfil a substantial and important part of the contract. They also asserted that the employee had been in breach of the implied duty of good faith in not informing them at her interview that she was pregnant, and that she would thus be unavailable to work the full six-month term of the contract. The ECJ, however, threw these arguments out and ruled that the employee had been the victim of unlawful direct sex discrimination. This would be the outcome, they stated, whether or not the employee's presence at work at a particular time was essential to the employer's business, and whether or not the employer would suffer a financial loss as a result of the employee's absence due to pregnancy. Furthermore, it was irrelevant to sex discrimination law whether the contract was a fixed-term contract or a permanent contract.

This area of employment law at least has the advantage of being clearly defined. The principle is simple. The employer must disregard a job applicant's pregnancy during every stage of the recruitment process, and especially when making the selection decision. To do otherwise will constitute direct sex discrimination, no matter what degree of inconvenience, or cost, might be created for the employer.

It should be noted that such decisions of the ECJ are binding on all EU member states, including the UK.

CASE STUDY

An employee working in the Ambulance Service became pregnant. She knew that the rules were that, as soon as she told her employers of her pregnancy, she would be assigned to desk duties because of the risks of her job. However, she really hated desk duties and decided to continue with her work and not tell anyone about the pregnancy.

Sadly, she was involved in helping patients in a road traffic accident, and in the process one of the patients fell on top of her. Later that day she miscarried. The doctors were unable to say whether the fall was the direct cause of the miscarriage, but it was likely that there was some link.

In this case, the employee did not attempt to take any action against her employer. However, if she had chosen to do so, do you think she would have been successful?

AGE DISCRIMINATION IN SELECTION

As noted in Chapter 2, at present there is no age discrimination legislation in the UK. However, there will be legislation from 1 October 2006, so it is important that employers start to think about how the legislation could affect their selection processes.

The Code of Practice on age diversity in employment (which is not legally binding) recommends that employers should not use age as a criterion in the recruitment process (nor in any other employment decisions). The Code recommends (among other things) that employers should:

■ not specify age limits or age ranges in job advertisements

■ avoid including age as a question on their application forms

■ try wherever possible to structure interview panels dealing with recruitment and promotion to consist of people of a variety of ages

■ ensure that age is not a barrier to training.

It is logical to conclude that the application of age limits or preferences in recruitment will severely restrict the pool from which selection can be made, and will often result in the most suitable person for the job being excluded from applying, being screened out during the early stages of recruitment, or being rejected after interview.

Although age discrimination is not at present unlawful, using an upper age limit as a criterion for selection for employment can in certain circumstances constitute indirect sex discrimination. This is particularly likely if the upper age limit is combined with a requirement for the successful applicant to have a specified minimum number of years' experience in a particular type of work. The discriminatory effect comes about because more women than men take career breaks in order to have children. Thus, the combination of an upper age limit and a requirement to have several years' experience will have a disproportionately adverse impact on women – as shown in the following case:

Price v Civil Service Commission (1978)

Price was a 35-year-old woman with two children. She applied for a job as a Civil Service executive officer, but found that there was an upper age limit of 28 years. She claimed that this was indirect discrimination against women because a significant number of women in their 20s take career breaks for childcare reasons. The EAT supported this view (and the Civil Service subsequently changed their policy).

It is therefore advisable to follow the guidelines set out in the Code of Practice and refrain from applying age limits in recruitment. Often, age limits are dreamed up by people based on their personal opinions or stereotypes, such as the notion that an older person will not fit in or will be inflexible. There is no evidence for these propositions, and the application of an arbitrary age limit may in practice have negative consequences for the organisation both from a legal and practical standpoint.

TASK

Ask your organisation, or an organisation with which you are familiar, how they have prepared for forthcoming legislation relating to age discrimination. Can you advise them on any additional arrangements that they should make?

MAKING SELECTION DECISIONS

Although there is nothing in any of the anti-discrimination legislation that obliges employers to appoint the best-qualified candidate for a particular job, they will place themselves at risk of discrimination complaints if they do not do so. If a candidate is rejected in favour of someone who, on the face of it, appears to have qualifications, experience and/or skills that are less suited to the requirements of the job and, if there is a difference in sex, race, religion or sexual orientation between the successful and the unsuccessful candidates, then a claim for unlawful discrimination may well succeed. The onus will be on the employer to show, to the tribunal's satisfaction, that the criteria for selection were not discriminatory or applied in a discriminatory way.

One effective and fair method of selection is to use a scoring system based on the skills, competencies, experience and training required for the job. It may help to give weightings to each individual element so that the assessment of candidates is made relevant to the specific job duties. This approach, if properly designed, can provide an objective aid to the evaluation of the candidates.

It is strongly recommended that employers should always keep a record of the interview process and the outcome of the recruitment exercise. In particular, it is essential to keep a record of the reason(s) for which the successful candidate was selected and why others on the short-list were rejected. In this way, if a claim for unlawful discrimination is brought to tribunal by one of the unsuccessful applicants, the employer will have some concrete evidence with which to defend themselves – ie show that the selection was based on merit and not influenced by sex, sexual orientation, race or religion. Conversely, an employer, who is facing a tribunal hearing without any documentary evidence of the recruitment programme or the reasons for the selection decision, will be in a very weak position when trying to persuade the tribunal that the recruitment procedure was carried out in an objective manner without any discrimination.

Employers should bear in mind that any documentation held on file may be the subject of an access request from the individual to whom the file relates (under the Data Protection Act 1998), and also that a court or tribunal may order the disclosure of documentation if it is considered necessary in the interests of justice.

There is no legal duty on an employer to inform an unsuccessful job applicant why their application was rejected. If, however, a job applicant is considering bringing a complaint of discrimination to an employment tribunal, they may serve a questionnaire on the employer which may ask (among other things) for the reasons the candidate was rejected. Printed forms are available under the various statutes for such an exercise, and the applicant may add their own questions, such as one about the criteria used to select the successful candidate. Where an employer receives such a questionnaire, it is advisable to complete it accurately and fully, although there is no statutory obligation to do so. However, if no response is provided, or if the response given is evasive or equivocal, this may lead the tribunal to infer that the selection decision was discriminatory.

ELIGIBILITY TO WORK IN THE UK

Employers are under a legal duty, since the implementation of the Asylum and Immigration Act 1996, not to appoint anyone who is subject to immigration control and does not have permission to live and work in the UK. To do so is a criminal offence subject to a fine of up to £5,000 per employee illegally employed. Employers therefore need to verify, before any offer of employment is confirmed, that the prospective employee has permission to work in the UK, and that their permission is current and valid in respect of the job in question.

The Asylum and Immigration Act 1996 applies only to new appointments and does not impose any requirement on employers to check up on their existing staff in relation to their ongoing right to reside or work in the UK.

The Asylum and Immigration Act 1996 does not apply to the employment of British citizens, Commonwealth citizens with the right of abode in the UK, or citizens of any country in the European Economic Area (EEA) and their spouses and dependant children under the age of 21. The EEA consists of the following countries: Austria, Belgium, Denmark, Finland, France, Germany, Greece, Holland, Iceland, Ireland, Italy, Liechtenstein, Luxembourg, Norway, Portugal, Spain, Sweden and the UK.

Ten further countries joined the EEA in May 2004 – namely, Cyprus, Czech Republic, Estonia, Hungary, Latvia, Lithuania, Malta, Poland, Slovakia and Slovenia.

In order to comply with the Asylum and Immigration Act 1996, employers should take the following steps in relation to anyone whom they are seriously considering employing:

- inspect the original of one or two documents relating to the job applicant indicating that they have the right to work in the UK
- retain a copy of such documents on record (throughout employment and for six months after employment has ended).

The law does not require employers to develop the expertise to verify the authenticity of any document produced by a job applicant. Responsibility extends only to viewing the original of the document, checking that it appears to relate to the individual in question, and retaining a copy of it. If, however, the employer knows, or has grounds to suspect, that the employment of a particular person would be illegal, or that the document produced is a forgery, then further checks should of course be carried out.

The Home Office issues a list of documents that may be used as evidence of a job applicant's right to work in the UK. For more details access their website on www.homeoffice.gov.uk.

The main difficulty in complying with the Asylum and Immigration Act 1996 is reconciling its requirements with the important requirement under the Race Relations Act 1976 not to discriminate against job applicants on grounds of nationality. The key point is to ensure that no foreign candidate is singled out for unfavourable treatment as a result of the employer's legitimate desire to check whether that applicant has the right to work in the UK.

The best way to avoid discrimination while meeting the requirements of the Asylum and Immigration Act 1996 is to adopt a policy of asking all candidates (whatever their actual or perceived nationality) to produce documentary evidence of their right to work in the UK at a specified stage in the recruitment process. This can conveniently be done at the time candidates are being invited to interview (or second interview) and can, for example, be combined with a request to produce documentary evidence of qualifications. In this way, no candidate can claim that they were treated differently from or less favourably than another candidate on grounds of race or nationality. Adopting a practice of demanding evidence of the right to work in the UK from one job applicant (for example, someone with a foreign surname), in circumstances where other applicants were not asked to provide such evidence, would give the applicant required to produce such evidence solid ammunition to bring a complaint of race discrimination to an employment tribunal.

The UK operates a work permit scheme, the objectives of which are to enable employers to recruit key people from outside the EEA to work in the UK while safeguarding the interests of UK nationals. Work permits are administered and issued on behalf of the UK Government by Work Permits (UK), part of the Home Office's Immigration and Nationality Directorate. A detailed account of the work permits scheme is beyond the scope of this book; however, the following represents a summary of some of the key provisions of the scheme:

■ If the person whom the employer wishes to appoint is not a UK national, a national of one of the EEA countries, a citizen of Switzerland, or a Commonwealth citizen who had a grandparent born in the UK, they may need a work permit. It is important to note that the criteria necessary for an individual to be granted a work permit are quite distinct from the criteria for permission to enter or remain in the UK.

■ Work permits are not issued directly to individuals but instead must be applied for by the employer who wishes to recruit the overseas national into a specific job. In most cases a fee is payable. A work permit is normally issued only if the job is one in which there is a known or proven skills shortage. Employers may not allow an overseas national who requires a work permit to commence work until a work permit has been obtained. The work permit will be issued for a specified, limited period (normally a maximum of five years).

■ Work permits are not transferable between employers or jobs. If an individual already holds a work permit in respect of a particular employment and wishes to move to a new job with a different organisation, the prospective new employer must apply for a new work permit for the individual.

KEY POINTS FROM THIS CHAPTER

■ There are various approaches that can be taken to selection, with a range of different validities.

■ When asking questions in selection interviewing, it is essential that the answers to any questions are not used to treat one group of people in a less favourable way.

- Research has shown that the different scores in intelligence tests seem to have some relationship to the ethnic origin of the person being tested.

- The responsibility lies with the employer, when interviewing a disabled candidate, to ask appropriate questions to establish the applicant's suitability for the job, and whether there are any reasonable adjustments to working arrangements, working practices or premises that they could reasonably make in order to facilitate the person's employment.

- The ECJ has consistently held that it is discriminatory and unlawful to refuse employment to a pregnant job applicant for a reason based directly or indirectly on the fact that she is pregnant.

- At present there is no age discrimination legislation in the UK, but there is a (non-legally binding) Code of Practice on age diversity in employment which recommends that employers should not use age as a criterion in the recruitment process.

- If a candidate is rejected in favour of someone who, on the face of it, appears to have qualifications, experience and/or skills that are less suited to the requirements of the job and, if there is a difference in sex or race between the successful and the unsuccessful candidates, then a claim for unlawful discrimination may well succeed.

- Employers are under a legal duty, under the Asylum and Immigration Act 1996, not to appoint anyone who is subject to immigration control and does not have permission to live and work in the UK.

EXAMPLES TO WORK THROUGH

1   You have been asked to recruit a security officer for a unit on an industrial park. The job involves working shifts, as the security cover has to be 24 hours a day. The Security Manager is concerned that one female applicant, with young children, might not be able to work the full range of shifts. He has told you that he wants to ask her about this in the selection interview. He is not saying that he will not recruit a woman, but he is concerned that she might not understand the full demands of the job. What advice would you give him?

2   As part of the selection process for recruiting graduate trainees to your organisation, all candidates undergo personality and aptitude assessment. This involves written assessments. One of the applicants is partially sighted, and has contacted you to express his concerns about taking these assessments. Consider the various approaches you could take to solving this problem, and determine which approach is best.

3   Mary is the only person who has applied for the job of solderer in the factory where you are the Personnel Manager. She has informed you that she is three months' pregnant. The Line Manager does not want to employ her, because he is convinced that she will be unable to do the job on health and safety grounds. What advice would you give him?

Issues Relating to Pay and Contracts

CHAPTER 8

OBJECTIVES OF THIS CHAPTER:

- to understand how discrimination can occur in the areas of pay and benefits
- to examine the detail of the Equal Pay Act 1970
- to outline how to develop non-discriminatory pay systems
- to consider how discrimination can occur when allowing time off work
- to examine how dress codes can be discriminatory.

EQUAL PAY

In 1970, when the Equal Pay Act was introduced, there was a gap of 30 per cent between the pay of men and women (according to the Women and Equality Unit). In 2003, that gap had reduced to 18 per cent. This means that women working full-time are currently paid, on average, 82 per cent of men's hourly pay. In 'The Gender Pay Gap' – a publication from the Equal Opportunities Commission (EOC) in 2001 – a number of reasons for this gap were suggested:

Differences in educational levels and work experience
Historically men had greater educational opportunities than women. Although this is no longer the case in the majority of instances, there might still be some impact of this among the older workforce. In addition, women are more likely to take career breaks for childcare reasons and this means that they have less opportunity to accrue work experience.

Part-time working
Although the statistical comparisons between pay allow for the differences in hours, part-time working still has an impact. This is because more women than men work part-time, and part-time jobs are often concentrated in lower paid areas of employment.

Travel patterns
Women are likely to be able to spend less time than men commuting (because of childcare and other caring responsibilities). Hence, women have a smaller pool of jobs to choose from, and there can be areas where there is a concentration of women looking for work which could push job rates down.

Occupational segregation
Sixty per cent of working women work in just 10 classifications of jobs. Typically jobs that are held primarily by women are lower paid jobs. Women are still under-represented in higher paid jobs.

Workplace segregation

Within the workplace, it is often found that the majority of women are concentrated in the lower paid jobs.

In 2001, Denise Kingsmill was appointed by the government to investigate the differences in pay between men and women. The 'Kingsmill Review' made a series of 14 recommendations, under the following five headings:

- improve the level of information available relating to the pay of women
- improve the level of reporting of relevant information
- increased research, particularly in the best use of women's skills
- the use of tax credits to encourage employers to recruit women, particularly to areas where women are under-represented
- improved rights of disclosure so that women can determine whether they are being paid fairly.

TASK

Read more detail of the 'Kingsmill Review'. Details can be found on the Women and Equality Unit website (www.womenandequalityunit.gov.uk) or the 'Kingsmill Review' website (www.kingsmillreview.gov.uk).

The government has recommended that organisations carry out regular pay audits – it is not uncommon for inequalities in pay to exist between men and women, but for the organisation to be unaware that the inequalities exist. However, despite the protestations from many trade unions, the requirement to carry out an equal pay audit is not currently compulsory.

CASE STUDY

An equal pay audit was carried out in an insurance company. It was found that men, on average, were paid 9 per cent more than women within each grade. The insurance company was very surprised by the results and investigated further. They found the following reasons for the disparities:

- More women than men worked part-time.
- To progress along a grade, employees were required to take exams giving them further qualifications within the insurance industry. More men than women were taking these exams – with women claiming that they had not got the time for the additional study (all of which had to be done in the employee's own time) because of childcare responsibilities.
- A significant proportion of women had taken time off to have children, and hence had not progressed along the grades as quickly as the men.

What should the organisation do now – and are the reasons that have been found acceptable explanations?

THE EQUAL PAY ACT 1970

The Equal Pay Act 1970 requires equality of treatment in pay and contractual terms (including pension benefits) between men and women doing 'like work', work rated as equivalent, or work of equal value. It should be noted that the Act cannot be used to found claims of unequal pay based on comparisons between employees of the same sex. It is also important to note that the Act only applies to perceived inequalities between men and women – it does not cover any perceived inequalities that have arisen on the grounds of such factors as race or disability. However, if there were such perceived inequalities, they could be covered under legislation such as the Race Relations Act 1976, or the Disability Discrimination Act 1995, as an occurrence of treating one group of people less favourably than another.

In order to succeed in a claim for equal pay, the complainant must identify a comparator of the opposite sex who is 'in the same employment' (hypothetical comparisons are not permitted). Normally, that will mean a comparator who works for the same employer or an associated employer at the same 'establishment' (ie the same unit or workplace), but the comparator may also be someone at another of the employer's workplaces, if substantially common terms and conditions of employment apply there. The comparator does not have to give consent to being named.

Recent case law has shown that an employee can make a comparison with someone beyond their own organisation in certain circumstances.

South Ayrshire Council v Morton (2002)

In this case, a female primary school headteacher in one education authority compared herself with a male secondary school headteacher in a different authority. It was found that the pay for all headteachers was determined by the Scottish Joint Negotiating Committee, and local education authorities actually had very little scope to alter a headteacher's salary. Although there were different education authorities involved, it was held that the pay of Morton and the comparator was actually attributable to a single source.

This point is further emphasised by the case of:

Lawrence & ors v Regent Office Care Ltd (2002)

Former employees of a county council, who had been transferred to a private firm following a competitive tendering exercise, claimed equal pay with employees of the council whose work had previously been rated as having equal value to theirs. The European Court of Justice (ECJ) ruled that the claim was invalid because, even though the employees were still performing the same work as before, their pay and that of their comparators was each determined separately and not governed by a single source.

Claims for equal pay can also be brought by using either a predecessor or a successor as the comparator, as shown in the following cases:

Kells v Pilkington plc (2002)

Kells was a research scientist and claimed that she did similar work to two male research scientists who had previously been employed by Pilkington, but was paid less than both of them. Although they had been employed more than six years earlier, she was still allowed to bring a claim in comparison to their pay.

Alternatively, it is possible to make a claim that a person replacing an individual is employed on a higher rate of pay:

Diocese of Hallam Trustee v Connaughton (1995)

Connaughton had worked as Director of Music from 1990 until she resigned in April 1994, her notice taking effect in September 1994. Her post was advertised at the salary of £13,434 per annum; however, she had been paid £11,138 per annum. Eventually a male was appointed to the role on a salary of £20,000 – taking up the position on 1 January 1995. The EAT ruled that she was allowed to bring a case, making a comparison with the pay of her successor.

The Equal Pay Act allows a claim to be brought if the man and woman (ie the claimant and the comparator) are employed on one of the following:

- like work
- work rated as equivalent
- work of equal value.

Like work

The legislation defines this as 'work of the same or a broadly similar nature'. Generally speaking, the Employment Tribunals will not be looking for work that is exactly the same; rather, they will be looking for a broad similarity. The Tribunal will also be looking at the typical tasks in the job, rather than incidental examples of similar tasks. The following case was brought on the basis of like work:

Capper Pass v Lawton (1977)

Lawton was a cook working 40 hours a week and preparing daily lunches for directors and their guests. She compared herself with two male assistant chefs who worked 40 hours per week with 5.5 hours of regular weekly overtime. They were responsible for cooking 350 meals per day for the employees, in two sittings. The Tribunal held that the skills and experiences required to do the two jobs were broadly similar, and the type of work carried out was also broadly similar. On this basis they decided that Lawton did similar work to the assistant chefs and allowed her claim.

Work rated as equivalent

If the organisation has an analytical job evaluation scheme (see section 'Job evaluation' on p. 162), then the approach of 'work rated as equivalent' can be used. An analytical scheme breaks jobs down into component parts and either gives jobs a 'value' by awarding points for the component parts, or makes comparisons between jobs. On this basis, jobs can be graded. If an employee can show that their job has been graded as equivalent to another job, they can potentially bring a claim of equal value although the actual jobs are very different:

Springboard Sunderland Trust v Robson (1992)

Robson compared her job of Team Leader to the job of a male Induction Officer. Robson's job had been evaluated at 410 points following a job evaluation process, and the Induction Officer's job had been evaluated at 428 points. The company grading scheme put all jobs between 360 and 409 points in grade three, and all jobs between 410 and 439 points in grade four. Despite this, Robson was treated as a grade three and the Induction Officer was rated as grade four. The EAT and the Employment Tribunal found that Robson's comparison was allowed because the two jobs were 'work rated as equivalent'.

Work of equal value

The concept of work of equal value was added to the legislation by the Equal Pay (Amendment) Regulations 1983. This was done to bring the legislation in line with the EC Equal Pay Directive. It is much more difficult to show that there is work of equal value. Typically the Employment Tribunal will appoint an 'independent expert' to examine any claim brought under this concept.

One way to obtain information from the employer in order to examine the claim of work of equal value is to issue an Equal Pay Questionnaire. Prior to the Employment Act 2002, employees could only issue such questionnaires once they had made an application to an Employment Tribunal. However, as a result of the Employment Act 2002, employees can issue questionnaires prior to bringing a claim. A sample questionnaire has been produced by the Women and Equality Unit (www.womenandequalityunit.gov.uk). The employer is required to respond to the questionnaire within eight weeks.

One example of work that was judged to be of equal value is shown in the following case:

Hayward v Cammell Laird (1984)

Hayward, a cook in the Cammell Laird shipyard, claimed her work was of equal value to painters, insulation engineers and joiners working on the same site. An independent expert was appointed by the Tribunal and investigated the claim. His conclusion was that there was evidence of work of equal value, and hence the claim was allowed.

TASK

Find out if your organisation, or an organisation with which you are familiar, uses job evaluation. If it does, look at the way in which jobs are graded and find out if jobs of the same grade receive similar pay and benefits. If they do not, find out how pay and benefits are determined. Have you identified anything that gives concern relating to work that is similar, like or equivalent?

CASE STUDY

A manufacturing organisation has two grading schemes. One grading scheme is for those employed in the actual manufacturing, and the other is for support staff. One grading scheme has ten grades (1-10) and the other scheme has five grades (A-E).

A clerical employee has made a claim that she does work of equal value to a light assembler. She has found a direct comparator – who is paid 13 per cent more than she is. The organisation is arguing that the two people are on separate grading schemes, and hence it is not possible to make comparisons between the two jobs. They are also claiming that the rather unpleasant manufacturing unit (smelly and dusty because of the nature of the products that are made) means that those who work there should be paid more money.

Despite these assurances, the employee has decided to go ahead with her claim, and the organisation has been informed that they must provide information about each job so that they can be evaluated and compared. The problem has yet to be resolved – what is the likely outcome?

DEFENCES TO AN EQUAL PAY CLAIM

The genuine material factor defence

An employer can defend a claim for equal pay by showing that there was a reason for the difference between the pay package of the man and the woman that represented a 'genuine material factor' unconnected with gender. The word 'material' in this context has been held to mean 'significant and relevant'. Factors such as qualifications, experience, performance and, in some instances, market forces may justify pay differences between a male and female employee. An employer will not, however, be able to defend an equal pay claim solely on the grounds that they cannot afford to pay the complainant more.

If the reason for an employee's lower level of pay is that they have shorter service than their chosen comparator, the employer must be in a position to justify operating a pay scheme based on length of service. To do this, they will need to demonstrate that length of experience in the particular job under review actually enables the employee to do the job more effectively.

Even if an employee expressly agrees to accept a lower rate of pay than someone else performing the same job or work of equal value, this will not prevent that employee from succeeding in an equal pay claim. It is not open to an employer to seek to contract out of their statutory responsibilities.

It is also worth bearing in mind that any female employee whose pay is dependent on length of service could claim under the Sex Discrimination Act 1975 that this practice was indirectly discriminatory against women. This would be based on the well-established argument that women generally have shorter service than men because more women than men take career breaks to raise a family. In the event of such a claim, the employer would have to satisfy a tribunal that the practice of basing pay on length of service was objectively justified.

Table 8 summarises a range of factors that may or may not justify differences in pay.

Table 8 *Examples of genuine material factors*

Potentially valid	Unlikely to be valid
Higher level of qualifications, enabling better or different job performance	Formal qualifications that do not affect job performance
More relevant experience, enabling better job performance	More experience where the type of experience is not directly relevant
Special skills relevant to the job	Special skills where these are not used in the job
Longer service, where this leads to enhanced job performance	Longer service that does not affect job performance
Significantly higher level of responsibility	Different job titles
Superior job performance as measured in an objective appraisal scheme	Alleged superior performance where this cannot be evidenced, for example where no objective appraisal scheme is in operation
The terms of a collective agreement that are gender-neutral	Historical practices that may themselves have been based on discriminatory assumptions
Time of work, eg a clearly defined premium aid for night shift working	Differences between the pay of men on night shift and women on day shift for traditional reasons
Place of work, for example an allowance paid to compensate for higher living costs in London	Different rates of pay in different branches of the same company because of separate collective bargaining procedures
Market forces where it is genuinely necessary to pay more to attract the 'right' person into the job	Argument that the organisation cannot afford to pay more to the claimant
Red-circling (ie temporarily maintaining an employee's higher salary upon transfer to a lower-graded job	Continuing indefinitely to pay an employee transferred to a lower-graded job a higher rate of pay

The following cases give examples of defences that might be allowed and disallowed by the Employment Tribunals:

Different negotiating groups

Enderby v Frenchay Health Authority (1993)

In this case, the health authority relied on the defence that the differences in the jobs that had been identified were as a result of the rates of pay being determined by different negotiating bodies. Enderby was a senior speech therapist and she claimed her work was of equal value to that of male principal grade pharmacists and clinical psychologists. The ECJ ruled that it was insufficient to rely on the differences resulting from different negotiating groups, and justifications for the actual differences had to be given.

Experience

Arw Transformers Ltd v Cupples (1977)

Cupples was aged 27 and paid £40.75 per week. She compared herself to a male colleague doing the same work (work study engineer) who was aged 53 and paid £60 per week. It was ruled that, although her colleague had more experience, the work that they were doing was the same and hence the differing level of experience was not a defence to the differences in pay.

Red-circling

If an employee is moved to a job at a lower level, organisations often 'red-circle' the rate of pay. This means that the pay is not reduced, but no increases are given until people doing the same work have reached the same level of pay.

Outlook Supplies v Parry (1978)

Parry was an accounts supervisor and she compared her pay to a male colleague who was also an accounts supervisor, but previously had been an accounts supervisor alongside being an assistant accountant. Due to ill health, the assistant accountant part of the role had been dropped and his pay had been red-circled. However, this had happened two and a half years earlier, and the tribunal ruled that red-circling was not a defence because it had gone on too long. Although the EAT agreed that red-circling should not go on for a prolonged period, it did not judge that two and a half years was too long and hence the employer's appeal was allowed.

Location

Navy, Army and Air Force Institutes v *Varley (1976)*

Varley worked as a clerk in Nottingham, working a 37-hour week. Colleagues doing the same work in London worked a 36.5-hour week. Varley argued that her hours should be the same as a male clerk working in London. However, she lost her claim because it was held that the difference was due to the location and not as a result of sex discrimination.

Where an equal pay claim reaches a tribunal hearing, the onus will be on the employer to establish that there was a genuine material factor that justified the difference in pay between the claimant and the comparator. An employer will be in a much stronger position to succeed in doing this if they operate a pay system that is transparent – ie a system in which the basis for determining pay rates is known and clearly understood by both managers and their employees.

Barton v *Investec Henderson Crosthwaite Securities Ltd (2003)*

Barton worked as a media analyst for the organisation (an investment bank). She and her colleagues were paid a base salary, a bonus, share options and long-term incentive plans. She brought a claim under the Equal Pay Act because her male colleagues had been paid substantially higher bonuses than her. In the tribunal, the chairman of the bank explained that the bonuses were discretionary, and there was little written explanation of how they were determined – this was not a transparent system. The EAT found that the employer had failed to discharge the burden of proof – because it was not able to show that the way the bonuses were determined were not discriminatory. The EAT also declared that it was unacceptable for an organisation to operate a bonus culture involving secrecy and/or lack of transparency.

TASK

Referring back to the earlier task, look at any differences in pay for work that seemed to be the same, like or equivalent. What defence might be given to the differences, and do you think those defences would be accepted by the Tribunals?

JOB EVALUATION

Where an employer elects to implement a job evaluation scheme and base employees' pay on the results of the scheme, it will be very important to make sure that the process of job evaluation is analytical, objective and based on factors that are not in any way discriminatory.

The overall purpose of job evaluation will be to establish a fair structure of job gradings on which the employer's pay system can be based. The key preliminary point to bear in mind is that a job evaluation scheme should be designed to evaluate jobs, and not the people doing the jobs. It is therefore advisable to assess and grade jobs on an anonymous basis whenever possible.

If a job evaluation scheme is to protect the employer against equal pay claims, it must be based on an analytical study – ie a detailed analysis of jobs that has been conducted in a structured, rational and objective way. This is demonstrated in the following case:

Eaton Ltd v Nuttall (1977)

Eaton was a female scheduler, and she compared her pay with a male scheduler doing like work. The difference in pay was justified by the employer on the grounds of the potential value of any errors made by the male scheduler (the errors had a potentially greater cost to the organisation). In making its judgement, the EAT provided some useful guidance in the methods of job evaluation that can be viewed as analytical. These fall broadly into two categories:

1   A scheme may be based on a points assessment system. Different numbers of points are attributed to different factors within each job according to a predetermined scale, and each job is then graded according to its total number of points. Different factors may be weighted differently according to their importance.

2   A factor comparison system, in which several benchmark jobs are selected on the basis that their existing rates of pay are considered to be fair. These jobs are then analysed in order to split them up into different factors, each of which is allocated a proportion of the total rate of pay for the job. Other jobs can subsequently be assessed by identifying which factors they contain, and adding together the rates of pay for each factor.

The EAT went on in the Eaton case to say that certain types of job evaluation study, such as job-ranking, paired comparisons and job classification systems, cannot be regarded as sufficiently analytical to justify a defence against equal pay claims. The key difference between an analytical and non-analytical scheme is that an analytical scheme breaks down each job, or at least representative benchmark jobs, into individual components, while non-analytical systems focus on comparing whole jobs that are then ranked in order of priority.

The specific factors that are usually used to evaluate jobs include:

- the knowledge required for effective performance of the job
- the interpersonal and communication skills required for effective performance of the job
- any physical skills relevant to the job (but employers should guard against attributing too much importance to such factors as physical strength, as this could discriminate indirectly against women)
- the physical, emotional and mental demands inherent in the job
- the amount of effort required to perform the job in terms of concentration, attention to detail, etc.
- the level of decision making and problem solving required in the job
- the job's overall level of responsibility – for example, responsibility for people, resources, finance, development and safety

- the amount of initiative, innovation and independence required for the job
- the working environment and conditions in which the job is performed.

Once jobs are evaluated, pay is usually determined by creating job grades or pay bands based on a points system, so that each job grade/pay band encompasses all jobs that score between a defined lower number and a defined upper number of points. This produces the inevitable consequence that each grade or band will contain a number of jobs with a range of points scores, some at the lower end of the scale and some at the higher. This may result in some practical difficulties, because an individual whose job falls at the top end of one grade may feel disadvantaged on account of not being placed in the next grade up. Nevertheless, it is reasonable to conclude that dividing lines have to be drawn somewhere, and the key requirement is to ensure that the exercise to draw the lines does not produce a discriminatory or perverse outcome.

Employers should ensure that they take account of the following in conducting job evaluation:

- ensure all job descriptions are written to reflect accurately the nature of the job as it is done
- eliminate any personal factors when evaluating jobs – eg disregard the employee's actual level of performance
- ensure the factors and weightings chosen for the job evaluation scheme contain no gender bias – for example, placing an inordinately high weighting on physical strength and a very low weighting on interpersonal skills
- endeavour to create a job evaluation panel that contains an equal mix of men and women
- ensure that the method of job evaluation is applied impartially and fairly to all jobs irrespective of who is performing them
- ensure job descriptions are regularly updated, and that any changes to the job are then reviewed to establish whether the job needs to be regraded (up or down)
- introduce an objective and fair procedure for dealing with complaints about job grading.

The EOC produced a revised Code of Practice on Equal Pay, which was implemented on 1 December 2003. Like other Codes of Practice, the Code is not legally binding on employers, although any failure to act on its provisions may be taken into account by a court or employment tribunal in the event of a claim for equal pay or sex discrimination taken against an employer.

The Code of Practice on Equal Pay provides useful practical guidance on how employers can ensure their pay practices are free from sex discrimination. The Code also recommends that employers should conduct equal pay reviews, and asserts that these are the most appropriate method for ensuring delivery of pay systems free from sex bias. The Code contains a section summarising the essential features of an equal pay review, including a five-step model for carrying one out.

TASK

Find further information on conducting equal pay reviews, and the Code of Practice itself, on the EOC's website at www.eoc.org.uk.

TIME OFF WORK

There are a number of situations in which an employee is entitled to take time off work. In this section we are going to examine how discrimination could occur if these entitlements are not handled correctly.

Time off for dependants

The Employment Rights Act 1996 entitles all employees to a reasonable amount of time off work (on an unpaid basis) in order to take care of, or arrange for the care of, a dependant who has been taken ill or been injured or assaulted. It also entitles employees to take time off in the event of the death of a dependant or the birth of a child to a dependant, or in the event of unexpected disruption to a dependant's care arrangements – for example, childcare.

'Dependant' is defined as an employee's:

■ spouse

■ child

■ parent

■ any person living in the same household as the employee (other than lodgers).

In light of the Employment Equality (Sexual Orientation) Regulations 2003, which require equality of treatment for gay and lesbian employees, the time off to care for dependants will be extended to allow for employees to take appropriate time off in the event of the death, illness or injury of a same-sex partner.

Time off for religious holidays

Following the implementation of the Employment Equality (Religion or Belief) Regulations 2003 in December 2003, employees are entitled not to be treated unfavourably on grounds of 'any religion, religious belief or similar philosophical belief'.

The Regulations do not expressly require employers to provide time off or special facilities for religious purposes, and no employer is obliged to accept unreasonable disruption to their business activities on account of employees' religious needs. However, if an employer unreasonably refuses to accommodate an individual's needs where doing so would be feasible, this could be in breach of the Regulations.

An employee's religious belief may involve practices associated with not working on a particular day of the week or on specified dates during the year. It follows that (for example) requiring a practising Christian employee to work on a Sunday, where that employee held strong religious views that Sunday working was unacceptable, would constitute indirect religious discrimination. Even though the employer might well apply the Sunday working requirement equally to all employees, it would nevertheless place people who shared the particular employee's religious beliefs at a disadvantage, thus constituting indirect discrimination. In order to be lawful, therefore, the employer would have to show that the requirement was proportionate to the achievement of a legitimate aim, taking into account all the relevant circumstances.

Employers may also face requests from Jewish employees or Seventh Day Adventists (for example) to be exempted from working on Saturdays (or requests from Jews to be permitted to leave work in time to be home one hour before sunset on Fridays, which is when their Sabbath begins). If not working on a particular day is genuinely a key facet of an employee's religious beliefs, then a refusal to accommodate the individual's request will be discriminatory. Similarly, the dismissal of an employee for refusing to work on Saturdays, where the refusal was on grounds of the person's religious beliefs, could constitute unlawful religious discrimination. Once again, the key question is whether a refusal to grant an employee's request was proportionate to the achievement of a legitimate aim.

Another potential problem is the payment of overtime premiums for Sunday working. Paying premium rates of pay for Sunday work could be challenged as discriminatory if the employer did not also pay the same premium rates for work performed on other religious Sabbath days – for example, Saturday.

The Employment Rights Act 1996 affords protection to shop workers and betting workers against detrimental treatment and dismissal on the grounds that they refuse to work on Sundays. This provision is not, however, connected with religion or religious beliefs, but is in place to protect people who do particular jobs.

Another conundrum for employers is how to deal with employees who wish to celebrate special religious days during the year and seek time off on those days instead of (for example) time off at Christmas or Easter. It could be argued that, if a Muslim employee (for example) was refused paid time off on an important Islamic festival in circumstances where the employer gave (Christian) employees paid time off on Christmas Day, this would constitute indirect and possibly direct religious discrimination. It could be indirect discrimination because a refusal to grant time off on the religious day in question would disproportionately affect Muslim employees compared with others, and direct discrimination on the grounds that the Muslim employee was refused a perk enjoyed by a Christian employee. While indirect religious discrimination can (potentially) be justified, direct discrimination cannot. Because the legislation in this area is relatively new, it will be necessary to wait until an appeal court or tribunal rules on this particular point in order to be certain whether such actions would be regarded as direct, or indirect, discrimination.

In view of these difficulties, it might be advisable for employers to review their programme of public holidays and, if necessary, take steps to make their policies or practices more flexible, so that employees who are not Christians are not denied the right to paid time off on the days or dates of the year that have special religious significance for them.

One option would be to introduce a policy under which there are no prescribed public holidays, but instead grant staff a predetermined number of floating holiday days each year (for example, eight days' paid leave over and above annual leave). The policy could provide that these days be taken either on traditional public holidays or (by agreement with management) on other days. This approach would benefit those who, as a result of their religion, do not celebrate Christmas or Easter and who might prefer time off at a time of the year that coincides with a date that is important to their faith.

Another option for employers who wish to promote diversity is to grant all employees who adhere to a religion or belief a set number of days holiday per year specifically for the purpose of celebrating religious holidays or festivals.

Time off to pray

Employees of certain religions may wish to pray at set times or at regular intervals during the day.

Muslims, for example, are required to pray five times a day for about 10 minutes each time, Jains are obliged to worship three times a day and Zoroastrians must pray five times during the day.

While there is no obligation in the Employment Equality (Religion or Belief) Regulations 2003 on employers to provide time off work or special facilities for employees for religious observance, employers may nevertheless wish to adopt a flexible approach towards the timings of rest breaks. Often the time off requested will be no longer than what is needed for a cup of coffee or a cigarette.

In order to promote equality and good will, the employer may also wish to set aside for employees a room in a quiet part of the workplace in which to pray or engage in private contemplation. The best way forward when considering this is to consult staff (or their representatives) to seek agreement on the room and its facilities, so as to ensure that employees of all denominations are equally catered for, and that the facilities provided are appropriate.

In light of the complexity of the subject of time off for religious reasons, employers should also:

- engage in dialogue with practising faith employees to increase understanding of their religious needs and endeavour to reach agreement to any adjustments they may seek
- devise training programmes to increase employees' awareness (in particular managers' awareness) of religious diversity
- be sensitive to the particular needs of any individual for whom a particular day or date has special religious significance
- aim to be flexible with individual employees and accommodate religious holidays and restrictions on days or hours of work whenever possible – for example, allowing flexibility in arrival and departure times, in the length and timing of lunch breaks, and permitting employees to swap hours or shifts
- be willing to compromise – for example, where the employee offers to work additional hours at another time
- adopt a flexible attitude towards lunch breaks, especially during Ramadan when Muslim employees are likely to be fasting until the end of the normal working day

■ if a request for time off for religious needs is refused, ensure the refusal can be justified in line with a legitimate aim of the business.

Time off for religious holidays – human rights implications

The Human Rights Act 1998 gives individuals the right to freedom of thought, conscience and religion (Article 9), and any breach of that right by a public authority could give rise to a further legal claim. Where the employer is a public authority, a breach of the Human Rights Act can form the basis of a stand-alone claim to a court or tribunal.

Although it does not overtly give employees the right to time off work to attend religious events or to pray, any refusal to grant such time off by a public-sector employer may nevertheless lead to a legal challenge under the Human Rights Act. To succeed in defending such a claim, the employer would have to show either that the employee had agreed contractually to work on the particular day or at the particular time (and had thus waived their 'right' to time off for religious reasons), or that the refusal was justified when balanced against the 'rights and freedoms' of the employer or the employees' colleagues. The employer could, for example, argue that they had the right to expect their employees to perform their contracts or to be available during peak periods of work. An employer would in no way be obliged under human rights law to grant excessive time off if this had an adverse effect on the business. This is illustrated in the following case:

Ahmad v Inner London Education Authority (1982)

Ahmad worked as a school teacher, and was a devout Muslim. His contract of employment was for a full-time job, but did allow him time off with pay on special religious days when his religion dictated that he should not work. He asked for permission to spend 45 minutes every Friday visiting the Mosque, but was refused. He resigned and claimed unfair constructive dismissal. The European Court of Human Rights (ECHR) found that there was no breach of Article 9 of the Human Rights Act because Ahmad had known of the requirements of the contract when he took the job.

The ECHR does take the view that employees are free (if they wish) to resign from an organisation if they consider that their rights to a belief or a religion are being infringed by an employer. This approach gives reduced protection to an employee, as is demonstrated in the following case:

Copsey v WWB Devon Clays Ltd (2003)

Copsey was dismissed for not agreeing to a new seven-day shift pattern which would include him working Sundays. The EAT found that, applying the approach of the ECHR, his claim failed because he did not have to work for the employer, he could resign, and hence his human rights had not been infringed.

NB: This occurred prior to the 2003 legislation relating to religion and belief. If the claim had been brought under this legislation, the ruling might have been different.

TASK

Find out how your organisation, or an organisation with which you are familiar, has adapted the time off provisions in light of legislation relating to discrimination on the grounds of religion or belief. Do you think that the adjustments that have been made are sufficient, or should further adjustments be made?

DRESS CODES

Another sensitive subject for employers and employees alike is the subject of dress codes. Employers should be aware that, if they impose company rules on dress and appearance (including any restrictions on hair length, jewellery, tattoos and body piercings), they will inevitably displease some, alienate others and run the risk of spawning claims for direct or indirect sex, race or religious discrimination. Nevertheless, employers may quite legitimately wish to introduce and maintain rules and standards of dress and appearance in order to ensure:

- health and safety
- hygiene (for example, in food-handling jobs)
- smartness (in order that the organisation can project a professional corporate image to clients, customers or the public at large)
- conventionality (in order to maintain good relations among staff and customers, and to avoid the possibility of causing offence).

Employers should be willing to consider any legitimate objections raised by an employee in relation to a particular aspect of the dress code and, where appropriate, make exceptions. In FME Ltd v Henry (1986), for example, an employee succeeded in a claim for unfair constructive dismissal when he was told that he would be sent home if he reported for work unshaven. The employee had objected to the rule that required men to shave on a daily basis because he developed a rash if he shaved every day.

There are two specific issues that may give rise to difficulties for employers who wish to implement or enforce a code on dress and/or appearance, and at the same time avoid sex discrimination. The first is the fact that men and women traditionally do not dress in the same manner or fashion, and rules on dress and appearance cannot therefore (logically) be identical for men and women. For example, it might be viewed as absurd for an employer to require female employees to wear a collar and tie to work. The second issue is that fashions, and what is acceptable to society at large, change over time and what was socially unconventional and possibly unacceptable 20 years ago may nowadays be regarded by the majority of people as 'normal'. For example, it is widely regarded as acceptable and 'normal' nowadays for a woman to wear a trouser suit to work, while this would have been unusual (and possibly frowned upon) 30 or 40 years ago (which is within the working lifetime of many people employed today).

The general principle developed by courts and tribunals is that it is an employer's dress code as a whole that stands to be judged, rather than the individual elements of the dress policy. There is no need for an exact item-by-item comparison, but it will be necessary to apply equal standards to men and women.

Case examples

Burrett v *West Birmingham Health Authority (1994)*

A nurse claimed indirect sex discrimination when she was disciplined for refusing to wear a cap as part of the prescribed female nurses' uniform. Male nurses were not required to wear a cap. The employment tribunal held that the existence of differing uniform requirements for men and women did not in itself amount to sex discrimination. The nurse had not been subjected to a detriment when compared with male staff because both male and female nurses were required to conform to a similar standard, and a male nurse would have been equally disciplined for refusing to comply with the rules.

Department for Work and Pensions v *Thompson (2004)*

In April 2002, the JobCentre Plus introduced a new dress code for staff. All staff were required to dress in a 'professional and businesslike' way. For men, this meant a collar and tie (although it could be removed in hot weather at the management's discretion) and women were required to adopt a similar level of dress. Thompson worked as an administrative assistant and did not meet the public. He refused to comply with the new code, and was given a warning. After that, he agreed to comply under protest, but made a claim of direct sex discrimination.

The tribunal supported his claim that he had suffered sex discrimination, because women had no prescribed form of dress, and hence had a range of choice that was not open to men. It awarded him £1,000 compensation. As a result of this, a further 6,950 cases were lodged at Employment Tribunals from male employees in a similar situation. The Department for Work and Pensions (DWP) appealed to the EAT.

The EAT found that the issue was whether Thompson had been treated unfavourably, not whether he had been treated differently. They also determined that the correct question to be answered was whether the required level of appearance could only be achieved by men wearing a collar and tie. If it was found that the required level of appearance could be achieved by allowing men more flexibility in their dress, then Thompson had been treated unfavourably. The case was referred back to another Employment Tribunal to consider the question, but in the meantime an agreement was reached between the DWP and the employees, with the DWP agreeing to amend the dress code.

Some racial and religious groups have rules, standards and customs that affect their dress and appearance. It follows that an employer's dress code may discriminate indirectly against people from a particular racial or religious group if the code prevents or restricts them from following their customs. Sikhs, Muslims, Hindus and Rastafarians are just some of the groups that may be adversely affected by employers' rules on dress and appearance. For example:

- Sikhs are required by their religion to wear turbans and have uncut hair and beards. It follows that a ban on beards at work would discriminate indirectly against Sikhs. Such a rule might be capable of justification on hygiene grounds if the job involved handling food (although a better solution would be for the employer to permit men to wear beards provided they cover them with a snood while at work).

- Orthodox Sikh men may wear a metal bangle called a Kora, which has a deep religious significance for them. Any rule that requires the removal of jewellery would have to be justified – for example, on safety grounds if the job involved working with machinery.

- Women from certain ethnic groups and some religions may be required to dress modestly – for example, to have their legs and/or arms covered at all times. Employers' dress codes should of course accommodate any need (or preference) for women to wear trousers.

- Women from some religious groups may wish to have their heads covered at all times, and a failure or refusal to accommodate this in a dress code may be indirectly discriminatory on grounds of race or religion.

- Orthodox married Hindu women may wear a nose stud to mark their married status. Any employer that imposes a blanket ban on facial piercings may find that this constitutes indirect religious discrimination. No employer would (presumably) ban women from wearing their wedding ring to work, unless there was a safety reason for such a rule.

- Some Hindu men wear neck-beads as a symbol of their faith.

- Some Hindu men wear a small, knotted tuft of hair tied at the back of their head like a ponytail as a symbol of their belief. A blanket ban on male employees having ponytails could thus be indirectly discriminatory on grounds of religion unless it can be justified.

- Orthodox Jewish men need to keep their heads covered at all times and may therefore require to wear a 'skull cap' to work.

Rules on dress and appearance – whether formal or informal, or specified by an individual manager or department – should be flexible enough to accommodate individuals' racial, religious or cultural customs, and employers should:

- avoid imposing rules rigidly without regard for individual employees' objections
- be willing to vary or adapt dress codes where possible to accommodate employees whose racial or religious backgrounds might prevent them from complying with the rules.

Employers may also wish specifically to consider:

- modifying health and safety wear to permit an employee to wear an item of religious dress safely
- providing beard bags or snoods if hygiene is an issue, rather than requiring a man to shave off his beard
- (where there is a company uniform) introducing specially designed outfits – for example, saris, turbans and hijabs.

Sikhs and turbans

Generally, Sikhs are subject to the same employment laws as any other racial or religious group, but with one major exception. The Employment Act 1989 (Section 11) contains a provision that permits male Sikhs to be exempted from the requirement to wear safety helmets on construction sites, providing a turban is worn instead. It is important to bear in mind that this dispensation applies only to Sikhs and only on construction sites. In other types of workplace, it will normally be lawful for an employer to insist that all employees, including Sikhs, wear protective headgear for safety reasons.

If a Sikh suffers an accident or injury on a construction site, any damages awarded against the employer will be limited to compensation for the injury that would have been sustained if the Sikh had been wearing a safety helmet.

In line with the Employment Act 1989, the Employment Equality (Religion or Belief) Regulations 2003 state that it can never be lawful to require a Sikh to wear a helmet on a construction site. The Regulations also state that the exemption for Sikhs contained in the Employment Act 1989 cannot give rise to a claim for unlawful discrimination by anyone else.

Article 10 of the Human Rights Act 1998 (the right to freedom of expression) will be another element affecting employers who decide to impose restrictions on what employees wear to work. The Act provides, however, that an individual's right to freedom of expression can be restricted 'for the protection of the reputation or rights of others'. 'Others' in this context includes the employer, the employee's colleagues and potentially members of the public with whom the employee might come into contact. So, for example, an employer who denied an employee the 'right' to wear a t-shirt sporting an animal rights slogan to work would not necessarily be in breach of Article 10, provided the employer had a proper reason for the restriction. Valid reasons might be a desire to ensure the employee projected a smart image to members of the public, or a concern that colleagues might be offended by the slogan or image on the t-shirt.

So long as a dress code is reasonable, not unnecessarily restrictive, and designed to achieve a legitimate business aim, it should not breach employees' rights to freedom of expression under the Human Rights Act.

TASK

Take note of the dress codes that different organisations appear to have. See if you can find any examples of dress codes that appear to be discriminatory in any way.

CASE STUDY

An airline commissioned a designer to develop a new uniform range for all its cabin crew. When the results of this were revealed, a number of Muslim women were very upset at the revealing nature of the uniform. It was agreed that they could adapt the uniform to ensure that they were covered in accordance with their religion.

A number of non-Muslim women also complained that the outfits were too revealing – the skirts being too short, and the blouses being too tight – and some of them were uncomfortable about wearing them. They had no religious grounds to object and hence they were instructed that they had to wear the uniform. Is there any legislation that they could use to fight the instruction?

KEY POINTS FROM THIS CHAPTER

- The Equal Pay Act 1970 requires equality of treatment in pay and contractual terms as between men and women doing 'like work', work rated as equivalent, or work of equal value.

- In certain circumstances, an employee may be able to make a comparison for equal pay purposes with someone beyond their own organisation if their pay and that of the comparator can be shown to be attributable to a single source.

- Pay systems should be transparent – ie a system in which the basis for determining pay rates (including bonuses) is capable of being understood clearly by all.

- If a man and woman are doing similar work but are paid differently, there must be a genuine material factor that justifies the difference in pay.

- An employer should respond as fully and honestly as possible to any equal pay questionnaire served by an employee, as any failure to respond or a response that is incomplete, evasive or equivocal may lead an employment tribunal to draw inferences that are unfavourable to the employer.

- The law does not expressly require employers to provide time off or special facilities for religious purposes, and no employer is obliged to accept unreasonable disruption to its business activities on account of employees' religious needs.

- An employee whose religious beliefs involve practices associated with not working on a particular day of the week, or on specified dates during the year, is protected in law against any unjustified refusal to allow time off on such days or dates.

- Employers may quite legitimately wish to introduce and maintain rules and standards of dress and appearance in order to ensure health and safety, hygiene, smartness or conventionality, but such rules and standards run the risk of generating claims for direct or indirect sex, race or religious discrimination unless they are proportionate to the achievement of a stated aim and applied even-handedly to both men and women.

EXAMPLES TO WORK THROUGH

1   Julie is employed as a call centre team leader, and in your grading system is classed as Grade 2. She is claiming that she should be paid the same as Fred who is an accountant and is also classed as a Grade 2. However, the Finance Director is arguing that this is nonsense because Fred has had to complete all his accountancy examinations before working as an accountant, and Julie has not taken any formal qualifications relating to her job. What advice would you give?

2   Four Muslim employees have approached the company asking for time off to celebrate their religious festivals. This has been refused. They are now arguing that this is direct discrimination because, each year, the organisation closes from Christmas Eve until 2 January. They argue that this closure allows all the Christian employees to celebrate one of their major festivals, and hence discriminates against employees of other religions who do not have a similar period of closure during their festivals. What would you advise?

3   You work for an airline company. The air stewardesses have complained that the skirts they are required to wear are too tight and uncomfortable, and have asked to have the option to wear trousers. The stewards are all required to wear smart trousers issued by the company. The company has refused the request, because they do not think that stewardesses wearing trousers promotes the image they want. The stewardesses are now claiming direct sex discrimination. What would you advise?

Equality and Diversity within Employee Development

OBJECTIVES OF THIS CHAPTER:

- to examine the impact of equality and diversity on training and development
- to consider specific issues relating to performance management and the use of appraisals
- to outline consideration that needs to be given to the transfer and promotion of employees
- to evaluate issues associated with performance-related pay.

ACCESS TO TRAINING AND DEVELOPMENT

Access to opportunities for promotion, transfer and training is expressly covered in the anti-discrimination legislation. Employers should aim not only to avoid any potentially unlawful discrimination, but also strive to ensure fairness and equality of treatment for all staff in relation to opportunities for development. Well designed, objective procedures should be used to deal with employee training and promotion, and employers should take care in particular to ensure that members of minority groups are not overlooked when deciding on promotions.

It is very important, when making decisions about employees' training and development, that managers should refrain from making assumptions about individuals based on generalisations or on their own past experiences of people with whom they have worked. For example, it would be sexually discriminatory to deny training to a female employee based on an assumption that the employee might leave in the near future to start a family, or to accompany her husband, should he be relocated to another area by his employer. Such assumptions about the likely behaviour patterns of women would be discriminatory if they placed a female employee at a disadvantage (ie led to her being denied or refused an opportunity for training). In contrast, if there was evidence that a particular woman did in fact plan to leave in the foreseeable future (whatever her reason), then that fact would constitute a valid, non-discriminatory reason for the employer to decline to invest in that employee's training. The outcome would obviously be the same in the event of a male employee whose plans to leave the organisation in the near future were known to management. This is illustrated in the following case:

> *Horsey v Dyfed County Council (1982)*
>
> Horsey took up a post as social worker for the Council, and agreed to attend a social work course at a university or polytechnic within one year as a condition of her appointment. The Council would pay for the course, but she had to commit to working for the Council for at least two years after the completion of the course. Sometime later,

her husband took a job in London, and Horsey received the offer of a two-year course in Maidstone. Horsey wanted to take this course so that she could live with her husband in the London area while studying. However, the Council refused permission for this because they were not satisfied that she would return to the Council once the course was completed. Horsey resigned, took a job in London and made a claim of unlawful sex discrimination against the Council. The Employment Appeal Tribunal (EAT) upheld this complaint because the Council had refused her permission to take the course in Maidstone on the assumption that a woman will leave her job to follow her husband.

Similarly, it would be discriminatory on racial grounds to refuse training to an employee of foreign nationality based on an assumption that the employee might decide to return to their own country soon after completion of the training. Such generalised assumptions may well be quite untrue in relation to a particular individual and may cause them a detriment on racial grounds. Instead of making generalised assumptions, the employer should consider the individual employee when deciding whether to offer training. For example, it would not be discriminatory to decline to nominate an employee for a training course on account of the employee's limited abilities or unwillingness to attend.

When organising internal training events, employers should pay heed to the likely diverse circumstances of their workforce in relation to the days of the week and times of day that individuals are likely to be available to attend the training.

Scheduling a training programme over a weekend, for example, may place female employees who work normal office hours at a disadvantage (as compared with male employees) on account of the greater likelihood of women having the predominant responsibility in the family for childcare. A female employee may be unable to attend a training event held at a weekend, particularly if she is a single parent. Training courses that extend into the evening may have the same detrimental effect on women more than on men (unless of course the employees in question normally work evening shifts). Such scheduling could therefore amount to indirect sex discrimination if a female employee was placed at a disadvantage by the scheduling of the training – for example, if she was unable to attend, or if she was to incur the overt disapproval of management for not attending.

An employer who insists on running internal training courses at weekends may also run the risk of claims of indirect religious discrimination from those whose religious beliefs mean that they cannot work on a Saturday or Sunday.

In order to avoid such problems and to ensure that valued employees are not thoroughly demotivated, the employer should seek to organise training programmes within the normal working hours of the employees who form the target audience of the training. If, however, there are strong business reasons for running training at times outside employees' normal working hours, the employer should make sure that employees are informed of the dates and times of the training well in advance so that they at least have an opportunity to make personal and domestic arrangements enabling them to attend. If, despite such advance notice, a particular employee cannot attend, that employee should not be penalised in any way.

Another consideration, where training spans whole days, will be to make sure that opportunities are available within the timetable for employees to take a break for the purposes of religious observance.

TASK

Look back at the training courses that have been arranged by your organisation, or an organisation with which you are familiar, over the past year. Given the information that you have just read, do you think that the arrangements for any of the courses were potentially discriminatory?

Both the Part-Time Workers (Prevention of Less Favourable Treatment) Regulations 2000 and the Fixed-Term Employees (Prevention of Less Favourable Treatment) Regulations 2002 provide that employers should not exclude part-timers or fixed-term employees respectively from opportunities for training on account of their part-time or fixed-term status. The Guidance Notes issued by the Department of Trade and Industry (DTI) to accompany the Part-Time Workers Regulations state also that training should be scheduled so far as possible so that staff, including part-timers, can attend. Neither set of Regulations places a positive duty on employers to offer training to part-time or fixed-term employees, but employers are instead under a duty not to exclude these categories of staff from training.

With respect to fixed-term employees, the Fixed-Term Employees Regulations impose an obligation on employers to treat a fixed-term employee, who has the same length of service as a comparable permanent employee, no less favourably than that permanent employee as regards access to training opportunities. In other words, it would be a breach of the Regulations to exclude from training a fixed-term employee with (for example) one year's service if a permanent employee with one year's service performing a comparable job would be offered the training, unless there is objective justification for the less favourable treatment of the employee engaged on the fixed-term contract.

Under the Disability Discrimination Act (DDA) 1995, an employee who is disabled has the right not to be treated unfavourably in relation to opportunities for training and development. Employers should therefore ensure that:

- disabled staff are given the same training and development opportunities as others
- negative assumptions about the abilities of disabled staff are not made
- arrangements for training do not place any disabled employee at a disadvantage
- training methods and scheduling are flexible enough to accommodate any disabled employee who is eligible to attend.

In order to comply with the duty to make reasonable adjustments in respect of a disabled employee whose disability would otherwise place them at a substantial disadvantage, employers may wish to consider making some of the following adjustments in respect of training:

- Move the training venue to a location with easier access for an employee who has limited mobility or who uses a wheelchair.

- Reschedule a training course to accommodate a disabled employee whose condition means that they need to attend a medical appointment or undergo medical treatment at a particular time.

- Ensure that tables, desks, chairs, etc. are suitable for an individual with a physical disability.

- Consider anyone who has a visual impairment when designing training – for example, by producing written training material in Braille or in extra-large print.

- Provide an induction loop for an employee who has a hearing impairment, so that they can use this in conjunction with their hearing aid at the training venue.

- Obtain a copy of the script of any video that is to be used during the training course for an employee with a hearing impairment (if this is possible).

- Redesign training – for example, by allowing a longer period overall and a slower pace for an employee with a mental impairment that affects their ability to concentrate, learn or understand.

- Design training with more frequent breaks, so that individual sessions are shorter for employees whose disability affects their span of concentration or who cannot sit for lengthy periods.

- Permit a disabled employee to be accompanied on the training programme by someone who can provide them with support or assistance.

- Provide special coaching or mentoring either before or after the main training event for an employee with learning difficulties.

An example of a case where an employer failed to make satisfactory adjustments is given below:

Huskisson v Abbey National plc (2000)

Huskisson was dyslexic and undertaking training to become a financial adviser. He encountered difficulties in conducting interviews and adapting his product knowledge to suit the needs of customers. He contacted his employers suggesting that his difficulties were related to his dyslexia. His employer took the decision to dismiss him because of his lack of progress, and because they did not think that any further training would be of any use. This was found to be unlawful disability discrimination because the employers had failed to consider making any reasonable adjustments, or to seek expert advice about the difficulties that Huskisson was facing.

When considering an employee with a mental impairment for training, managers should beware of making negative assumptions about an individual's potential to learn or develop. An employee with learning difficulties, for example, may be quite capable of learning if they are afforded extra time to assimilate the necessary information, or given extra coaching or support.

One of the most important forms of training for any organisation (and one that is often afforded only lip-service) is induction training for newly employed staff. If a new employee is not made to feel comfortable and confident during the first few days or weeks of their employment, there will be a higher-than-average chance that they will leave. This will result in a considerable waste of time, energy and money for the employer, who will inevitably have to repeat the recruitment exercise.

Starting a new job is stressful for most people. They may initially feel 'out of place', uncomfortable and under pressure to make a positive impression to a range of people whom they do not know. A new employee who belongs to a minority group (for example, a woman in a predominantly male environment, or an employee from a minority ethnic group) may feel particularly out of place when thrown into a completely new environment, because they may, over and above these ordinary stresses, have to cope with the worry of being perceived as 'different'.

To improve the process of induction, employers may wish to:

- design induction so that new employees are offered a range of different introductory sessions with different people in different departments
- avoid cramming induction into the first day or two of the new employment
- endeavour to give the new employee something useful and productive to do as early as possible in their employment
- make it clear to all new employees during induction what people need to do in order to make progress within the organisation
- make sure induction includes information about the informal processes that exist within the organisation, as well as the official policies and procedures
- nominate an individual in respect of each new start (for example, a mentor) from whom the employee can seek specific guidance or advice, or to whom they can take any problems they experience in becoming integrated into the organisation
- ensure that managers who carry responsibility for induction training are properly trained themselves.

TASK

Review an induction programme that you have taken part in. Do you think that it made all employees equally welcome to the organisation? What improvements could have been made?

POSITIVE ACTION

While positive discrimination in employment is not permitted by UK law, certain forms of positive action are allowed provided the action taken is in the form of encouragement to members of an under-represented or disadvantaged group to take up opportunities for employment or training. In effect, positive action will widen the pool for development, promotion or selection.

The circumstances in which positive action may be taken are, however, limited. Specifically, positive action in relation to gender and race may be undertaken only when either men or women, or people from a particular racial group, are under-represented in the organisation as a whole or in a particular type of employment. The equivalent provisions related to religion and sexual orientation permit employers to take steps to encourage people of a particular religion (or sexual orientation) to take advantage of training opportunities, provided such action is carried out to prevent or compensate for disadvantages linked to religion (or sexual orientation) suffered by those of that religion (or sexual orientation).

Positive action in training is therefore a lawful means of attempting to redress an existing imbalance, and is specifically aimed at helping to equip employees from an under-represented or disadvantaged group for particular work.

It is important to note, however, that offering training to an employee just because they belong to a minority group is not permitted in UK law. What is permitted is training set up specifically and exclusively for people from an under-represented or disadvantaged group. Furthermore, although single-sex training or training restricted to members of a particular racial or religious group is permitted under the positive action provisions, where training is made generally available by an employer, the employer may not then give priority to members of a minority group. In other words, the positive action provisions affecting training dictate an 'all or nothing' approach. For example, in an organisation where women are under-represented in management positions, it would be lawful for the employer to offer management training exclusively to female employees in order to encourage more women to progress into management. Where, however, the employer elected to offer management training to all employees (ie both men and women), it would not be open to them to give priority to a female employee in the process of deciding who was to be nominated for a particular training course.

Positive action can include (for example):

- offering training to people who have been out of full-time employment because of domestic or family responsibilities, to enable them to get back into work (this is expressly permitted in the Sex Discrimination Act 1975)
- designing focused training for people from groups that are under-represented in a particular type of work – for example, to increase the chances for promotion into supervisory or management posts for women or people from minority racial groups
- offering training to overseas nationals who are not ordinarily resident in Britain and who are not expected to remain in Britain – for example, if the training will be needed when they return to their home country (this is expressly provided for in the Race Relations Act 1976)
- encouraging ethnic minority employees to apply for promotion or transfer opportunities
- promoting flexible working practices (which are likely to benefit all staff), and training managers in how to manage flexible working and work-life balance.

TASK

Draft an advertisement that is to be placed on internal notice boards asking employees to put their names forward if they are interested in a specific training course. Be careful to ensure that nothing about the advertisement is discriminatory.

CASE STUDY

New technology was being introduced into a call centre. It was essential that all the call-centre operators learnt how to use this within a two-week period, because it was then going to be used on a daily basis. The timescale was acknowledged to be very short – but this was due to difficulties there had been with developing new software.

Over 60 per cent of the workforce in the call centre did not work full-time and hence ensuring that everyone attended for the training was logistically very difficult. After some complicated timetabling, everyone was assigned to one of three training sessions. This meant that some employees would need to come in when they would not normally be working, but they were told they would be paid for the extra hours.

Three employees did not attend the last training session. They phoned in just before it was due to start and informed the Supervisor that their childcare arrangements had fallen through, and they would not be attending. The training session had been arranged at a time that they would not normally be working. The Supervisor informed them that they would have to wait for a training session that was being run at another call centre two weeks later and that, until they had attended that session, they should not come to work. They claimed unfair sexual discrimination. Although this case never went to the Employment Tribunal, a local solution being found, would they have been successful?

PERFORMANCE MANAGEMENT

Performance management should be a continuous process operating within an organisation. It involves identifying the vision, goals and strategies of an organisation and converting them into individual objectives. The individual objectives need to be agreed with employees and regularly monitored, typically through an appraisal system.

The setting of objectives is a key task for management, and it is useful to refer to the SMART acronym in considering how objectives can promote diversity, and how to avoid discrimination:

Specific
It is important that the employees understand exactly what they are required to do. If the employees are working within teams, then the operation of the team will be more successful if everyone understands their objectives. It is important that any limitations of the employees are considered when setting specific targets. For example, if an employee is working part-time, it is not reasonable to expect them to have targets relating to the same volume of work as a full-time employee.

Measurable
If the employees understand how their performance is to be measured, there are likely to be fewer accusations of discriminatory behaviour in the appraisal process. If targets are clear, then both the employer and the employee should have the same conclusion about whether a target has been met. In this case, the employee is less likely to accuse an employer of marking them down on the basis of a discriminatory factor.

Achievable
It is essential that any objectives that are set are achievable. If an employee is disabled, for example, then the employer must consider whether any adjustments need to be made to

make the objectives achievable. It is also important that the employer does not use the setting of unachievable objectives as a means of confirming unfound prejudices.

Realistic

Once the objectives have been outlined, the employer must consider whether the achievement of the objective is realistic for that employee. If the employee has a disability, does not work full-time, or has any other restriction on the potential achievement of the objective, then this must be taken into consideration.

Time-bound

Just as it is important to have clearly measurable expectations, it is also important for the employee and the employer to have a common understanding of when the objectives are to be completed.

As with other aspects of the employment relationship, performance appraisal should be conducted without any direct or indirect discrimination against individuals on grounds of gender, marital status, race, religion or belief, sexual orientation, age or disability.

The starting point for ensuring a fair and non-discriminatory appraisal scheme is to review the scope of the scheme and make sure that no-one is excluded from appraisal on any of the prohibited grounds.

If appraisal is offered to some groups of employees and not others (for example, to 'white-collar' staff and not 'blue-collar' workers), this could lead to indirect discrimination if the gender or racial composition of each of the two groups is different. If fixed-term employees are excluded from appraisal, this would in most cases be unlawful under the Fixed-Term Employees (Prevention of Less Favourable Treatment) Regulations 2002, unless their exclusion could be objectively justified. The same principle applies to part-time employees under the Part-Time Workers (Prevention of Less Favourable Treatment) Regulations 2000. Excluding part-timers, and even possibly casual workers, from appraisal could also amount to indirect sex discrimination if the majority of part-timers or casuals in the organisation are women.

One particular pitfall to avoid is the inadvertent exclusion from appraisal of a woman who is absent from work on maternity leave. Once the employee has returned to work, her manager should ensure she is given a full opportunity to undergo an appraisal that is as equal as possible to the standard appraisal offered to other staff (taking into account that she has been absent from work for a period of time).

In the French case of Caisse Nationale d'Assurance Vieillesse des Travailleurs Salariés v Thibault (1995), a female employee successfully claimed before the European Court of Justice (ECJ) that she had been the victim of sex discrimination when she was denied an annual performance assessment, and along with it the chance of promotion, because she had taken maternity leave. The reasoning of the ECJ was that, had the employee not been pregnant and taken maternity leave, she would have been given a performance appraisal, and could have therefore qualified for promotion. Since pregnancy and maternity leave are exclusive to women, the employee's exclusion from the annual performance assessment for reasons related to maternity leave amounted to direct sex discrimination.

Having ensured that no employees are unreasonably excluded from the appraisal process, the next step for management should be to examine the assessment criteria of any existing scheme to ensure these do not discriminate indirectly against any group of employees. For example, if employees' performance is measured in terms of flexibility (ie flexibility in terms of availability to work additional hours at short notice), this would discriminate indirectly against female employees, who are less likely than male employees to be able to comply with any request to work overtime at short notice.

Criteria used for assessing job performance should be job-oriented and measurable, and not person-oriented (which would allow the appraiser's opinion of the appraisee as a person to be the determining factor). Criteria could, for example, be based on tasks completed, standards achieved and targets met, rather than factors such as 'attitude', 'reliability' or 'flexibility', which would allow the appraiser's subjective view of the individual's personal qualities to take precedence. If an assessment of the employee's communication skills forms part of the appraisal, care should be taken not to discriminate against employees of foreign nationality whose first language is not English.

Appraisal interviews are notoriously difficult to conduct effectively. One barrier may be the appraiser's personal opinions about the appraisee, their work or future potential. It is important that those conducting appraisals have been properly trained in the art of appraisal interviewing. Such training should include awareness training on prejudice and stereotyping based on such factors as sex, marital status, sexual orientation, race, cultural background, religion, appearance, age and other factors.

CASE STUDY

A banking organisation carried out an annual appraisal of all employees, and the employee's individual bonuses were paid according to the outcome of this appraisal. The appraisal of each employee was graded A (extremely effective) to E (not at all effective).

One employee had chronic arthritis and was registered as disabled. Although she performed competently in her job, her speed of work was slow due to her disability. For three years she was given a 'C' grade, largely because of the slowness of her work. She claimed that this was unlawful discrimination, because there was no hope of her ever getting a grade above 'C' however hard she worked. The organisation argued that the appraisal had to be applied consistently to all employees because of the link to the bonus. Hence, very strict guidelines were given to all assessors and, if the employee did not meet certain criteria, they were restricted on the grade they would receive.

The disabled employee successfully argued that this was unlawful discrimination, and the criteria were adjusted accordingly.

TASK

Look at the appraisal form used by your organisation, or an organisation with which you are familiar. Examine it to see if there are any potentially discriminatory factors.

PERFORMANCE-RELATED PAY

Performance-related pay is the payment of a bonus or an element of the base pay in accordance with the performance of an individual. The approach of performance-related pay became particularly popular because it pays people for their performance, and hence is thought to motivate people to achieve higher levels of performance.

The main difficulty with performance-related pay is the measurement of performance. In some jobs it is reasonably easy to make measures – for example, the number of calls handled in a call centre, or the number of items made on a manufacturing line. However, even these seemingly clear measures have their problems – are people sacrificing quality for the sake of quantity, and what if the quantity produced is disrupted by events out of the control of the employee?

However, most jobs do not have such clearly definable targets, and hence there is an inevitable element of subjectivity in assessing performance. This can lead to the possibility of discriminatory factors having an influence on the assessment that is made.

One approach used by some organisations is to have a quota system – whereby a set percentage of employees achieve each level of award. This does allow an easy analysis of the system to see if one group of employees is under-represented at one level. However, the quota system can result in someone receiving a lower level of award than they are seen to deserve because no more awards at a particular level are allowed.

In his book, *Employee Reward*, Michael Armstrong refers to the report from the First Division Civil Servants at the 1991 Trades Union Congress. It was alleged that 52 per cent of male civil servants in grades 5–7 had qualified for extra performance-related payments, whereas only 38 per cent of women had done so.

The use of performance-related pay can also perpetuate pay differences, which can arise to claims under the Equal Pay Act 1970, as explained in Chapter 8. Presume, for example, that a man and a woman doing the same job are both paid £20,000 per annum. At the end of the first year, the woman receives a 5 per cent increase in pay based on performance, and the man receives a 10 per cent increase. If the same happens the next year, the differences in pay are now £24,200 compared with £22,050.

It is important, therefore, that, in setting up a performance-related pay scheme, safeguards are put into the scheme to guard against the pay system becoming discriminatory.

Safeguards should include:

■ thorough training of all those who will be involved in determining performance related pay awards

■ a regular monitoring of the payments made, analysed by factors such as gender, race, disability, etc.

■ ensuring clear agreement between the employee and employer about the objectives that have been set and how they will be measured.

An interesting judgement from the ECJ was given in the following case:

Handels-og Kontorfunktionaerernes Forbund I Danmark v Dansk Arbejdsgiverforening (acting for Danfoss) (1991)

An equal pay claim was brought by a Danish trade union on behalf of two of its female members who compared their pay with male colleagues doing the same work. Although the women and their comparators worked within the same grade, the pay within the grade could be increased according to flexibility, seniority and vocational training. Statistical evidence showed that, on average, women were paid 6.85 per cent less than men in the same grades.

The ECJ ruled that flexibility in the scope of quality of work was a justifiable criterion for pay, but it was inconceivable that women consistently performed at a lower level than men. However, if flexibility related to adapting to different work schedules, then this could be indirectly discriminatory against women as they could find it harder to adapt their work schedules because of other responsibilities outside of the workplace.

This ruling shows that any factors that are used to give additional payments for performance, or related criteria, must be justifiable.

There are alternatives to performance-related pay that could be considered. There is increased popularity of the use of skill-based pay and competence-based pay. Although these two approaches also have their disadvantages, they are often preferred because the assessment is less subjective than the assessment of performance.

Skill-based pay is a system of paying for the skills that the employee has gained. This has the benefit to the employer of raising the skill base within the organisation, having employees who are able to complete a wider range of tasks, and hence being able to operate with a leaner workforce.

For skill-based pay to be a motivator, there must be opportunities for employees to learn new skills, so that their pay can progress and increase. This goes back to the comments we made at the start of this chapter – all employees must have equal access to training and development to ensure that the pay system does not become discriminatory.

Similarly, competence-based pay is a system of paying for the competencies that the employee has. As defined by Boyatzis (1982), a competency is:

> **" an underlying characteristic of an individual which is causally related to effective or superior performance. "**

It can be very time-consuming to set up a competency-based pay system because of the time required to identify competencies required in each job. The assessment of whether an employee has actually achieved a particular level of competency can be somewhat subjective, and hence give opportunities for allegations of discrimination.

It is particularly important that the competencies identified do not have some sort of discriminatory bias. For example, in determining the competencies that are required for a manager, it is important that the competencies do not inadvertently favour a more masculine style of management. It is also important that the competencies do not discriminate against particular racial characteristics.

TASK

How are you paid? Do you think that there is any aspect of the way your pay is determined that is unfair? Do you think that there is a better approach that could be taken?

PROMOTION OPPORTUNITIES

The duty to ensure equality of treatment in promotion is similar in principle to the duty not to discriminate during the process of recruitment and selection. The genuine occupational qualifications (GOQs) and genuine occupational requirements (GORs) that are permissible in recruitment to new posts are also permissible in respect of selection for promotion or transfer.

Specifically, the anti-discrimination legislation provides that employers must not discriminate in the access afforded to opportunities for promotion. This wording clearly covers a wide range of situations involving the availability of opportunities for promotion as well as the employer's decisions as to whom to promote. For example, an employee who was allocated only menial or unchallenging tasks could argue that this practice restricted or prevented them from gaining access to opportunities for promotion. If the allocation of menial tasks could be shown to be linked to discrimination on grounds of sex, race, etc., then a case for unlawful discrimination in opportunities for promotion could be made out.

As in the process of recruitment, it is important, when operating procedures for selection for promotion, to ensure that any criteria applied to the promoted post are not indirectly discriminatory. This is illustrated in the following case:

Falkirk Council v Whyte and ors (1997)

A prison employee, who had been unsuccessful in an application for promotion to a management post, claimed indirect sex discrimination on account of the employer's policy of applying 'management training and supervisory experience' as 'desirable' criteria for the post. She argued that female prison officers were less likely than male officers to have the requisite management training and experience, and that she had suffered a disadvantage when she was rejected because of the application of these criteria.

The employer argued at tribunal that because the management training and supervisory experience criteria were not applied to the selection process as essential factors, the employee's rejection for the post could not have been discriminatory. However, the evidence was that the employer had in fact applied these criteria as decisive factors. The employee who had been rejected for the promoted post had therefore suffered a disadvantage as a result of the imposition of the requirement to have management training and supervisory experience. The EAT took the view that the imposition of this requirement was not objectively justified in the particular case.

Employers should therefore think twice before specifying requirements based on length of service, length of experience, flexibility, mobility and full-time working as either necessary or desirable criteria for promotion to a particular post. Such provisions can discriminate indirectly against women, who are more likely than men to be disadvantaged by them as a result of family and childcare responsibilities. It is important, if a particular criterion is to be applied in the selection decision, that it can be objectively justified as relevant or necessary for the effective performance of the job in question.

Discrimination on grounds of marriage is unlawful under the Sex Discrimination Act (SDA) 1975, as demonstrated in the case of the Chief Constable of Bedfordshire Constabulary v Graham (2002), described in detail in Chapter 4.

It often happens that an individual is selected for a promotion without any formal procedure having been undertaken by the employer. While this practice may be convenient for the employer who may have earmarked a particular employee for a particular post, it does run the dual risk of:

- alienating other employees who would have valued the opportunity to apply for the promoted post

- being an arbitrary practice capable of being challenged as indirectly discriminatory against, for example, women or ethnic minority employees who may be vulnerable to being overlooked for promotion. If, say, a woman on maternity leave could show that she had more suitable experience or qualifications in relation to the promoted post than the person selected, the employer would have great difficulty at tribunal in defending a claim for sex discrimination.

Even if the employee who is appointed to the promoted post is the most suitable candidate, making an appointment without first affording the opportunity to apply for the job to other employees, who may consider themselves capable of performing it, will breach the inherent principle of equal opportunities and send out the wrong signals. Conversely, adopting a policy of making opportunities available to all employees to apply for all promoted posts will act to promote equality and diversity throughout the organisation, and will minimise the likelihood of appointments being perceived as unfair or discriminatory.

The case of Visa International Services Association v Paul (2004) quoted in Chapter 4 illustrates this point. In this case, a vacancy for which Paul had trained, and in an area in which she had expressed an interest in working, arose while she was on maternity leave. By not giving Paul the opportunity to apply for the job, discriminatory behaviour was judged to have occurred.

It follows that, to promote equality and diversity, all available vacancies should be widely advertised internally, using all available methods – for example, notice boards, internal magazines, e-mail and any company intranet. Managers should take steps to make sure that employees at different branches or locations are also informed of vacancies. Arguably, it is only where people from all sectors of the organisation are given every opportunity to be considered for promoted posts that the aims of diversity can fully be achieved.

The Fixed-Term Employees (Prevention of Less Favourable Treatment) Regulations 2002 contain a specific provision that entitles employees engaged on fixed-term contracts to receive information from their employer about any suitable available vacancies that arise in the establishment. Furthermore, fixed-term employees have the right to be treated equally in comparison to permanent employees with the same length of service with regard to the opportunity to obtain permanent employment. These provisions would entitle fixed-term employees to be considered on an equal footing to comparable permanent employees in relation to any available promoted posts.

The Part-Time Workers (Prevention of Less Favourable Treatment) Regulations 2000 provide that employers must not subject part-time workers to any detriment on account of their part-time status. This principle would be breached if a part-time employee was refused a promotion just because they worked part-time, unless the employer was able to justify the refusal on objective grounds unrelated to the individual's existing part-time status. Managers should not assume that part-timers do not want promotion or are unsuitable for promotion, whether the promoted post is part-time or full-time. Instead, all staff should be given an equal opportunity to apply for the promoted post in question.

Checklist for good practice in dealing with promotions:

- Review, and if necessary revamp, promotion procedures to ensure that each stage of the procedure, including vacancy notification, interviewing, assessment and final selection, is being carried out objectively and without discrimination on any ground.

- Ensure that procedures for promotion are communicated to all staff (including fixed-term and part-time workers) so that everyone understands the process used to identify and assess internal candidates for promotion.

- Scrutinise any traditional routes to promotion into supervisory and management posts to make sure the employer's practices do not indirectly discriminate against female employees or those from minority racial or religious groups.

- Review and if necessary change any rules that restrict or preclude transfers between certain jobs.

- Think carefully before specifying the criteria for selection into a promoted post to ensure that they can be objectively justified.

- Ensure all job vacancies are advertised internally at all the employer's branches and locations so that all employees are consistently informed about promotion opportunities.

- Ensure that fixed-term and part-time staff are given fair and appropriate consideration for promoted posts.

- Introduce a process whereby unsuccessful internal candidates are given feedback explaining why their application for a promoted post was unsuccessful, and giving positive guidance on how they might improve their chances of promotion in the future.

- Monitor promotions to provide a record of the numbers of men/women and members of different racial groups who are promoted. If any imbalances are identified relative to the total numbers of people employed, explore the causes and take appropriate steps to eliminate them.

CASE STUDY

The promotion system among a group of medical staff within a hospital is based on the range of experience that they can demonstrate on the job. It is not allowed to apply for a senior job unless the applicant has worked in at least six different departments, and has spent at least one year in each department.

The senior employees within this group are almost entirely men, and the rigid promotion system is blamed for this. It is argued that the promotion system is indirectly discriminatory against women because they are more likely to have breaks in their career for childcare reasons.

However, the hospital have argued that the matter is one of safety for patients. At a more senior level, the employees have greater patient responsibility, and hence they need the greater level of experience. Promoting people earlier might leave them responsible for making critical life and death decisions that they do not have the experience to make.

The argument rumbles on – what do you think the solution should be?

TASK

Find out how promotions are decided in your organisation, or an organisation with which you are familiar. Think of any ways that the process could be improved, particularly with a view to safeguarding against potential discrimination.

MOBILITY

It is common for employers to include mobility clauses in the contracts of employment of certain staff, typically senior management and project employees in large national organisations. However, a blanket policy to incorporate a clause into employees' contracts requiring them to agree to relocate to a different UK (or overseas) location at the employer's request is not advisable, as it would discriminate indirectly against women. This principle was established in the case of Meade-Hill & anor v British Council.

Meade-Hill & anor v British Council (1995)

The employee, who had been promoted, was issued with a new contract which included a wide-ranging mobility clause requiring her to agree to work anywhere in the UK at the employer's discretion. Even though this clause did not immediately affect the employee (who was not being required to relocate at the time in question), she applied to a court seeking a declaration that it was unenforceable on the grounds that it amounted to indirect sex discrimination. Her argument was founded on the principle that a larger proportion of women than men are secondary wage earners, and consequently fewer women than men can in practice comply with an employer's instruction to relocate.

On appeal, the Court of Appeal upheld the employee's complaint, ruling that the mobility clause had been 'applied' immediately the contract had been entered into, and that its application was not objectively justified in all the circumstances of the case.

It is not, in any event, sensible for an employer to try to force an employee (whether male or female) to move to a different location against their will. A much better policy would be to seek to agree mobility requirements individually with employees as and when the need to fill a vacancy arises, without any pressure being placed on a particular employee to move, whether permanently or temporarily. Even though mobility may be a justifiable requirement in some jobs, it is important to consider the employee's personal circumstances at the time a transfer is being mooted, and not penalise an employee who, for family or other personal reasons, cannot, or does not wish to, move to a different location.

In contrast, a limited mobility clause requiring employees to agree to move to a different location within reasonable distance of their home would be helpful to an employer in the event that they decide to move premises or transfer employees between different workplaces in the same city or district.

KEY POINTS FROM THIS CHAPTER

- Scheduling training programmes over a weekend or during evenings may place female employees who work standard office hours at a disadvantage as compared with men, and should therefore be avoided in these circumstances.

- Both the Part-Time Workers Regulations 2000 and the Fixed-Term Employees Regulations 2002 provide that employers should not exclude part-timers or fixed-term employees respectively from opportunities for training on account of employees' part-time or fixed-term status.

- Positive action in training is a lawful means of attempting to redress an existing imbalance (for example, in the proportions of men and women in a particular type of work), and is specifically aimed at helping to equip employees from an under-represented or disadvantaged group for particular work.

- Performance management systems should be based on objectives that are clearly understood by both the employer and the employee.

- The starting point for ensuring a fair and non-discriminatory appraisal scheme is to review the scope of the scheme and make sure that no-one is excluded from appraisal on any of the prohibited grounds.

- It will be unlawful to exclude part-time or fixed-term employees from appraisal purely on grounds of their part-time/fixed-term status, although the exclusion of a particular individual may be objectively justified.

- Criteria used for assessing job performance should be job-oriented and measurable (for example, against agreed targets) and not person-oriented (which would allow the appraiser's subjective view of the individual's personal qualities to be the determining factor).

- The use of performance-related pay requires some level of subjectivity in assessment, and hence there is the potential for discrimination to occur. Approaches such as skills-based pay and competence-based pay have less potential for discrimination to occur.

- Anti-discrimination legislation provides that employers must not discriminate in the access afforded to opportunities for promotion, which means a wide range of situations involving the availability of opportunities for promotion, as well as the employer's decisions as to whom is to be promoted, are covered.

■ Adopting a policy of making opportunities available to all employees to apply for all promoted posts will promote equality and diversity throughout the organisation and minimise the likelihood of appointments being perceived as unfair or discriminatory.

■ A blanket policy to incorporate a clause into employees' contracts, requiring them to agree to relocate to a different UK location at the employer's request, is not advisable as it would discriminate indirectly against women.

EXAMPLES TO WORK THROUGH

1   To improve the success of teamwork within your organisation, it has been decided to have a series of weekends away for each team. The weekend will include a mix of work-based and social-based activities, all designed to help the members of the team to work together more effectively. Due to customer demands, it is not possible to take the whole team away from work during the normal weekly working day. Two members of one team have stated that they will not attend because they have young children and want to spend the weekend with them. What should you do?

2   Following a recent round of appraisals, you notice that the scores for men in one department are significantly higher than the scores given to the women. How would you investigate this?

3   Your organisation has a very clear process for determining promotions, including psychometric assessment, interviews and a review of appraisal ratings over the last three years. An equal opportunities audit has shown that significantly more men than women, and significantly more people of a white ethnic origin than all other origins, have been promoted over the past two years. What actions would you propose to take, if any?

Discrimination at Termination of Employment

10

OBJECTIVES OF THIS CHAPTER:

- to understand how discrimination can occur in the termination process
- to examine the fair approach to disciplinary procedures and dismissals
- to outline particular issues associated with the dismissal of disabled employees
- to understand how factors used to select employees for redundancy can be non-discriminatory
- to understand potential issues associated with age discrimination
- to consider specific issues associated with the giving of references

THE LAW RELATING TO DISMISSAL

According to the Employment Rights Act 1996 (section 98), there are five potentially fair reasons for dismissal:

- conduct
- capability
- redundancy
- statutory ban
- some other substantial reason.

In order to bring a claim of unfair dismissal to the Employment Tribunal, the employee must have at least one year's continuous service with the employer. However, in situations where the dismissal is automatically unfair, no qualifying period of service is required.

The situations in which a dismissal will be automatically unfair include those where the dismissal relates to:

- the employee's membership (or non-membership) of a trade union
- the employee's pregnancy or any maternity-related issue
- a transfer of undertaking
- the refusal of a retail employee to work on a Sunday
- a conviction that is, according to law, deemed to be 'spent'

- activities carried out in the role of health and safety representatives
- asserting a statutory right
- making a protected disclosure under the Public Disclosure Act
- asserting the right to be paid in accordance with the National Minimum Wage Act 1998
- disclosing fraud or corruption.

If an employee considers that the reason for the dismissal, or the motive or the process of the dismissal, was discriminatory, then they can bring two separate claims to the Employment Tribunal. If they have at least one year's continuous service, they can bring the claim of unfair dismissal under the Employment Rights Act 1996. Regardless of their length of service, they can also bring a claim for discrimination under the relevant legislation (depending on the nature of the discrimination). The claim will be of unlawful discrimination, and the act of discrimination will be the dismissal or a particular aspect of the dismissal.

In addition to the requirement to have a fair reason for dismissal, the employer must apply a fair procedure, and in particular must follow the statutory dismissal and disciplinary procedure (DDP) that was introduced to UK law on 1 October 2004. The detail of the procedure can be read at www.dti.gov.uk/, but the primary requirement is to follow a three-stage procedure:

1   Write to the employee setting out the circumstances that have led the employer to consider dismissing the employee (for example, alleged misconduct or proposed redundancies), and explaining the basis for the employer's thinking. The letter should also invite the employee to attend a meeting.

2   At the meeting, give the employee a full and fair opportunity to answer the case against them or make representations, as appropriate. The employee must be granted the right to bring a colleague or trade union official along to the meeting, if they wish. The outcome should afterwards be communicated to the employee in writing.

3   Allow the employee the right to appeal to a more senior level of management if the employee is not satisfied with the outcome of the meeting.

TASK

Go to the Department of Trade and Industry (DTI) website, www.dti.gov.uk, and read more detail about the statutory disciplinary procedure. Can you identify any ways in which discrimination could occur in this procedure?

The Employment Relations Act 1999 gave the right for workers to be accompanied by a fellow worker or trade union representative to any disciplinary or grievance hearing that is formal in nature or likely to lead to formal action.

SEX DISCRIMINATION IN THE TERMINATION PROCESS

Discrimination at the time of the termination of a person's employment could be linked to the reason for dismissal, the motive behind it, the process for redundancy selection or the manner in which the dismissal or redundancy was carried out. A discriminatory dismissal will always be unlawful.

Employers should therefore ensure that the reason for an employee's dismissal is not related in any way to gender, trans-gender status, marital status, race, religion, sexual orientation or (unless it can be justified) disability. They should also take care to ensure that all procedures and processes that lead, or might lead, to termination of employment are carried out objectively and free from discrimination.

Whenever an employer has grounds to invoke their disciplinary procedure (whether or not this is thought likely to lead to the employee's dismissal), it is essential that the processes must be free from all forms of discrimination.

A difficult area is dealing with an employee who is unable, or unwilling, to be flexible as regards hours of work – for example, when it comes to shift working or a requirement for overtime. This may be because of family commitments, in particular childcare responsibilities. Another example could be an employee who refuses to work on a particular day of the week, or date during the year, possibly for reasons related to their religion or belief.

There may be a tendency for some managers to view an apparent unwillingness to work long or unsocial hours, or different shifts, as a negative factor, possibly justifying disciplinary action in the event of an outright refusal to work at the required times. This could, however, create a problem for the employer if the employee in question is a woman with caring responsibilities, because any unfavourable treatment of the woman in such circumstances would be likely to constitute indirect sex discrimination. This is because courts and tribunals have, over many years, accepted the general principle that fewer women than men can work long hours or unsocial hours owing to their childcare responsibilities. The Sex Discrimination Act (SDA)1975 states that any provision, criterion or practice that is likely to be to the detriment of a larger proportion of women than men, and which places a particular woman at a disadvantage, will be indirect sex discrimination and unlawful unless the employer can justify it. The following case illustrates this point:

London Underground Ltd v Edwards (1998)

The employer changed their rostering system in such a way that Ms Edwards, a train driver, could not comply with a requirement to start work at 4.45am on some mornings. This was because she was a single parent. Ms Edwards succeeded in her claim that the new arrangements were indirectly discriminatory against her as a woman, and the Court of Appeal held that it was not justifiable for the employer to have insisted that she comply with the early morning start time. While there was nothing inherently unlawful about the new rostering system, the employer, as a large organisation, could have exempted Ms Edwards from the requirement to do the early shift, or made alternative arrangements to accommodate her needs without causing any difficulty in terms of the efficiency of the business.

Similarly, any disciplinary action, or dismissal, of a woman on the grounds of a refusal to work longer hours or unsocial hours (or even full-time hours as opposed to part-time hours) will be indirect sex discrimination unless the requirement to work the hours or shift pattern in question can be shown to be objectively justifiable based on the needs of the business, and it can also be shown that the employer was justified in applying the requirement to the woman as an individual.

If a female employee is dismissed in any of the following circumstances, it is likely that her dismissal would be judged to be sex discrimination by an employment tribunal:

- dismissal for any reason linked to the fact that the employee is pregnant
- dismissal on account of the inconvenience the employee's impending absence on maternity leave was thought likely to cause
- enforced retirement at an earlier age than that at which a man in similar circumstances would have been compelled to retire
- termination on the grounds that the woman has raised a genuine complaint of sexual harassment
- dismissal because the employee cannot work shifts, work extensive overtime or work full-time, criteria that place women at a disadvantage as compared with men
- selection for redundancy based on lack of flexibility as regards hours of work or shift working
- dismissal for any reason where a man would not have been dismissed in similar circumstances.

In the previous section we noted a list of situations in which dismissal will be automatically unfair. This included the situation where an employee is dismissed on the grounds of pregnancy or a maternity-related issue. This is illustrated in the following case:

Brown v Rentokil (1998)

The employee (a service driver) was absent from work continuously after she became pregnant. The employer operated a contractual policy under which any employee who exceeded 26 weeks' continuous sickness absence would be dismissed automatically. The employee in this case was dismissed in accordance with the policy once her sickness absence reached 26 weeks (at which time she was still pregnant). The European Court of Justice (ECJ) held that the treatment of the employee amounted to direct sex discrimination despite the existence of the policy which, the ECJ held, was largely irrelevant because no comparison with a man off sick could legitimately be drawn. The ECJ did not criticise the employer's policy in a general sense, but their judgment made it clear that the employer should have disapplied the policy in the case of an employee who was absent for a pregnancy-related reason.

TASK

Ask your organisation, or an organisation with which you are familiar, for a summary of the reasons why employees have been disciplined or dismissed over the past year. Can you see any examples of potentially discriminatory actions?

RACE DISCRIMINATION IN THE TERMINATION PROCESS

As already noted, any dismissal that is specifically related to, or motivated by, one of the areas covered by discrimination legislation will be unlawful discrimination. However, it is often difficult to be certain what exactly has motivated the decision to dismiss. An important indicator is the consistency of treatment. If there is evidence that employees of a different race would have been treated differently, and there is evidence that the treatment given to an employee is unfavourable, then there is a potential case of unlawful discrimination.

The following case illustrates this example:

Atrari v PK Stationery Ltd (1991)

Atrari, a Moroccan, was dismissed on the grounds that his accent made him incomprehensible. However, the tribunal held that his accent made him no less intelligible than a pronounced British regional accent. On that basis, they held that an influencing factor in the dismissal was his race.

However, if it can be shown that all employees would be treated in the same way irrespective of race, then it is unlikely that the conclusion can be drawn that discrimination has taken place:

Sidhu v Aerospace Composite Technology Ltd (2000)

Sidhu was involved in a fight following a racially motivated attack on him by other employees. The employer's disciplinary policy clearly stated that, when violence occurred, provocation would not be taken into account. All the employees involved in the fight, including Sidhu, were dismissed. The Court of Appeal held that the employer had not discriminated against Sidhu because there was no evidence that the policy was applied differently to employees of different races.

It is also important for the employer to consider the impact of any policies that could be deemed to be indirect discrimination if dismissal occurred as a result of them. Possible examples are:

- dismissing an employee for failing to wear a uniform that contravened clothing standards required due to their religious beliefs
- dismissing an employee for failing to reach a prescribed standard in English, when it cannot be shown that the prescribed standard is required in the job
- dismissing an employee for refusal to work on specific holy days
- dismissing an employee for refusing to be clean shaven (if the employee's religion required him to grow a beard).

DISABILITY DISCRIMINATION IN THE TERMINATION PROCESS

The Employment Rights Act 1996 permits employers to dismiss employees who are not capable of performing their jobs – for example, on account of ill-health or injury. Such dismissals are thus capable of being fair under that Act, provided the employer has properly applied the statutory DDP prior to the employee's dismissal, and acted reasonably in an overall sense in the manner of carrying out the dismissal.

The question of whether such a dismissal would be in breach of the Disability Discrimination Act (DDA)1995 is, however, quite a separate matter. The burden of justifying the dismissal of an employee on grounds related to disability is a high one. The dismissal of a disabled employee should only be contemplated after the employer has:

- made all possible reasonable adjustments to facilitate the ongoing employment of the disabled employee

- established that there is no alternative work within the organisation that the employee could reasonably do (after training)

- reasonably concluded that there are no other adjustments that could reasonably be made to support the employee

- obtained appropriate medical advice confirming the effects of the employee's condition on their ability to perform their job, and indicating that there is little or no likelihood of a material improvement in their condition in the foreseeable future

- concluded that, despite any adjustments that have been made, the employee's disability, or its effects (for example, excessive absence from work), is causing the employer a substantial problem

- satisfied themselves that lack of capability is a substantial reason for dismissal under the Employment Rights Act 1996

- acted reasonably throughout the process of considering termination of the employee's employment.

It is worth referring back to the case of Mid Staffordshire General Hospitals NHS Trust v Cambridge (2003) here (which was explained in detail in Chapter 5). In this case, the hospital dismissed Cambridge, but it was found to be an unfair dismissal because they had not given reasonable consideration to all the adjustments that could reasonably be made to support the employee.

One particularly difficult area is dealing with an employee whose conduct or performance is unsatisfactory and where, additionally, the employee has a stress-related illness that is causing absence from work. A stress-related illness may, depending on how it affects the employee, amount to a disability in law, as shown in the following example:

Rowden v Dutton Gregory (2002)

The employee, who was a secretary in a firm of solicitors, had been absent from work with a stress-related illness. A disciplinary hearing had been convened but, when the employee was unable to attend, her employer went ahead without her and subsequently took the decision to dismiss her on grounds of various types of misconduct, poor timekeeping and excessive sickness absence. The employee brought claims for unfair dismissal and disability discrimination to an employment tribunal. The employer conceded the unfair dismissal claim before the tribunal, but the disability discrimination claim went on to appeal.

The Employment Appeal Tribunal (EAT) held ultimately that the actions of the employer in holding a disciplinary hearing, while the employee was absent from work with an illness that amounted to a disability, had caused the employee a detriment and thus constituted disability discrimination. The employer had also failed in their duty to make reasonable adjustments by not making alternative arrangements in relation to the disciplinary hearing in order to prevent the process from placing the employee at a substantial disadvantage.

The EAT also held that, since two of the reasons for the employee's dismissal – namely, poor timekeeping and excessive sickness absence – were related to the employee's disability, and since these two reasons had a significant impact on the employer's decision to dismiss, the dismissal itself was discriminatory. The employee therefore succeeded in showing that both the disciplinary process and the decision to dismiss amounted to disability discrimination.

It may be advisable, therefore (depending on the circumstances), not to proceed with disciplinary action against an employee who is signed off work with a stress-related illness, but instead to wait until the employee returns to work before dealing with the matter. Alternatively, the employer could ask an occupational doctor to advise on whether the employee is fit to attend a meeting (even though they may not be well enough to work).

Where the stress-related illness has arisen following the instigation of disciplinary proceedings and the employer suspects that the employee's absence is an avoidance tactic, caution must still be exercised. The employer should:

- refrain from making automatic assumptions that the employee is deliberately trying to evade disciplinary action

- inform the employee in writing that the disciplinary action will be postponed for a reasonable period in order to allow them to recover sufficiently to take part in the proceedings

- seek the employee's consent to contact their GP or seek advice from an occupational doctor as to whether the employee is well enough to attend an investigatory or disciplinary meeting

- make it clear to the employee in a firm but non-threatening way that the disciplinary investigation or action (as the case may be) must be dealt with, and that it is in everyone's interests to deal with it as soon as possible

- give the employee the option (if it is considered appropriate) to appoint a representative (for example, a colleague or trade union official) to attend a meeting on their behalf.

A dismissal on the grounds of disability can potentially be justified if the grounds for the dismissal are material and substantial, as shown in the following case:

A v *London Borough of Hounslow (2001)*

In this case, the employee had recently begun work as a physics/IT technician at a secondary school. Soon after he began work, the results of a medical examination (upon which his offer of employment was dependent) disclosed that he had schizophrenia and that, although his condition was stable, there was no guarantee that he would never suffer a relapse. Although the chances of a relapse were small, the advice from the school's occupational health specialist was that, if it were to occur, the employee could pose a serious risk to himself, the other staff and the pupils. As a result of this advice, the school dismissed the employee, who subsequently asserted that this course of action amounted to disability discrimination.

It was clear from the facts of the case that the employee's condition amounted to a disability, and that his dismissal was for a reason related to disability. The question was whether the dismissal could nevertheless be justified on grounds that were material and substantial. The EAT held that, even though the employee's condition had been under control for a number of years, the prospect of a relapse and the danger it might create for pupils and teachers amounted to 'an incalculable risk'. They thus found that the employer's actions were justifiable.

A further case is also of interest here:

Allen v *H Hargarve & Co (1999)*

The employee was a butcher who, owing to tenosynovitis (inflammation of the tendons owing to repetitive action), had been on long-term sick leave and could no longer perform his job. The work in the employer's slaughterhouse was physically heavy and involved working at speed and under pressure. The only possible alternative position was tray-washing but, in order for the employee to be able to perform this work, the employer would have had to make alterations to the machine that would have prevented other employees from using it. In any event, the company had no vacancies at the time in question either in tray-washing or cleaning. Taking into account all these circumstances, the EAT judged that the dismissal of the employee was justified. The reasons for the dismissal were material and substantial – because they related to the employee's physical condition, his inability to perform his job, the machinery and the non-availability of other jobs.

It can be seen from the above cases that dismissal for a reason related to an employee's disability is not automatically unlawful. Such a dismissal must, however, be justified by factors that are material and substantial if a claim for unlawful disability discrimination is to be avoided or defended successfully. The main criterion is that the employer must first have exhausted all possible avenues as regards their duty to make reasonable adjustments to support the disabled employee prior to considering termination of employment. If there are further adjustments that the employer could have made, but failed to make, then the dismissal will not be justified.

It is important to note also that the responsibility to make adjustments lies with the employer, and it is not up to the disabled employee to offer suggestions (although they should of course be encouraged to do so). If the employee does make suggestions, then the employer should give them due consideration, as shown in the following case:

Fu v London Borough of Camden (2001)

Fu was employed as a district housing officer. Following a series of accidents, she was absent for a lengthy period of time. The Occupational Health Unit told the employer that it was unable to say when Fu would be able to return to work, and she was offered the choice between ill-health early retirement or dismissal. However, Fu had made a number of suggestions of adaptations that could be made to her workplace to enable her to work. These included a voice-activated computer, easy access shelving, a hands-free telephone and a specially adapted chair. The EAT judged that the employer should have considered the adjustments suggested by the employee and the extent to which they could have helped to overcome her medical symptoms and facilitate her return to work. Failing to take this approach meant that the actions of the employer amounted to unlawful disability discrimination.

Another example of an employer not giving due consideration to potential adaptations is given below:

London Borough of Hillingdon v Morgan (1999)

The EAT upheld an employment tribunal decision that the employer had unlawfully discriminated against the employee by refusing to allow her to work part-time from home for a temporary period. The employee, a service information officer, had been absent from work for eight months on account of myalgic encephalomyelitis (ME), and her doctors (including an occupational doctor) had recommended that this type of arrangement would help her to ease back into full-time employment. Despite the doctors' recommendations, the employer refused to agree to the home-working arrangement and, when the employee did return to work, took no steps to support her. As a result, she was unable to cope with the stresses of the job and consequently resigned.

The EAT found that there was no objective reason why the employer could not have permitted the employee to work on a part-time basis from home initially. The employer had thus failed to fulfil their duty to make reasonable adjustments.

Nevertheless, if the employer is in a position where there is no action, or further action, that they can reasonably take to enable the disabled employee to cope adequately with their job (or another suitable job), or to return to work, then dismissal may be a lawful option. The point may come where, even though management have adopted a supportive approach towards the employee to date, the employee's absence(s) from work may have become excessive or job performance may have dropped well below the standard that is acceptable. In such circumstances, dismissal may eventually be the only course of action that realistically remains open to the employer. In this case, the employer should proceed according to the checklist below:

■ Review the employee's job performance and/or sickness and absence record to assess whether it is sufficiently unsatisfactory to justify dismissal, taking care not to assume automatically that recent poor performance or a recent high level of absence will continue indefinitely.

■ Review the feasibility of altering the employee's job duties, or offering the employee alternative work, including part-time work.

■ Consider what reasonable adjustments, or further adjustments, could be made to the employee's working arrangements or conditions to facilitate better performance or a return to work, and discuss these with the employee.

■ Keep in regular touch with an employee who is absent from work to discuss how they are, and the likely length of time they expect to be absent.

■ Discuss with the employee how they feel about their employment and (if the employee is on sick leave) the likelihood of a return to work, and what type of work they think they may be capable of doing on their return.

■ Seek expert medical advice from an occupational doctor, a specialist in the employee's condition or (with the employee's written consent) their GP (better still, seek medical advice from more than one source).

■ Inform the employee of any time limits that have been set for appraising the situation.

■ Review whether the employee is receiving statutory or occupational sick pay, and for how much longer payment is set to continue (so as to avoid any breach of contract claim).

■ Tell the employee, as soon as it is thought to be the case, that their continued employment may be at risk, and the reasons for taking that view.

■ Ensure the necessary steps of the statutory DDP are followed as this procedure applies to ill-health dismissals.

■ Adopt a supportive approach towards the employee at all times.

As we have noted in earlier chapters, the employer has a duty to consider reasonable adjustments that can be made to the workplace. When assisting an employee who has been absent from work for a lengthy period of time, or an employee who is no longer capable of performing their job, the following points should be considered:

■ offering the employee a phased return to work – for example, the possibility of part-time working, whether temporarily or permanently

■ agreeing to permit the employee to do some or all of their work from home as a step towards returning to office-based employment

■ discussing the possibility of redeployment into a different job – for example, a less demanding role

■ providing training or coaching on the employee's return to work – for example, a mini-induction to help the employee to become re-integrated into the workplace (especially if the employee's absence has been a long one)

- providing a mentor for the employee who can be assigned to provide general support and keep an eye on how the employee is coping with being back at work

- agreeing (within reason) to a higher than usual tolerance of job performance, conduct or attendance that is falling short of the organisation's normal standards

- suggesting a transfer to alternative work, if a suitable post is available – for example, where the employee, although incapable of handling the job they are employed to do, could adequately perform a different job (obviously any transfer should only be with the employee's consent)

- allowing the employee to transfer to another job at the same or a higher grade without the requirement to undergo competitive interviews

- altering the employee's job duties – for example, by transferring some of the duties that the disabled employee can no longer manage to other employees (again, only after full consultation with all those affected)

- reducing the employee's working hours (with consent), or exempting the employee from shift working or overtime working

- agreeing to permit regular time off work for hospital appointments, rehabilitation or medical treatment

- providing training, coaching or supervision

- providing special equipment to help the employee perform their duties.

As was shown in the case of Archibald v Fife Council (2004) (quoted in detail in Chapter 7), it is not acceptable to require the employee to undergo a series of competitive interviews for alternative employment when the employee is no longer able to do their original job because of disability.

It is essential for the employer to consult the disabled employee fully about the prospect of adjustments to working conditions, job duties and any other arrangements before coming to any final decision. Such discussions should have, as their main objective, the aim of establishing a way of facilitating the continued employment of the employee if at all possible.

TASK

Talk to the HR Manager in your organisation, or an organisation with which you are familiar, and ask about cases of long-term absenteeism. Ask how the cases have been managed, and how the DDA was taken into consideration when deciding on the actions to take.

DISMISSAL ON ACCOUNT OF A GENUINE OCCUPATIONAL REQUIREMENT (GOR)

There are limited exceptions to the general principle that it is never lawful to dismiss an employee for reasons that relate to one of the factors covered by discrimination legislation. In certain limited circumstances, an employer may dismiss an employee on racial or religious grounds, or on grounds of sexual orientation based on the argument that being of a particular race, religion or sexual orientation is a GOR for the specific post. For the GOR to apply, however, it must be genuinely necessary, in order to ensure effective performance of the job in question, for the job-holder to be a person from a defined racial group, someone who belongs to a specific religion, or someone of a particular sexual orientation. In these circumstances, it is lawful for the employer to decline to offer employment or promotion, or dismiss the employee, provided also that the race/religion/sexual orientation requirement is proportionate in the particular case.

It is important to note that the GOR exception applies (at present) only to dismissals that are on grounds of the individual's race, ethnic origins, national origins, religion or sexual orientation (and not yet to gender).

Dismissal could be lawful (ie not discriminatory), for example, where an employee changed their religion to one that made them unsuitable in relation to the performance of the job in which they were employed. Another example could be where being of a particular sexual orientation was a GOR for a particular post and it was discovered that the post-holder was not of that particular sexual orientation. The exceptions are narrowly drawn, however, and would apply only in very limited circumstances. Employers should note also that, even if a GOR can legitimately be applied, this does not mean that the employee's dismissal will be fair under the Employment Rights Act 1996. The fairness of any dismissal will depend on a wide range of factors – for example, whether there was a reasonable alternative to dismissal, such as transfer to another job.

DISCRIMINATION IN THE REDUNDANCY PROCESS

In order to comply with the various anti-discrimination laws, an employer undertaking a programme of redundancy must ensure that all employees are treated consistently irrespective of their sex, trans-gender status, marital status, racial group, sexual orientation, religion or disability. This would apply at all stages of the redundancy programme, impinging for example on:

- the process of consultation
- the treatment of employees who volunteer for redundancy
- the criteria used to select individuals for redundancy
- consideration for any alternative employment
- any redundancy payments granted over and above the statutory minimum.

When an employer, through the process of consultation, has confirmed the jobs that are to be made redundant, they need to identify which employees will be affected by the redundancy. If a job that is identified as redundant is a job that is only performed by one employee, then the decision is usually straightforward. However, if the employer employs several people doing the same job, and only a limited number of those jobs are to be made redundant, then some process of selection must take place.

One approach that can be used is to base the selection purely on the length of service of employees – this is known as LIFO (last in, first out). Clearly this is a completely objective process, and hence reduces the opportunity for any discriminatory factors to enter the selection process. However, it can be to the employer's detriment if the process results in the loss of new employees recruited for their fresh ideas and recent qualifications. LIFO may also discriminate indirectly against women, as it is often the case that women tend to have shorter service than men.

A more common approach that is used is to develop a selection matrix, covering a range of factors that are seen as being important to the job. This could include such factors as skills, experience, knowledge, length of service, etc. Although this approach means that the employer does not lose the best performing employees, it does allow for discrimination to occur because a number of factors require some level of subjective judgement.

To reduce the possibility of discriminatory factors, a number of safeguards must be in place. This is illustrated in the following case:

Williams v Compair Maxam (1982)

In this case, the employers were criticised for the subjectivity of the selection factors that they used. Employees were selected for redundancy on the basis of three departmental managers listing those whom they felt should be retained for the best long-term viability of their departments and the company. The EAT found that the criteria were completely subjective and that there had been no attempt to agree objective criteria with the trade union. In making their ruling, the EAT listed the following safeguards that should be in place to ensure a fair selection:

- Give as much warning as possible of impending redundancies.
- Consult over the selection criteria, with the aim of reaching agreement over the criteria.
- The criteria must be checked objectively (eg against attendance reports, or records of performance).
- The criteria must be applied fairly.
- If possible, alternative employment must be offered in preference to redundancy.
- Those who carry out the assessment must know all the employees in the selection pool.
- Assessors must be able to assess all the criteria correctly.

In addition to the guidelines laid down in this case, there are other points that an employer should consider:

- Use a range of criteria, rather than just one.
- Ensure that the criteria are objective, ie based on factors that are capable of being evidenced.
- Aim to identify criteria that are fair and reasonable in all the circumstances, but which allow the employer to retain those employees whose skills, experience and talents will best meet its future needs.
- Use only criteria that are capable of being applied objectively and fairly.
- Establish a procedure under which no single manager can take redundancy selection decisions alone.
- Treat part-time and fixed-term employees in the same way as full-time and permanent staff.

It is also important to ensure that selection criteria do not directly breach any legislation, as shown in the following case:

> **Whiffen v Governing Body of Milham Ford Girls' School & anor (2001)**
>
> The employer's policy was to select teachers engaged on fixed-term contracts for redundancy first (before any permanent staff were considered). The Court of Appeal judged that this was indirectly discriminatory against women, because more women than men were on fixed-term contracts. However, it should be noted that such a policy used today would, in any event, be in breach of the Fixed-Term Employees (Prevention of Less Favourable Treatment) Regulations 2002.

In addition to ensuring that selection criteria are as objective as possible, there are criteria that could potentially be directly discriminatory. Examples of these are:

- Using absence records might be discriminatory against a disabled employee who, as a result of their disability, has needed time off work for rehabilitation or ongoing medical support.

- Taking other forms of absence into account could discriminate against women – for example, sickness absence during pregnancy or absence on account of childcare problems.

- Using mobility as a criterion could discriminate indirectly against women, who in general are less likely than men to be able or willing to move to a different location with their job.

- Insisting on using qualifications as a factor in the selection process could be racially discriminatory where the qualifications specified were not strictly necessary for the jobs in question, and where it could be shown that employees of foreign nationality were less likely than British employees to possess them.

- Using LIFO as a determining factor can discriminate indirectly against women (or employees from ethnic minority groups) who, statistically, tend to have shorter service than men.

- Applying a requirement for flexibility in terms of hours and shift working would discriminate indirectly against women, who are less likely than men to be able to work long or unsocial hours owing to childcare responsibilities.

- Applying flexibility as a criterion could also discriminate indirectly against people from certain religious groups who, as a result of their religious beliefs, may not be able to work on certain days or dates.

- Placing strong emphasis on skills that tend to be possessed more often by men than women (or vice versa) – for example, giving marks for physical strength, would place women at a disadvantage.

- Using communication skills, levels of assertiveness or perceived ability to 'fit in' as criteria, as these may indirectly disadvantage employees from certain racial or religious groups – for example, people who have been brought up in a culture where assertiveness or outgoing behaviour are not valued or encouraged.

- Using age as a criterion in the redundancy process – for example, selecting those who are near to retirement age for compulsory redundancy first, before applying other criteria to the workforce at large. Depending on the gender make up of the workforce, this could be indirectly discriminatory against men (or women).

- Selecting part-time or fixed-term employees for redundancy first, which would be in breach of the Part-Time Workers Regulations 2000 and the Fixed-Term Employees Regulations 2002 respectively, and would also potentially be indirectly discriminatory against women.

TASK

Find an example of a redundancy selection matrix. Look at the criteria and consider how objective the measurements of the criteria are. Can you see any potential problems with the use of the matrix?

When considering how to execute a redundancy programme, employers should make sure that any employee on maternity leave is treated no less favourably than employees at work and, if alternative work is available or becomes available while the employee is absent, that she is offered the work as an alternative to dismissal.

When reviewing whom to select for redundancy from among a group of employees doing the same or similar work, employers should take particular care not to overlook the requirement to consult an employee who is absent from work on maternity leave. A failure to consult an employee over prospective selection for redundancy, because she is absent on maternity leave, is likely to be regarded as direct sex discrimination. This is what happened in the following case:

McGuigan v T G Baynes & Sons (1998)

Ms McGuigan was on maternity leave when her employer decided there was a need to make one employee out of three in her department redundant. Ms McGuigan's two colleagues were both male. A points-scoring exercise was carried out, as a result of which Ms McGuigan was selected. None of the three employees was consulted about the selection process, nor were they informed as to how the redundancy decision had been arrived at. Ms McGuigan subsequently complained to an employment tribunal of unfair dismissal and sex discrimination. Both complaints were ultimately upheld.

The employer attempted to defend their actions by asserting that they had not consulted any of the employees in the department, and that Ms McGuigan's treatment had therefore been no less favourable than that of her male colleagues. The EAT, however, held that the employee's absence on maternity leave had been an 'effective and predominant' cause of the employer's failure to consult her. This was despite the fact that the other employees had not been consulted either. Case law had clearly established that less favourable treatment on grounds of pregnancy or maternity leave will entitle a woman to succeed in a case of direct sex discrimination without comparing her treatment to that of a male colleague.

Employers undertaking a redundancy exercise must ensure that the methods used to select staff for redundancy do not place any disabled employee at a disadvantage. Managers should take care when reviewing staff's abilities not to view an employee's disability in a negative light, or allow the fact that an employee is disabled to count against them in any points-scoring exercise. Equally, it will be important to exclude from consideration the effects of an employee's disability. Specifically, employers should avoid applying the following criteria to disabled employees:

- sickness absence, where much of it has been on account of the employee's disability
- breadth of skills, as this could cause a detriment to an employee whose disability meant they were incapable of performing certain tasks
- flexibility, as this criterion could work to the disadvantage of an employee who could not work at certain times on account of their disability
- productivity, where a disabled employee's impairment had the effect of slowing down their work performance to a rate below the average
- physical fitness or level of energy, which would discriminate against any employee with a physical disability.

A number of employers adopt the approach of offering redundant employees suitable alternative employment in preference to any applications from employees who are not facing redundancy. However, the following case shows that an employer is not allowed to give preferential treatment to redundant employees over disabled employees who are also seeking redeployment because they are unable to continue in their current job.

Kent County Council v *Mingo (1999)*

Mingo worked as an assistant cook but, following a back injury, was unable to continue in this role. He was certified as fit for work, as long as the role did not involve any heavy lifting. The Council had classifications of groups of employees who were seeking redeployment. Category A were employees who were at risk of, or had been given notice of, redundancy. Category B were employees who sought redeployment on the grounds of incapacity/ill health. Mingo was placed in Category B. Mingo worked in a series of temporary placements and was eventually dismissed. He claimed unlawful disability discrimination because any vacancies that had occurred had gone to Category A employees. The EAT and the Employment Tribunal held that the Council had not made any reasonable attempt to find Mingo another role and hence avoid his dismissal.

DISCRIMINATION IN RETIREMENT AND POST-EMPLOYMENT

Most employers are aware that it is unlawful to operate different retirement ages for men and women. A retirement age specified by the employer for a job or group of jobs can (as the law stands at the moment) be any age, so long as there is no differentiation between male and female employees (and no discriminatory impact on other grounds, such as race).

It is, however, permissible to operate different retirement ages for different groups of employees provided no discrimination results from the application of the policy. Where an employer has decided to do this, it is important to:

- ensure there is a valid, objective reason for the difference in retirement ages
- check to make sure the groups of workers to whom different retirement ages apply do not have a substantially different gender (or racial) profile.

If, for example, a group of employees in one part of the organisation consisted predominantly of women, and if that group had a retirement age that was higher or lower than a group of employees elsewhere that comprised mainly men, a claim for unlawful sex discrimination could potentially be brought to tribunal. In these circumstances, the burden of proof would be on the employer to prove to the tribunal's satisfaction that the difference in retirement ages could be objectively justified on grounds unrelated to sex.

An employee who is aged 65 or over, or who is over their employer's normal retirement age, is, as the legislation stands at present, precluded from taking claims for unfair dismissal or redundancy pay to an employment tribunal. These provisions are conditional on the existence of a retirement age that is the same for men and women. This limit on taking a claim for unfair dismissal or redundancy pay was challenged in the following case:

Rutherford and anor v Secretary of State for Trade and Industry (2004)

Rutherford claimed that the age limit of 65 years was indirectly discriminatory against men. He was 67 years old at the time of his dismissal due to redundancy. He argued that, among employees aged between 55 and 74, there were significantly more men than women in the workforce. As retirement was a greater issue for this age group than the whole of the working population, he argued that this disparity was indirect discrimination against men, and hence was unlawful.

However, the Court of Appeal decided that the correct comparison should be the whole workforce (aged from 16 to 79), and found that there was no significant difference in the numbers of men and women affected when this comparison pool was used. Hence, on that basis, the age limit of 65 years was judged to be non-discriminatory.

When age discrimination is added to the legislation in 2006, the upper age limit for taking unfair dismissal and redundancy payment claims will be removed, and such claims from employees over retirement age will be subject to the usual legal principles. It is not clear at the time of writing, however, whether the government, as part of the new age discrimination law, will abolish compulsory retirement ages or introduce a default retirement age (subject to justification) of 70.

TASK

During your studies, ensure that you keep up to date with any developments in the drafting of legislation relating to age discrimination. The DTI website (www.dti.gov.uk) is a useful source of information.

Discrimination after an individual's employment has ended is now unlawful under all the anti-discrimination laws as a result of two entirely separate developments. The first was the implementation of legislation – specifically, amendments to the Race Relations Act (RRA) 1976 and the SDA 1975 to that effect were implemented in July 2003, and a similar amendment to the DDA 1995 was made in October 2004. Equally, the Employment Equality (Religion or Belief) Regulations 2003 and the Employment Equality (Sexual Orientation) Regulations 2003 both expressly provide that discrimination and harassment after an employment relationship has ended will be unlawful whenever 'the discrimination or harassment arises out of and is closely connected to that relationship'.

The legislation does not specify any time-based limitation on the right not to suffer post-employment discrimination. It would seem, therefore, that the right applies indefinitely after an individual's employment has ended, so long as the ex-employee can show a connection between their treatment and their employment.

Examples of post-employment discrimination are:

- a refusal to give a reference
- the provision of an adverse reference
- a post-dismissal appeal hearing in which (for example) sexist or racist remarks were made
- refusal to grant the ex-employee benefits such as admission to sports and social facilities where other ex-employees have been granted these benefits, provided these actions were on grounds related in some way to the ex-employee's gender, race, religion or sexual orientation.

In a separate development, the House of Lords ruled (in six conjoined cases, the lead case being D'Souza v London Borough of Lambeth [2003]) that an employment relationship can outlast the existence of the contract of employment, and the right for ex-employees to bring claims of unlawful discrimination against their ex-employer must be applied to all forms of less favourable treatment, including direct and indirect discrimination, victimisation and harassment. Thus, discrimination perpetrated against an ex-employee is covered by the relevant legislation, provided the employee's treatment arose out of their employment relationship and caused them a detriment on grounds of gender, race or disability.

D'Souza v London Borough of Lambeth (2003)

D'Souza was dismissed and successfully brought a claim of unfair dismissal to the Employment Tribunal. The employer was ordered, by the Employment Tribunal, to reinstate D'Souza, but they refused. As a result, they were ordered to pay additional compensation to D'Souza. However, D'Souza brought a further claim that the refusal to reinstate him was race discrimination and victimisation (because an element of his earlier claim had related to race discrimination). Although D'Souza was no longer an employee, the House of Lords ruled that the treatment related to the earlier contract of employment, and hence the claim was allowed.

This decision took place prior to the implementation of the Employment Equality (Religion or Belief) Regulations 2003 and the Employment Equality (Sexual Orientation) Regulations 2003 but, since both sets of Regulations expressly outlaw post-employment discrimination and harassment, this is largely irrelevant. The point is that any form of post-employment discrimination on any of the prohibited grounds will be capable of challenge at an employment tribunal provided there is some connection between the ex-employee's treatment and their previous employment.

THE GIVING OF REFERENCES AND THE TERMINATION OF FIXED-TERM CONTRACTS

As discussed in the previous section, discrimination on any of the prohibited grounds after an individual's employment has ended will be unlawful if the treatment of the person is in any way connected to their previous employment. Employers should therefore take great care in the compilation of references requested in respect of a previous employee to ensure that nothing is stated that could put the person at a disadvantage on grounds of gender, race, religion, etc. Three particular areas where risks may occur are in respect of:

- a disabled ex-employee whose performance was below standard for reasons related to disability
- a female employee who, owing to childcare responsibilities, was unable to be flexible in terms of working time
- an employee who was unable to work on certain days or dates owing to their religion or belief.

Employers should take care not to make any negative statements in a reference about any ex-employee in any of these areas. For example, if a Jewish employee had, while employed, been unwilling to work on Saturdays (the Jewish Sabbath) owing to their religious beliefs, the employer should avoid presenting this information as a negative element in a reference. It could be discriminatory under the Employment Equality (Religion or Belief) Regulations 2003, for example, to describe such a person as 'inflexible', or as 'unwilling to work at weekends', as this type of reference would put the person at a disadvantage compared with others for whom references may be given. Similarly, it would be sex discrimination to describe a previous female employee as inflexible if, owing to childcare responsibilities, she was unable to work variable hours.

The expiry of a fixed-term contract without renewal is regarded as a dismissal in UK law. This is despite the fact that the employer and employee will have agreed at the outset that the contract will terminate on a particular date or on a particular occasion. The dismissal will be by reason of redundancy, or possibly on the grounds of 'some other substantial reason' (SOSR).

Normally, the dismissal because of the expiry of a fixed-term contract will be fair in law, but in certain circumstances an employment tribunal may take the opposite view, for example if:

- the employer recruits a replacement for the fixed-term employee shortly after the expiry of the contract (suggesting that the reason for the fixed-term employee's dismissal was not in fact the expiry of the contract, but in reality some other reason – and matters could be even worse if the replacement employee was of the opposite sex or a different race)
- there was another job into which the fixed-term employee could have been transferred on the expiry of their contract, but the employer did not discuss this opportunity with

the fixed-term employee to establish whether such a transfer would have been of interest to them

- the employer in some other way acted unreasonably in terminating the fixed-term employee's contract.

The new statutory DDP must also be applied to dismissals on the grounds of the expiry of a fixed-term contract. This means that the employer must, prior to the proposed termination date, write to the employee setting out the circumstances and inviting them to attend a meeting. The meeting must allow the employee to make representations about their employment and, if the decision to dismiss goes ahead, the employee must be granted the right of appeal.

To ensure fairness in termination therefore, the employer should first review (in consultation with the fixed-term employee) whether the employee can be offered alternative work (whether permanent or fixed-term). If no alternative work is available, the employer should still be certain that the real reason for the proposed dismissal of the fixed-term employee is (for example) that the term has expired, the work is complete or the person whom the fixed-term employee replaced has returned to work.

KEY POINTS FROM THIS CHAPTER

- Disciplining or dismissing a female employee because she is unable or unwilling to be flexible as regards hours of work may be indirectly discriminatory on grounds of gender unless objectively justified.

- The dismissal of an employee on grounds of incapability is potentially fair under the Employment Rights Act 1996 (provided fair procedures have been followed) but the question of whether such a dismissal would be in breach of the DDA 1995 is an entirely separate matter.

- A dismissal on grounds related to disability must, if it is to be lawful, be justified by factors that are material and substantial.

- If there are any adjustments, or further adjustments, that an employer could reasonably have made for a disabled employee, but failed to make, the dismissal of that employee will not be capable of justification.

- The responsibility to make adjustments for a disabled employee lies with the employer, and it is not up to the disabled employee to offer suggestions (although they should of course be encouraged to do so).

- In certain limited circumstances, an employer may dismiss an employee on racial or religious grounds or on grounds of sexual orientation, based on the argument that being of a particular race, religion or sexual orientation is a GOR for the specific post and the race/religion/sexual orientation requirement is proportionate in the particular case.

- Employers undertaking a redundancy exercise must ensure that the methods used to select staff for redundancy do not place any disabled employee at a disadvantage – for example, by allowing the disability to count against the employee in a points-scoring exercise.

- A retirement age specified by the employer for a job or group of jobs can (as the law stands at the moment) be any age, so long as there is no differentiation between male and female employees and no discriminatory impact on other grounds such as race.

- Discrimination after an individual's employment has ended is unlawful under all the anti-discrimination laws whenever the discrimination or harassment arises out of and is closely connected to the employment relationship.

- The expiry of a fixed-term contract without renewal is regarded as a dismissal in UK law by reason of redundancy or on grounds of SOSR.

EXAMPLES TO WORK THROUGH

1   Due to customer demand, it has become essential to extend the current working hours of the call centre where you are the HR Manager. All employees are to be asked to move from working 9am-5pm to alternating shifts of 6am-2pm and 2pm-10pm. Three female employees have informed you that they are unable to work either of the shifts due to childcare responsibilities. The Line Manager wants to dismiss any employee who does not agree to the new shifts, because he believes it will cause difficulties within the teams if some people work the new shifts, while others remain on the old shifts. What would you advise?

2   James has worked for many years as a labourer on a building site. Following a serious road traffic accident, he is no longer able to walk more than half a mile, stand for longer than 10 minutes or lift any moderate to heavy loads. He appears unable to do any jobs on the building site. What should you do?

3   Your organisation has announced a redundancy of 100 jobs, and there will need to be a selection process. The management team propose using a matrix including the following criteria: attendance, length of service, skills, flexibility, knowledge and experience. Comment on the criteria they have selected, with particular reference to potential discriminatory issues.

Harassment as Discrimination

HARASSMENT AND LEGISLATION

Harassment of any kind in the workplace can have devastating effects, both on the well-being of its victim and on the morale (and consequent effectiveness) of the workforce generally. Harassment can undermine an employees' confidence, make them feel demeaned and degraded, create enormous stress (leading potentially to mental illness) and ultimately have a seriously detrimental impact on the productivity not only of the victim, but also on other employees who find themselves working in a culture of fear and resentment.

The law governing harassment has developed substantially in recent years, both as a result of court and tribunal decisions that have interpreted harassment as a detriment under discrimination law, and as a result of new legislation which has, for the first time, provided a statutory definition of harassment.

Anti-discrimination legislation is not yet entirely consistent as regards its approach towards the interpretation of harassment. Most of the differences will disappear in time as a new statutory definition of harassment is introduced to the various strands of discrimination law. The Race Relations Act (RRA) 1976 was amended in July 2003 to include a statutory definition of harassment (see p. 213), although this definition applies only to harassment on grounds of race, ethnic origins and national origins, and not to harassment on grounds of colour or nationality. The Disability Discrimination Act (DDA) 1995 was amended in October 2004 to include a definition of harassment; that has altered the previous need for there to be a comparator in order for a claim to be made. The new definition is explained on p. 218 in this chapter.

The Sex Discrimination Act (SDA) 1975 is expected to be amended in 2005 to include a similar statutory definition of harassment. The newer legislation – namely, the Employment Equality (Religion or Belief) Regulations 2003 and the Employment Equality (Sexual Orientation) Regulations 2003, both contain a parallel statutory definition.

TASK

Details about legislation and practical guidance relating to harassment can be found in a specific guidance document on the ACAS website. Access and read this document (www.acas.org.uk/publications).

RACIAL HARASSMENT

The RRA 1976 was amended in July 2003 to make specific provision to render harassment on grounds of race or ethnic or national origins unlawful, and to introduce a statutory definition of racial harassment.

The definition in the RRA 1976 is:

> **" A person subjects another to harassment where, on the grounds of that other's race or ethnic or national origins, he engages in unwanted conduct which has the purpose or effect of –**
>
> **(a) violating that other's dignity, or**
>
> **(b) creating an intimidating, hostile, degrading, humiliating or offensive environment for that other. "**

The amended Act also states that:

> **" Conduct shall be regarded as having the effect specified in paragraphs (a) and (b) if, and only if, having regard to all the circumstances, including, in particular, the perception of that other, it should reasonably be considered as having that effect. "**

Thus, the principle that employees are entitled to decide for themselves what conduct they perceive as unwanted and offensive has been introduced to statutory law as a free-standing ground of unlawful discrimination, with the proviso that treatment that has an alleged discriminatory effect must also be capable of being interpreted as harassment by a reasonable person. This provides an objective dimension and a yardstick of reasonableness for judging whether or not conduct that has had an alleged detrimental effect on the person experiencing it amounts to unlawful harassment. The person's subjective perception of the alleged harassment stands to be balanced against an objective, reasonable viewpoint, taking into account all the circumstances of the particular case.

For example, if an over-sensitive Afro-Caribbean employee unreasonably took offence at a one-off innocent remark about black people, but most reasonable people would not have perceived the remark as offensive in the circumstances in which it was made, then a complaint to a tribunal alleging unlawful racial harassment would be unlikely to succeed. On the other hand, if, for example, a Pakistani employee was genuinely offended on account of racist banter in the workplace in circumstances where their British colleagues found the same remarks amusing, then the Pakistani employee would nevertheless be able potentially to succeed in a claim for racial harassment. It has been established for some time, as a result of court and tribunal decisions, that it is for each individual to determine individually what they find offensive.

CASE STUDY

In the post-room of a large organisation, there was a supervisor of white ethnic origin and three assistants. One of the assistants was of Asian ethnic origin, and two were of white ethnic origin. For as long as anyone could remember, there had been banter between the supervisor and the assistants, much of it focused on the racial origin of the Asian employee. A lot of employees who had cause to come to the post-room were somewhat shocked by the nature of the banter but, if they commented, the assistant of Asian ethnic origin laughed and said she 'gave as good as she got!'

One day, the Asian assistant went to see the Personnel Officer in floods of tears. She had decided that the banter was offensive, and she wanted it stopped. As she explained her complaint, she admitted that nothing had changed, she had just decided that the supervisor's behaviour was harassment and therefore unacceptable. She wanted him disciplined.

When the supervisor was questioned by the Personnel Officer, he admitted that all the banter took place but said it had been happening for years. Although that might not excuse the banter, he had never been aware that it had caused any offence. He would stop it immediately, but he would not accept that he had harassed the employee, and would fight any disciplinary action. His trade union representative supported him in this.

What should the organisation have done?

An interesting element of the definition of harassment is the concept that a complaint of harassment can be brought on the grounds that an employee's working environment is intimidating, hostile, degrading, humiliating or offensive to them. One consequence of this approach is that it will be possible for an individual to succeed in a claim for unlawful harassment even where the conduct complained of was not directed at them personally.

One inconsistency in the legislation, however, is that the provisions in the RRA 1976 governing harassment apply only to harassment on grounds of race, ethnic origins or national origins. This means that harassment on grounds of colour or nationality will stand to be dealt with under the 'detriment' provisions of the Act as interpreted by the courts and tribunals over the years.

TASK

Try to gain an understanding of behaviour that people find acceptable and unacceptable in the workplace. Talk to a range of colleagues and friends, and see if you get similar responses from different people.

RELIGIOUS HARASSMENT

Since the implementation of the Employment Equality (Religion or Belief) Regulations 2003, which contain a statutory definition of harassment as a distinct form of discrimination (parallel wording to that contained in the RRA 1976 – see earlier), employees are expressly protected against any harassment on grounds of their religion or belief. For example, if a Muslim employee was incessantly teased about their beliefs or religious practices, this could amount to harassment. The law prohibiting religious harassment is also likely to impinge on behaviour in workplaces where employees have allegiances to football clubs linked to sectarian rivalry, such as the rivalry between Rangers and Celtic supporters in Glasgow. It is possible that the wearing of clothing displaying football slogans with a sectarian significance could create an offensive working environment for some employees.

HARASSMENT ON THE GROUNDS OF SEXUAL ORIENTATION

The implementation of the Employment Equality (Sexual Orientation) Regulations 2003 made it unlawful to harass someone at work on the grounds that they are, or are thought to be, gay, lesbian or bisexual (or heterosexual). One difficulty with this strand of the discrimination legislation is that an employer will be less likely to possess the knowledge as to whether a particular individual is gay or lesbian. Such lack of knowledge will not, however, allow an employer to escape liability for any unlawful harassment that takes place in the course of the individual's employment.

SEXUAL HARASSMENT

UK sex discrimination legislation does not (as yet) contain a definition of sexual harassment. As early as 1986, however, the courts and tribunals recognised that sexual harassment at work could amount to a detriment and hence be a form of direct discrimination. The case that set the precedent was Strathclyde Regional Council v Porcelli:

Strathclyde Regional Council v Porcelli (1986)

Porcelli had been subjected to a campaign of inappropriate touching and suggestive remarks by two male colleagues who resented her and wanted to force her out of her job. The Scottish Court of Session ruled that the behaviour meted out to the woman would not have occurred if she had been a man, and that it therefore amounted to less favourable treatment under the SDA 1975. They further stated that harassment need not be based on a sex-related motive for it to constitute unlawful sex discrimination, and that, provided the unfavourable treatment to which the woman was subjected included a significant sexual element to which a man would not be vulnerable, it would be regarded as direct sex discrimination.

The Employment Appeal Tribunal (EAT) held, in the following case, that a series of verbal incidents may become a discriminatory detriment if persisted in, irrespective of whether the employee expressed an objection at the time the individual remarks were made. In the same case, the EAT held that an employer will not be able to defend a claim for sexual harassment on the basis that vulgar comments and sexual remarks were made equally to both men and women. They took the view that, even though both sexes were subjected to the same remarks, women were likely to find the remarks more intimidating than men, and hence the effect of the remarks was to place women at a disadvantage as compared with men.

Driskel v Peninsula Business Services & ors (2000)

Driskel worked for Huss, and during the time that she worked for him was subjected to a lot of sexual repartee. She applied for a promotion, and he was to be the interviewer. The night before the interview, he told her to wear a short skirt and a see-through blouse, showing a lot of cleavage, to the interview. She ignored the comment, just pointing out the next day that she had not done as he had asked. She subsequently made a complaint of sex discrimination. There was a rather prolonged investigation and eventually Driskel told the employer that she would only work if Huss were moved elsewhere. She was told that this was impractical and she would be dismissed if she did not work with her department head. This happened, and Driskel successfully claimed unfair dismissal and sex discrimination.

Although there is as yet no definition of sexual harassment in UK law, the EC Code of Practice on the protection of the dignity of women and men at work (www.europa.eu.int) provides a framework for defining it, by stating that:

- sexual harassment is 'unwanted conduct of a sexual nature, or other conduct based on sex affecting the dignity of women and men at work'
- sexual harassment can consist of 'physical, verbal or non-verbal conduct'
- conduct of a sexual nature will amount to sexual harassment where it is 'unwanted, unreasonable and offensive to the recipient
- it is for each individual to determine what behaviour is acceptable to them and what they regard as offensive.

It is important to note that the sexual harassment does not have to be a series of events (as in the Porcelli case). If one single incident is sufficiently serious, it is possible for this to be classed as harassment, as shown in the following case:

Bracebridge Engineering Ltd v Darby (1989)

On one occasion, Darby was stopped by two male supervisors as she went to wash her hands. She had been criticised on a number of occasions for leaving early, and it was thought that she was again attempting to do so. They carried her forcefully into a darkened room where they sexually assaulted her and made lewd comments. She complained to a manager, but it was decided to take no action against the supervisors. She resigned and claimed sexual discrimination and harassment. The employers argued that the incident was an isolated event and hence it could not constitute harassment. However, the EAT determined that a single event could constitute harassment if, as in this case, it had been sufficiently serious. It was also found that the treatment Darby suffered would not have been suffered by a man and hence this was an incident of sexual discrimination and harassment.

It can be seen from the EU's approach to harassment (which has been observed and upheld for many years by UK courts and tribunals) that the decision as to whether particular conduct amounts to sexual harassment lies with the victim. It follows that managers responsible for staff should take care not to view behaviour purely subjectively, as this may lead them to view an allegation of sexual harassment as insignificant in circumstances where the recipient of the behaviour has been genuinely offended. The important criterion is whether the recipient of the conduct finds it offensive, and not whether the manager regards the same conduct as trivial or a joke. More recently, the EAT confirmed in the following case that it is up to the recipient of the conduct in question to decide what type of conduct is acceptable and what is offensive:

Reed and another v Stedman (1999)

Stedman worked as a secretary, until she resigned and subsequently made a claim for sexual discrimination and harassment. In her complaint, she listed 15 separate complaints, primarily relating to Reed. The tribunal, in reaching its decision, relied on just four of the complaints. They accepted that no individual event, on its own, amounted to sexual harassment, but ruled that when added together they were evidence of ongoing conduct that amounted to sexual harassment. They also found that the organisation should have investigated the situation. Although Stedman never made any formal complaints, several informal complaints were made to colleagues, and the conduct also had a negative impact on her health. The employer appealed, primarily on the grounds that the behaviour did not amount to sexual harassment; however, the EAT upheld the tribunal's decision.

The key factor in determining whether harassment constitutes unlawful sex discrimination is whether it can be shown that the victim was treated unfavourably on grounds of their sex (as opposed to some other reason unconnected with gender). Bullying at work that has no sexual motive, or that is not sex-based or sexual in nature, cannot give rise to a complaint under the SDA 1975 (although the victim may – if the bullying is sufficiently serious – be able to resign and claim constructive dismissal, provided they have a minimum of one year's continuous service with their employer).

In the Reed case, the EAT expressed the view that some conduct will be of such a nature that it will be obvious it was unwanted from the victim's perspective, while in other cases behaviour may be borderline. In the former case, the employee will not have to provide evidence to a tribunal that they were disadvantaged by the treatment meted out to them, as this will be accepted at face value. In the latter case, however, the employee would have to show (in order to prove detriment) that the conduct continued after they had made it clear to the perpetrator that it was unwelcome. The EAT stated that, provided any reasonable person would understand the victim to be rejecting the conduct in question, its continuation should be regarded as harassment. This approach is in line with the EC Code of Practice, which states:

> **Sexual attention becomes sexual harassment if it is persisted in once it has been made clear that it is regarded by the recipient as offensive.**

An interesting development occurred in the case of Shamoon v Chief Constable of Royal Ulster Constabulary (2003) (the details of this case were given in Chapter 3) in which the House of Lords approved the principle that an employee may be subjected to a detriment even though the action or behaviour complained of caused no physical or economic consequence.

DISABILITY HARASSMENT

In October 2004, the DDA 1995 was amended to include the following definition of harassment:

> " **Harassment occurs where, for a reason which relates to the disabled person's disability, a person engages in unwanted conduct which has the purpose or effect of:**
>
> **(a) violating the disabled person's dignity, or**
>
> **(b) creating an intimidating, hostile, degrading, humiliating or offensive environment for the disabled person.** "

In looking at this definition, it is first important to note that the conduct has to be 'unwanted'. Again, this depends on what the employee sees as being unwanted – it is not necessary for the employee to have previously indicated that any specific conduct is unwanted. The tribunal will usually be required to make a decision of fact as to whether the conduct was unwanted.

It is also important to note the word 'or' at the end of clause (a). The conduct is only required to violate the employee's dignity or create an environment as described. However, in most situations the two will be heavily interlinked.

As in the definition of racial harassment, whether the conduct complained of constitutes harassment will depend on the perception of the complainant. However, if the tribunal considers that the perception of the complainant would be perceived as unreasonable by any reasonable person, given the circumstances, there will be no harassment. (Note: the tribunal is not allowed to substitute its own judgement for that of the complainant.)

A complaint of discrimination can be taken to tribunal as a result of either a single serious incident of harassment or a series of relatively minor incidents which, when viewed collectively, can be classed as a campaign of conduct amounting to unlawful harassment or causing detriment to the victim.

Two examples where disabled employees have been subjected to harassment come from the following tribunal cases:

Blowman v Lumonics Ltd and another (1998)

Blowman suffered from chronic fatigue syndrome. His colleagues regularly called him 'Joe Wickes' or 'Wicksey' after an Eastenders character who suffered from schizophrenia. It was found that this amounted to harassment as it was a sustained pattern of conduct.

Verma v Herbie's Pizzas Ltd (2000)

Verma was profoundly deaf, unable to lip-read and unable to read or write English. With support from his social worker, he gave evidence that he had been subjected to harassment and bullying. The tribunal upheld his claim, and also found that he was unable to take any measures to stop the bullying and harassment because of his inability to communicate. It was also found that the employers had taken no action to stop the conduct towards him.

TASK

Find out how your organisation, or an organisation with which you are familiar, addresses the issue of harassment in the workplace. Do they have specific policies, guidelines or training for managers?

HARASSMENT AS A CRIME

In addition to the employment laws that protect workers from harassment, the implementation of the Criminal Justice and Public Order Act 1994 in England and Wales made it a criminal offence for an individual to commit an act of deliberate harassment against another person. This Act does not apply in Scotland. To be covered by the Act, however, the harassment must be shown to have been intentional. This contrasts with the discrimination laws, under which a claim can be made irrespective of whether there was a deliberate intention to harass the victim.

More specifically, it is an offence under the Criminal Justice and Public Order Act intentionally to commit an act that causes another person harassment, alarm or distress either by:

■ using threatening, abusive or insulting language or behaviour, or disorderly behaviour, or

■ displaying any writing, sign or other visible representation which is threatening, abusive or insulting.

The Act covers all forms of harassment, irrespective of the motive behind it, and so harassment on grounds of sex, race, religion, sexual orientation, etc. are prohibited, as well as harassment on other grounds not covered by employment law, such as harassment motivated by personal dislike or difference in political opinion. Thus, an employee who is being intentionally harassed by a colleague at work may have recourse to justice by complaining directly to the police, over and above the potential right to bring a complaint against their employer to tribunal alleging discrimination on one of the prohibited grounds.

Another criminal law governing harassment which applies throughout the UK is the Protection from Harassment Act 1997. This Act makes it a criminal offence to pursue a course of conduct that amounts to harassment, or which causes a person to fear that violence will be used against them, on at least two occasions. The principal objective of this Act was to provide protection to individuals who were the victims of stalking. There is no requirement under this Act for the behaviour in question to be intentional for it to be an offence.

Furthermore, the Anti-terrorism, Crime and Security Act 2001 created an offence of religiously aggravated harassment. The Act amended the Crime and Disorder Act to include a new category of 'religiously aggravated criminal offences'. Thus, harassment or hostility at work, based on a person's membership of a religious group, could be a criminal offence, as well as affording the victim the opportunity to bring a claim against their employer for unlawful harassment under the Employment Equality (Religion or Belief) Regulations 2003. A 'religious group' is widely defined in the Act as:

> " **a group of persons defined by reference to religious belief or lack of religious belief.** "

CASE STUDY

Within a large branch of a retail chain, there were allegations that an employee of Asian ethnic origin was subjecting an employee of Afro-Caribbean ethnic origin to a sustained process of harassment. This included name-calling, but also demeaning him in front of customers.

The management became aware that the problem had spilled over to outside working hours. The two employees lived near each other, and regularly drank at the same pub. One night, police were called when the taunting developed into a fight between the two employees.

Although the management then became aware of the extent of the harassment at work, they took no action, taking the view that the matter was now in police hands and none of their business. Was this a correct decision to make?

DIFFERENT FORMS OF HARASSMENT

Harassment can take many forms, some blatant and others more subtle. In general, harassment may be physical, verbal or non-verbal. Many types of conduct will be capable of being interpreted as unlawful harassment if the conduct is 'on grounds of' sex, marital status, sexual orientation, gender re-assignment, race, religion or belief, or disability (and – after October 2006 – age), and if it has had the effect of making the victim feel distressed in some way, or has created a working environment in which the employee has been made to feel uncomfortable.

Where an employee is physically abused by a colleague, there is unlikely to be any doubt that the abuse constitutes a detriment, or that it amounts to harassment under the anti-discrimination legislation, provided only that the physical abuse can be shown to have been on grounds of gender, race, disability, etc.

Forms of physical harassment include:

- unwelcome fondling, patting or touching
- threatened or actual sexual assault
- physical assault motivated by race
- pranks played against (for example) a disabled employee.

A case illustrating physical harassment (and verbal) is Jones *v* Tower Boot Company (1996), described in detail in Chapter 3.

According to the 2002 Report by the Wainwright Trust (an educational and research charity, www.wainwright.trust.btinternet.co.uk), verbal harassment, including sexist and racist 'banter', is the most common form of harassment. Verbal harassment includes a wide range of behaviour, such as:

- language that is of a sexual nature or racially offensive, whether oral or in writing – for example, derogatory remarks made about a colleague in an e-mail
- office gossip, or detrimental speculation about an employee's private sexual activities or religious practices
- sexist or racist remarks made to or about an employee, or jokes or banter based on sex, race, religion, sexual orientation or disability
- calling someone by a name based on sex or race – for example, calling a female colleague 'blondie' or an Asian employee 'Paki', both of which might be regarded as demeaning or insulting
- offensive terminology such as the word 'wog' when referring to a black employee, 'cripple' when describing a disabled person or 'lezzie' said to a lesbian
- deliberate isolation of someone at work, or non-co-operation on grounds of gender, race, religion, sexual orientation or disability
- teasing directed at an employee on account of the fact that they have a same-sex partner or a son or daughter who is gay or lesbian
- teasing on the subject of religious convictions or religious practices
- persistent sexual advances or pestering for sexual favours.

When considering terminology related to an individual's race or disability, it is worth bearing in mind that language evolves, and words that were once acceptable may now be regarded as derogatory.

An example of verbal harassment is given in the following case:

Insitu Cleaning Company Ltd and another v *Heads (1995)*

This case actually relates to a single incident when a manager of the organisation made a comment referring to the size of Head's breasts. She complained, but he then denied making the remark. The employer asked her to invoke the grievance procedure but she refused. Her claim for unlawful sexual discrimination was upheld, because the tribunal concluded that the manager had made the remark and it was sufficiently offensive to constitute unfavourable treatment.

TASK

Over the next few weeks, listen to the general banter that goes on at your place of work. Do you hear anything that a reasonable person could conclude constitutes harassment? What is the reaction of colleagues to any such banter?

In addition, there is non-physical and non-verbal harassment. Some examples are:

■ sexually suggestive gestures

■ leering at someone in a manner that is overtly sexual

■ the display of pin-up calendars or pictures of naked women (or men)

■ the display of racist publications

■ sexually explicit or racist material displayed on computer screens

■ the conspicuous display of a tattoo or the wearing of a badge that contains a slogan that is racist or offensive to people of a particular religion

■ gestures that are derogatory or demeaning towards gay or lesbian people

■ the wearing of clothing displaying football slogans that have a sectarian significance.

The above lists of examples are, of course, not exhaustive but they demonstrate the scope of behaviour that could, depending on the context, be viewed as unlawful harassment.

A recent ruling relating to non-verbal and non-physical harassment comes from the following case:

Moonsar v Fiveways Express Transport Ltd (2004)

Moonsar (a female) complained that, on three occasions, men with whom she worked in the same office had downloaded pornography on to their computer. The pornography had not been shown to her, but she was aware of what was happening and subsequently argued that it led to an intimidating atmosphere and offended her dignity.

The EAT found that downloading and displaying pornographic images where a woman could see them amounted to less favourable treatment for the purposes of sex discrimination legislation. They commented that such behaviour, carried out by male workers in the presence of a female worker, whether or not actually directed towards her, was an obvious affront to her dignity and would constituted a detriment. The behaviour therefore amounted to direct sex discrimination.

The definition of harassment as a distinct form of unlawful discrimination has implications for employers who condone banter in their workplaces. Legislation on race, disability, religion and sexual orientation clearly states that, where unwanted conduct has the effect of 'creating an intimidating, hostile, degrading, humiliating or offensive environment' for an employee, it will be regarded as unlawful harassment. Sex discrimination legislation will be amended in the future to contain similar wording. If the working environment is one in which sexual or sexist remarks, coarse or vulgar humour, racial, racist or homophobic banter or jokes about religious practices are commonplace, and if any individual employee genuinely finds this type of environment degrading, humiliating or offensive, the employer may find themselves facing claims at an employment tribunal for unlawful harassment. The fact that other employees are being subjected to the same banter or jokes will be irrelevant, provided only that the remarks and banter are capable of causing offence in the mind of a reasonable person. In addition, it is not necessary for an individual to show that the remarks that caused offence were directed at them personally, as the legislation requires only that the conduct in question created an uncomfortable environment for them.

An example could be where one or more employees regularly engage in racist banter at work and a black employee (for example), who works within earshot of the banter, feels demeaned by the jokes or finds the terminology used offensive. If the conduct occurs regularly, the employee who is upset by it could be said to have been subjected to a working environment that is degrading or humiliating, simply by being required to work in the presence of such banter. It may be that those engaging in the banter had no malicious motive, did not intend to cause offence and were unaware that they were doing so. Nevertheless, provided the employee in question genuinely finds the conduct unwanted, and assuming it is sufficient to reasonably be considered to have a detrimental effect, it will be capable of giving rise to a claim of unlawful race discrimination.

It may be helpful to bear in mind that an employee who is feeling upset by banter in the workplace may not feel comfortable about the prospect of telling their colleagues that they find the banter unacceptable, or about complaining to management about it. They may feel that working relationships may be damaged, that they will be seen as a trouble-maker, ostracised by their colleagues or not taken seriously. These fears are understandable, and management should not assume in the absence of any complaints that no problems of this nature exist. The key is to put in place policies, procedures and practices designed to prevent discriminatory harassment, including offensive banter, rather than waiting to deal with a problem after it has arisen.

It is strongly advisable, therefore, for employers to review the culture in which their employees work and take steps to actively discourage any banter that could be viewed as discriminatory, in order to avoid the risk of claims for unlawful harassment from an employee offended by it. This may involve introducing guidelines for all employees explaining the parameters of the laws on harassment and providing examples of what is, and is not, acceptable conduct.

As noted previously, under the new statutory grievance procedure, an employee must raise a written grievance before being eligible to take their complaint to an employment tribunal. However, where an employee has suffered harassment and has reasonable grounds to believe that raising a grievance would lead to further harassment, this requirement can be waived.

EMPLOYER'S RESPONSIBILITIES

Employers are liable in law for any act of discriminatory harassment carried out by one employee against another in the course of their employment. Liability cannot be avoided by pleading ignorance of the fact that the harassment was taking place, or by asserting that there was no deliberate intention to offend the victim.

This is shown in the case of Jones v Tower Boot Company (1996) quoted earlier. The employer argued that it was not responsible for the discrimination, because it had come from two specific employees who had not been authorised to behave in the way they did. However, the EAT found that the actions of the colleagues had occurred 'within the course of their employment' and hence the employer was responsible.

Even where the employer has taken steps to prevent discrimination – for example, by introducing an anti-harassment policy – a tribunal will examine whether there were any further preventative steps at all that the employer could have taken that were reasonably practicable, as shown in the case of Canniffe *v* East Riding of Yorkshire Council (2000).

Canniffe v *East Riding of Yorkshire Council (2000)*

Canniffe claimed that she had been subjected to a series of sexual assaults and threats of assault by a colleague. Her employer showed that they had a series of policies regarding discrimination and harassment, and that these had been brought to the attention of all employees. However, the EAT found that Canniffe's supervisor and other employees had been aware of what had been going on and had not acted on this, or done anything specific to stop the incidents occurring. It found that having policies in place, although laudable, was not sufficient for the employer to demonstrate that they had taken every reasonable step to stop the harassment.

In the event of a serious incident of harassment, or a series of events that might collectively be viewed as a course of conduct that creates an uncomfortable working environment, the employee could succeed in a claim for unlawful discrimination at an employment tribunal. A complaint would be particularly likely to succeed where the employee had already made management aware that the behaviour of a colleague was causing them offence or distress, and the complaint had been ignored, dismissed as trivial or inadequately dealt with.

There is no minimum length-of-service requirement to bring a case of discrimination to a tribunal, and no age limit. In most cases, the employer will be ordered to pay the complainant compensation for injury to feelings and for financial loss (if any).

TASK

Find out how your organisation, or an organisation with which you are familiar, attempts to ensure that employees are not involved in any behaviour that could be deemed to be harassment in the 'course of their work'. Do you think that the measures that are being taken are sufficient?

An employee who is being seriously harassed at work may also be able to succeed in a complaint of unfair constructive dismissal.

In order to show that there has been an unfair constructive dismissal, an employee must show that:

- There was a fundamental breach of the contract by the employer.
- The breach of the contract caused the employee to resign.
- There was no significant delay in resigning.

Serious harassment, or a failure on the part of management to deal adequately with a genuine complaint of harassment, would in most cases be regarded by the courts as a breach of trust and confidence, a duty that exists within every contract of employment. If there is a fundamental breach of trust and confidence and this causes the employee to resign without significant delay, it is likely that a claim for constructive dismissal will be successful.

Morrow v Safeway Stores plc (2000)

Morrow was a bakery production manager in a Safeway's store. There had been a number of complaints against her due to low levels of bread stocks on the shelves. On one day, there was a special promotion of a particular type of bread, but her manager found that there was none of this type of bread on the shelves. He gave Morrow a severe reprimand in the store, in front of customers and other employees. She was very distressed and discussed the situation with the HR Manager. She agreed to think about the situation during an imminent holiday, but chose instead to resign and claim constructive dismissal.

The EAT found that the public nature of the reprimand had fundamentally breached the mutual trust and confidence within the contract of employment. This was the reason why Morrow had resigned, and she had resigned without significant delay. Hence, she was successful in her claim. The EAT held that a breach of the implied term of trust and confidence would always amount to a fundamental or repudiatory breach of the employee's contract.

Employees do, however, require a minimum of one year's service to bring a complaint of unfair constructive dismissal to tribunal.

ADDRESSING CLAIMS OF HARASSMENT

Over and above the impact on the employer of any financial award they are ordered to pay to an employee following a campaign of harassment, there may be serious consequences for morale. Harassment of any kind can have devastating effects on the person subjected to it, and will also create a working atmosphere of fear in which employees will not be enabled to give of their best. An individual who is the victim of harassment may lose their confidence and feel anxious and unhappy; the stress caused by the harassment may even cause them to become seriously ill.

It is very important for employers to take any complaint of harassment seriously in the first instance, and deal with it promptly, effectively and fairly. It is, however, understandably difficult to tackle such a complaint, for a host of reasons. The personal nature of the behaviour complained of, the fear of emotional reactions or unpleasant confrontation, the worry that working relationships might be damaged and even a fear that, if the matter is looked into, more problems might be reported, are all likely to create anxiety for the manager responsible for dealing with a complaint. Nevertheless, these difficulties must be tackled if the problem is to be solved, as it is the unarguable responsibility of management to make sure that all complaints are dealt with without either procrastination or excuses.

The first step in dealing with a complaint of harassment in the workplace will always be to conduct an investigation into the alleged incident(s). The investigation should of course be as thorough as possible, and must be unbiased. For this reason, the person dealing with the investigation should have no connection with the allegations.

Confidential meetings will be needed, first with the complainant and subsequently with the alleged harasser. At these meetings, the person being interviewed should be allowed to bring a colleague or trade union representative along with them if they wish. It may also be appropriate to hold meetings with any witnesses to the incident(s) of alleged harassment in order to gather relevant information.

The aim at this stage is to gather as much evidence as possible about what happened so as to be able to give the person accused of harassment an opportunity to respond fully to the complaint against them. It should of course be borne in mind that, however serious or credible an employee's complaint may seem, there are always two sides to every story. The employee accused of harassment must also be treated fairly, and in an unbiased and non-accusatory manner.

The following represents a checklist of how a manager should proceed to investigate an employee's complaint of harassment:

- Hold a confidential meeting with the employee who has raised the complaint of harassment to discuss the details of their complaint. Specific examples of what was said or done (and the manner and tone in which things were said or done) should be sought, with times and dates of relevant incidents, if possible.

- Give the employee the opportunity to be accompanied by a colleague or trade union representative at the meeting if they wish.

- Write to the alleged harasser (ensuring confidentiality), explaining that there has been a complaint of harassment made against them, and inviting them to attend a meeting to establish the facts. It should be made clear that this meeting will be an investigatory meeting and that the employee is not being accused of any wrongdoing.

- Hold the meeting with the alleged harasser at which they should be given the opportunity to be accompanied by a colleague or trade union representative of their choice (if they wish).

- Give the alleged harasser full details of all the allegations that have been made against them – in other words, the specifics regarding the behaviour that has allegedly caused offence. It is important that they are given all the facts and allegations so that they have a fair opportunity to defend themselves.

- Listen to the alleged harasser's side of events, and allow them to provide a full explanation of their conduct and the reasons (if any) behind it. Ask probing questions, if necessary, to get at the truth.

- Try to establish whether the person accepts, partly accepts or completely refutes the allegations made against them.

- Be prepared to adjourn the meeting for further investigation if the alleged harasser provides new information that needs to be checked out.

- Once discussions are concluded, inform the employee what will happen next and within what timescale.

- Keep a confidential record of the key points discussed at each meeting.

If, following investigations, there are reasonable grounds to believe that the allegations of harassment are well-founded, the employer will, in most instances, decide to instigate disciplinary action against the employee who perpetrated the harassment. The disciplinary process should, however, be dealt with as a separate set of proceedings and, if possible, carried out by someone other than the person who conducted the investigations.

Any employee who has been the victim of harassment at work will inevitably have suffered distress and anxiety as a result of the way they have been treated. In particular, if the harassment has been going on for a period of time, the adverse effect on the employee may be substantial. It may also have taken a considerable amount of courage for the employee to come forward with the complaint.

It follows that it will be very important, once it has been established that the employee has indeed been the victim of harassment, for the employer to offer the employee their full support. This will include reassurance that the problem will be fairly and thoroughly dealt with, and a firm commitment to put a stop to the harassment, but it may also involve the need to provide moral support to help the employee come to terms with what has happened.

CASE STUDY

A female employee in a media organisation was being subjected to a series of harassment by her line manager. This included comments of a sexual nature and, on a number of occasions, inappropriate physical contact. The employee was told by her line manager that she could not complain, because all grievances had to be addressed to him.

Eventually the employee approached the Personnel Department, asking for advice. The department she worked in was very specialist, and there was no opportunity for her or her manager to move to another department. She said she just wanted the harassment to stop.

Unfortunately the Personnel Department did not think through the situation carefully, and they immediately approached the line manager asking for his version of what was happening. He denied everything, and then (when alone with the employee) launched a violent verbal attack on the employee which she found very frightening.

She then went to see her GP and was given a medical note for one month on the grounds which specified 'stress'. At the end of that month, she decided that she could not face returning to work, and she resigned. She made a claim to the Employment Tribunal of sex discrimination which was eventually settled out of court. How should this situation have been handled?

One excellent way of providing moral and practical support is to appoint an appropriate person to fulfil the role of employee counsellor. This may be done either by appointing a member of staff who has received professional training in counselling techniques, or by providing employees with access to an external confidential advice service through an independent counselling organisation.

If a counsellor is appointed, their role could include:

■ providing a sounding-board to employees, who believe they are being harassed, to help them view the problem objectively and decide what to do

- offering information and guidance to employees on the courses of action open to them and the likely outcomes

- helping the employee to plan how they might go about making an informal direct approach to the harasser to explain that certain behaviour is unacceptable, and asking for it to stop

- accompanying an employee to an informal meeting with the alleged harasser to help the employee explain their case (if that is the course of action the employee decides upon)

- talking to the alleged harasser (in confidence), if the victim of the harassment feels unable to make a personal approach, to explain that a particular aspect of their behaviour is causing offence or upset, and why the victim finds it unacceptable

- supporting an employee who wishes to raise a formal complaint, if this is the course of action the employee would prefer (especially in the event of serious allegations)

- counselling both parties as to future behaviour once the complaint has been discussed and resolved.

Harassment of any kind in the workplace is a serious issue, and one that should always be treated seriously by management. In some cases, instances of harassment will provide solid grounds for the perpetrator of the harassment to be dismissed, while in other cases a formal written warning may be appropriate. Any warning issued should make it clear that any further type of harassment or victimisation of the employee, or any other employee, is likely to lead to the employee's dismissal. By contrast, in cases where the individual was genuinely unaware that their conduct was causing offence, an informal warning may suffice so long as the person clearly understands and accepts that the conduct causing offence or embarrassment must not recur.

It is important for the person dealing with the alleged perpetrator of harassment to refrain from making accusations, showing emotion or jumping to premature conclusions. The person accused of harassment has as much right to be treated fairly as the person complaining of the harassment. As with any form of alleged misconduct in the workplace, it is important that the manager responsible for handling it should act fairly and reasonably in dealing with the problem.

Once a problem of harassment has been uncovered, it may be difficult, if not impossible, for the alleged harasser and the victim to continue to work together. Furthermore, if the allegations of harassment are established as being well-founded, it may be inappropriate to allow the harasser to continue to work anywhere near their erstwhile victim.

If there has been a complete breakdown in trust or where, despite reassurances that the problem has been resolved, the employee flatly refuses to continue to work alongside the harasser, the employer may have to consider transferring one or other of the employees involved to another job or even another department.

Caution should be exercised, however, if consideration is being given to transferring the employee who has been the victim of harassment, as a transfer may be viewed as a further detriment (and thus discriminatory). If, however, the employee genuinely wishes to move, and provided the transfer in question is on terms and conditions at least as favourable as the employee's current terms, this may provide a satisfactory solution. The employer should discuss the option of a transfer with the employee with a view to exploring whether it is a viable option, rather than imposing a transfer unilaterally.

A more appropriate course of action may be to transfer the harasser to another post (but only after it has been established that the allegations of harassment were well-founded). Once again, however, the matter would have to be discussed and agreed with the employee, otherwise a transfer to a different job could amount to a breach of the employee's contract (irrespective of the motive behind the transfer).

In contrast, in circumstances where the harassment has been of a relatively minor nature, and provided the employer has taken appropriate steps to deal with the matter, the employee should be encouraged to continue in the same job, with the reassurance that there will be no further instance of the behaviour complained of. An unconditional apology from the erstwhile harasser would be a welcome step towards a viable future working relationship. In a case of this nature, counselling might be helpful.

If, following the conclusion of proceedings to deal with a complaint of harassment, the harasser and the person whom they harassed continue to work in the same part of the organisation, an appropriate manager should follow up by monitoring the situation to ensure that:

- the working relationships between the various people are now harmonious and no further instances of harassment have taken place
- neither party is engaging in recriminatory behaviour against the other
- the complainant is not being victimised (whether by the harasser or by colleagues) on account of the fact that they complained.

Following any disciplinary action taken, whether in the form of a warning or dismissal, the employee must be allowed the right of appeal. The appeal should, if the size of the organisation allows it, be dealt with by someone who has not been involved in either the investigation or the disciplinary proceedings. It should also, ideally, be held by someone more senior than the person who dealt with the disciplinary hearing.

Finally, the employer should keep confidential records of all meetings held in connection with the allegations of harassment, and the process used to address and resolve the complaint and the outcome. In so doing, it will be important to adhere to the relevant provisions of the Data Protection Act 1988.

TASK

Review the policy on harassment that your organisation, or an organisation with which you are familiar, has written. If there is no such policy, make an attempt to write one.

KEY POINTS FROM THIS CHAPTER:

- The Race Relations Act 1976 was amended in July 2003 to make specific provision to render harassment on grounds of race or ethnic or national origins unlawful, and to introduce a free-standing statutory definition of racial harassment.
- Conduct at work may be regarded as unlawful harassment if it violates another person's dignity, or creates an intimidating, hostile, degrading, humiliating or offensive environment.

- Employees are expressly protected by statute against any harassment in the course of their employment on grounds of race, religion or belief, disability or sexual orientation.

- Although UK sex discrimination law does not (as yet) contain a definition of sexual harassment, courts and tribunals have consistently held that sexual harassment at work can amount to a detriment and hence be a form of direct discrimination.

- The EC Code of Practice on the protection of the dignity of women and men at work defines sexual harassment as 'unwanted conduct of a sexual nature, or other conduct based on sex affecting the dignity of women and men at work', and further states that conduct of a sexual nature will amount to sexual harassment where it is 'unwanted, unreasonable and offensive to the recipient'.

- A complaint of sex discrimination can be taken to tribunal as a result of either a single serious incident or a series of relatively minor incidents which, when viewed collectively, can be classed as a campaign of conduct causing detriment to the victim.

- An employee who is being seriously harassed at work may bring a claim of unlawful harassment to tribunal, and may also be able to succeed in a complaint of constructive dismissal if they have resigned because of the harassment, provided they have a minimum of one year's service.

- In most cases, instances of harassment will provide solid grounds for the employer to take disciplinary action (including dismissal in serious cases) against the perpetrator of the harassment.

EXAMPLES TO WORK THROUGH

1   A female employee has complained that some men in the office where she works have calendars on their desks portraying semi-naked women. She says she finds this offensive and has asked for them to be removed. However, everyone else in the office (including other female employees) has complained that she is over-reacting. What would you do?

2   A male supervisor came across one of his female employees sitting outside the factory (but on company premises) crying. He sat down beside her and asked her what was wrong. In a bid to comfort her, he put his arm around her shoulders. She told him about her problems, which related to the break-up of a relationship with her boyfriend. The supervisor thought he had been a good boss – but he has now been told that she has complained that he touched her inappropriately. He is very upset by the allegation. What would you advise?

3   You have been made aware that two of your employees are involved with a group, outside work, which is blatantly offensive towards people who are not of white ethnic origin. As a result of this, a number of employees from ethnic minorities have asked for the two employees to be moved to another section because they fear that they will be harassed. However, the two employees argue that they have never made comments about their beliefs during their work, and that to move them away from the area where they work will constitute harassment against them – on the grounds of their beliefs. What do you do?

Preventing Discrimination and Promoting Equality and Diversity

CHAPTER 12

> **OBJECTIVES OF THIS CHAPTER:**
>
> ■ to understand how discrimination can be prevented in the workplace
> ■ to explore ways of promoting equality and diversity
> ■ to outline the requirements prescribed by legislation
> ■ to consider model procedures that could be implemented.

As we have seen through the various aspects of diversity and discrimination that we have studied, discrimination in the workplace has a number of negative consequences for the organisation. Ultimately, there is the potential penalty of substantial compensation. However, the poor working atmosphere that can be caused by discrimination has much wider impacts. If employees are not comfortable in the workplace, there will be higher absenteeism and increased turnover of staff. There is also likely to be a reduction in motivation that has a direct impact on productivity.

Most employers accept that discrimination must be stopped, and many employers are starting to understand the benefits of diversity. In this chapter, we are going to explore actions that can be taken to achieve this in the workplace.

On their website (www.eoc.org.uk), the Equal Opportunities Commission (EOC) outline a series of steps that can be taken by employers to achieve true equal opportunities. It is those steps that will give the framework for this chapter.

EQUAL OPPORTUNITIES POLICY

The purpose of an equal opportunity policy is to focus on a commitment to equal opportunities, and to make that commitment public. Leighton (2004) comments that recent research suggests that there is a perception among senior policy makers that anti-discrimination law has already been very effective and there is a declining problem. This attitude can lead to managers not seeing any need for policies to be developed.

Thus, the adoption of appropriate policies and procedures represents a very important first step in the journey towards protecting the employer from liability for claims of unlawful discrimination. Articulately written policies will not, however, be enough on their own to provide the employer with protection against liability. In the event of a claim to tribunal for unlawful discrimination, the tribunal will also wish to examine closely whether:

- the policies and procedures genuinely have full management commitment and support
- the policies and procedures have been communicated properly to all staff in ways that ensure clear understanding
- management and (where relevant) staff have received adequate training in equal opportunities
- disciplinary procedures have been amended so as to include acts of discrimination and harassment as serious misconduct.

Colley v British Road Services Ltd (1994)

In this case, an employee claimed racial harassment, and in its defence the organisation showed that it had an equal opportunities policy. The tribunal agreed that the policy was 'excellent', but found that the organisation had taken no steps to put the policy into practice, and hence it was found that the organisation was liable for the harassment.

Although there is no legal requirement for employers to put an equal opportunities policy in place, there will be many benefits in doing so. The objectives of an equal opportunities policy could include:

- to ensure that no employee or job applicant is treated unfavourably on grounds of sex, race, religion, etc.
- to increase general awareness of the importance of equal opportunities in the workplace, and make it clear why discrimination or harassment of any kind is unacceptable
- to set out minimum standards of behaviour expected of workers and what workers can expect from the organisation
- to help towards the creation of an environment in which workers feel comfortable and confident that they will be treated with respect and dignity
- to enable all workers to perform at their best
- to make it clear that the employer takes equality and the prevention of discrimination seriously, and that anyone who acts in breach of the policy will be liable to disciplinary action up to and including summary dismissal.

Over and above an effective equal opportunities policy and anti-harassment policy, it will be important to have an accompanying complaints procedure, designed specifically to provide a route for workers who are the victims of discrimination or harassment to report the problem and receive support from the employer. The employer's normal grievance procedure will not normally be adequate for this purpose, simply because it often happens that the perpetrator of discrimination or harassment is the worker's supervisor, who will also be the person to whom grievances must be taken under the grievance procedure. It is best to have a separate complaints procedure that is designed specifically to deal with instances of alleged discrimination and harassment.

Where proper preventative measures are introduced, they will place the employer in a relatively strong position to defend any claims of unlawful discrimination or harassment taken against them. This is because all the anti-discrimination laws include the statement that an employer facing a claim for unlawful discrimination will have a defence if they can show that they 'took such steps as were reasonably practicable to prevent' the discrimination in question (see the Sex Discrimination Act [SDA] 1975, Race Relations Act [RRA] 1976, Disability Discrimination Act [DDA] 1995, Part-Time Workers [Prevention of Less Favourable Treatment] Regulations 2000, Fixed-Term Employees [Prevention of Less Favourable Treatment] Regulations 2002, Employment Equality [Sexual Orientation] Regulations 2003, and the Employment Equality [Religion or Belief] Regulations 2003). This means that, if an employer can provide evidence to a tribunal that they did everything they reasonably could to prevent discrimination in the workplace, they may be held not liable for any discriminatory conduct that does occur despite the measures taken. The burden of proving this defence is, however, a high one, and tribunals will not only scrutinise the employer's policies and procedures, but will examine the extent to which they were actually put into practice.

Examples of what should be covered in such policies are included at the end of this chapter.

TASK

Find out if your organisation, or an organisation with which you are familiar, has an equal opportunities policy. If it has, read a copy of the procedure. Can you think of any ways in which it could be improved? If there is no policy, talk to the person responsible for equal opportunities and discuss how a policy might be beneficial to an organisation.

CASE STUDY

Following a successful discrimination claim against it, the management of a haulage firm decided that they would write an equal opportunities policy. They gave the task to a new graduate trainee within the organisation.

The graduate trainee was encouraged to gather a group together to discuss what should be in the policy – the group included a representative from each gender, every race represented in the organisation, a disabled employee and the manager who had been involved in the discrimination claim.

The policy was readily accepted by the whole workforce once it was written, because it was seen as a joint piece of work from all groups within the workforce. Since the writing of the policy, there have been no further discrimination claims, and the management report a great improvement in teamwork and general work attitudes.

A PERSON RESPONSIBLE FOR EQUAL OPPORTUNITIES

The EOC recommend that the most senior person in the organisation is named as the person responsible for equal opportunities. If this is not possible for any reason, then the person who is named as being responsible should report regularly to the most senior person. It is also important that the trades unions are involved in the development of an equal opportunities policy – because they are the representatives of the employees. If there are no recognised trades unions, then elected employee representatives should be involved.

Despite a senior person having overall responsibility for equal opportunities, the day-to-day responsibilities have to be delegated to personnel and line managers for practical reasons. All those who have responsibility must be clear about what they are required to do and not do.

As we have already noted, the employer is responsible for acts of discrimination carried out in the course of work by its employees (vicarious liability). Although the person responsible for equal opportunities cannot listen to every conversation and monitor every event, it is essential that they do everything possible to promote a culture where discrimination is not allowed. It is also important to note that this responsibility extends to acts of discrimination carried out by a third party, as in the case of Burton and Rhule v De Vere Hotels (1996), described in detail in Chapter 3.

TASK

Find out who, in your organisation or an organisation with which you are familiar, is responsible for equal opportunities. Talk to them about their duties and responsibilities.

ENSURE EMPLOYEES KNOW ABOUT THE POLICY

The EOC recommends that the equal opportunities policy should be published and should be made known to all employees. It also suggests that the policy should be made known to relevant third parties, such as job centres and recruitment agencies that are used by the organisation.

In the case of Canniffe v East Riding of Yorkshire Council (2000),explored in detail in the Chapter 11, the Employment Appeal Tribunal (EAT) considered whether there were any preventative steps that had been taken by the employer, and whether there were any further preventative steps that the employer could reasonably have been expected to take. In considering these points, the EAT found that the employer had taken preventative steps, in the form of having relevant policies and bringing them to the attention of all employees. However, they also found that there was more that the employer could have done – ie they could have taken direct steps to stop the assaults and threats of assaults, because other employees were aware that they were taking place.

HOW IS THE POLICY TO BE IMPLEMENTED?

As shown in the case of Canniffe v East Riding of Yorkshire Council, it is not sufficient to simply state that there is a policy in place – it also needs to be carefully implemented. Approaches that could be taken are:

■ the setting up of a working party to monitor the successful implementation

- a series of briefings/training sessions that all employees are required to attend
- the circulation of the policy for all employees to read
- the posting of the policy on the company intranet (although this would not be sufficient to conclude that all employees had actually read the policy!).

Alongside the implementation of the policy, an organisation also needs to consider how legislation relating to discrimination is to be taught to all line managers, and maybe the key points communicated to all employees. If employees do not realise that actions they are taking breach legislation, then there are more likely to be claims of discrimination for the organisation to defend. Ignorance of the law is no defence.

For example, a line manager might decide to refuse the application of an employee who is disabled because, in the opinion of that line manager, the employee would be unable to carry out the job. However, the line manager is required by law to consider any reasonable adjustments that could be made in order to allow the applicant to do the job. If the line manager was unaware of that requirement, it would not make the rejection of the applicant lawful.

EQUAL OPPORTUNITIES COMMITTEE

The EOC recommends that an organisation sets up an equal opportunities committee with the following main aims:

- to analyse the information provided by the monitoring of equal opportunities in an organisation
- to assess the findings against the objectives of the equal opportunities policy to identify how the policy is actually working
- to put forward suggestions to remedy any failures
- to assess the success of the proposed remedies over time.

If the employer recognises a trade union, then it is important that there is a representative from the trade union on the committee. Regardless of this, it is important that the committee represents a cross-section of people of different levels of seniority and the different groups within the organisation (eg each gender represented, a range of ethnic origins represented, disabled employees represented, etc.). Without having a range of representation, there is a danger that the committee becomes very narrow in its focus.

TASK

Talk to a range of employees within your organisation, or an organisation with which you are familiar, asking them about the equal opportunities policy within the organisation. Are they aware of the main requirements of the policy? Do they know where there is a copy of the policy?

CASE STUDY

Within a manufacturing organisation, equal opportunities had always been an agenda item at the end of the monthly management and trade union consultation meeting. However, it was decided that it was not being given sufficient attention, and a meeting was arranged to discuss equal opportunities exclusively.

The meeting was not a great success because no-one had anything of any substance to say. It was decided, therefore, to seek volunteers to be members of the committee. The management were rather unsure about this idea, concerned that the people who would volunteer would be those who wanted to make complaints! However, it was decided to give the idea a try. After some initial problems with deciding a clear agenda, the committee was very successful, making a number of useful suggestions to the organisation.

PROVIDING TRAINING IN EQUALITY, DIVERSITY AND THE AVOIDANCE OF DISCRIMINATION

In order to ensure that the employer's equal opportunities policy and anti-harassment policy are put into practice, and to minimise the likelihood of instances of discrimination or harassment, full training in equality, diversity and the avoidance of discrimination should be provided to all staff. Training is especially important for managers, supervisors and anyone who is responsible for recruitment and promotion decisions, as it is clearly vital that people in positions of authority understand how the various laws impact upon their actions. Employers may wish also to make awareness training in equal opportunities matters available to all staff on a voluntary basis.

Equal opportunities training should aim to achieve the following objectives:

- to provide information about the fundamental principles of UK discrimination legislation, and the concepts of direct and indirect discrimination, victimisation and harassment
- to identify the different grounds on which discrimination can occur, eg grounds of gender, sexual orientation, part-time status, colour, religion, etc.
- to identify the types of behaviour that can constitute unlawful discrimination, eg failure to promote, pay differences, discriminatory questions at interview, etc.
- to clarify the many forms that harassment can take, eg physical, verbal and non-verbal
- to provide examples of the types of joke, banter and casual remark that may cause offence and therefore constitute unlawful harassment
- to explore the meaning of equality and diversity, and identify the barriers to achieving them
- to encourage all employees to adopt a positive attitude towards equality and diversity
- to encourage employees to recognise, understand and reject stereotyped assumptions, prejudice and negative attitudes towards certain people or groups
- to raise awareness of the employer's policies and procedures relating to equality and the prevention of discrimination, and their underlying values
- to identify actions and behaviours that promote equality and diversity in the workplace.

The importance of training is illustrated in the following case:

Haringey Council (Haringey Design Partnership Directorate of Technical and Environmental Services) v Al-Azzawi (2000)

Al-Azzawi was a senior architect of Iraqi Arabic ethnic origin. He was present at a discussion about a forthcoming union quiz evening when a co-worker referred to 'bloody Arabs', whom he claimed had disrupted a previous event. Al-Azzawi complained and the co-worker was suspended while the incident was investigated. The co-worker was found to be guilty of misconduct, rather than gross misconduct, and was given a written warning that remained live on his record for a period of two months; he was also required to write an apology to Al-Azzawi. Al-Azzawi brought a claim that the Council was vicariously liable for the remark made by the co-worker.

The tribunal upheld Al-Azzawi's claim, but this finding was overturned by the EAT. The EAT considered whether the employer had taken all reasonable steps to prevent the discriminatory comment. The employer had policies on racial awareness, all employees received training in racial awareness (and the co-worker in question had received this training) and all employees who violated the policy were disciplined. On this basis, the EAT concluded that the employer had done everything possible to prevent the discrimination occurring.

TASK

Talking further to the employees you identified in the last task, ask them if they have had any training relating to equal opportunities. What benefits did they gain from this training?

EXAMINE EXISTING POLICIES, PRACTICES AND PROCEDURES

In Chapters 6 and 7, we looked in detail at the policies and procedures relating to recruitment. We have also looked at policies and procedures relating to issues such as pay, benefits and termination of employment. The EOC recommends that all such policies should be regularly reviewed to ensure that they are meeting the aim of promoting equal opportunities. This is particularly relevant if it can be shown, through the monitoring of equal opportunities, that there is some evidence that equality is not being achieved.

As well as examining the content of all procedures, it is also important to examine the language and the illustrations used. For example, if a company brochure shows only pictures of white male employees, this could indicate an underlying attitude of discrimination.

It is also important that application forms are reviewed alongside policies, practices and procedures. As well as ensuring that no potentially discriminatory questions are being asked, it is important to consider how the information that is gathered is being used, as shown in the following case:

> ### *Glynn* v *London Transport (1998)*
>
> Glynn completed an application form when applying for a job with London Transport. In the section headed 'Equal Opportunities Information', there was a statement that the information provided would only be used to monitor the equal opportunities policy. Glynn declared that he had no sight in his left eye, but did not see that as a disability. He was subsequently rejected for employment on the grounds of that information. London Transport accepted that they had unlawfully discriminated against Glynn. The tribunal also made a declaration that the organisation was not allowed to use information that it had gathered to monitor the equal opportunities policy for any purpose other than that monitoring.

MONITORING EQUAL OPPORTUNITIES

The purpose of monitoring is to determine whether the equal opportunities policy is working. Areas to look at include the profile of employees:

- who have been recruited into the organisation, compared to those who have been refused positions
- who have been promoted within the organisation
- at each level of the organisation and in certain job categories
- who have been selected to attend training and development events, or who have been supported through the gaining of further professional qualifications
- at different levels of salary, and the allocation of benefits at these different levels
- who have been taken through the disciplinary procedure
- who have brought a grievance against the organisation
- who have resigned from the organisation
- who have been made redundant from the organisation
- who have been dismissed from the organisation.

By looking at the profile, an organisation should be considering the gender, ethnic origin and disability of the employees. If other information is gathered, such as age, religion or sexual orientation, this should also be examined.

If an organisation has truly adopted equal opportunities, then there should be a reasonable balance of employee profiles in each of the areas listed. However, the statistics do need to be analysed with care.

For example, when looking at the ethnic origins of employees who have been recruited into the organisation, consideration needs to be given to the population of people who can reasonably have been expected to apply for the vacancy. If the vacancy is a job where it is unlikely people would travel a long distance or would relocate, then the local population is the area to consider. If the organisation is located in an area with a high proportion of residents from ethnic minorities, then that should be reflected in the proportion of ethnic minority people employed by the organisation. However, if the organisation is located in an area with very few residents from ethnic minorities, it is reasonable to expect that the population of the organisation will reflect this.

The following case demonstrates how data from such a monitoring exercise could be used to support a claim of discrimination:

West Midlands Passenger Transport Executive (WMPTE) v Singh (1998)

Singh was an inspector with the WMPTE and applied unsuccessfully for the post of senior inspector. He believed that the reason he had not been promoted was based on his race, and he sought disclosure of data showing the numbers of white and non-white applicants for promotions and their success rate. The Court of Appeal confirmed that he was allowed access to this information. It noted that it is particularly difficult to show that discrimination has occurred in the recruitment process and, if the statistics did demonstrate any particular person of behaviour, then it was justifiable that they should be disclosed.

TASK

Ask your organisation, or an organisation with which you are familiar, if you can look at their statistics relating to equal opportunities. If you are allowed access, analyse the statistics to identify if any difficulties are identified from those statistics. Talk to the person responsible for equal opportunities about your findings.

ACTION TO REMEDY PAST DISCRIMINATION

It is very important for an employer to take prompt and decisive steps to deal with any instance of discrimination or harassment as soon as they become aware of it. Taking appropriate measures to deal promptly and effectively with discriminatory conduct will not remove the employer's liability for the discriminatory act in an overall sense, but it will play an important part in convincing a tribunal that, because the discrimination was promptly remedied, the employer had taken such steps as were reasonably practicable and necessary.

Another important approach to remedying past discrimination is the implementation of positive action policies. As outlined in Chapter 6, positive discrimination is not lawful, but employers are permitted, if they wish, to take certain measures (known as 'positive action') to encourage people from under-represented or disadvantaged groups to apply for employment or access training. As well as considering positive action, the employer might wish to take the following steps:

- supporting employees in gaining further qualifications that they were not able to do at an earlier age due to discrimination in the education process at the time
- ensuring that all employees have equal opportunities to gain the experience that is necessary to achieve promotion
- providing training in particular skills that are required to progress in an organisation.

However, it must be clear that in promoting the interests of a group that is under-represented, discrimination against other groups is not occurring, as happened in the following case:

Riyat v London Borough of Brent (1983)

Riyat was a women of white Polish origin. She worked as an employment assistant in the careers office. The Brent Council were concerned that, despite having a clear and well-written equal opportunities policy, Council officers were not pursuing it with sufficient vigour. Some councillors decided to become involved in the recruitment processes, which resulted in a number of internal candidates being removed from short-lists and replaced with less well-qualified external candidates of different ethnic origins.

Riyat applied for the job of senior employment assistant and a councillor of West Indian origin removed her from the short-list, replacing her with an alternative candidate of West Indian origin (J). The Principal Careers Officer protested and Riyat was put back on the list, along with J. When Riyat was interviewed, she was questioned intensely on her views on positive discrimination. At the end of the interview round, the interviewers were unable to decide between J and Riyat and hence the job was re-advertised. On the second attempt, Riyat, J and four others were interviewed. Again, Riyat was questioned closely on her views on positive discrimination, and felt a certain hostility towards her. It was decided to appoint J because it was determined that Riyat did not understand or did not support the equal opportunities policy.

Riyat successfully claimed that she had been subjected to race discrimination. It was found that she had said nothing in her interview that had suggested that she did not support the equal opportunities policy. It was also found that the equal opportunities policy was good, but the councillors had extended it by removing white candidates from short-lists, and hence people were being selected on the basis of their ethnic origin. This was unlawful race discrimination.

Despite taking all the steps listed, it cannot be guaranteed that discrimination will not occur. The CIPD briefing, 'Discrimination and the Law' (Leighton 2004), ends with the following quote from Sayce (2003):

" Do not get seduced by the naïve view that 'informing' or 'educating' people will change attitudes, let alone their behaviour: why should it unless you have carefully analysed their motivations? Do not make the opposite error – that law alone will bring the depth of change sought. Why should it when it is framed and interpreted in the context of a discriminatory culture? "

CASE STUDY

After a successful discrimination claim made against, it a retail organisation decided to make equal opportunities awareness part of the induction training.

Now, all employees – whatever their level in the organisation – have the basic legislation explained to them, and are told what is considered to be unacceptable behaviour. They are also made aware of some of the main features of the religions and races represented among the employees, to make them more aware of the cultural issues that exist.

This training is very popular among the employees, who have found it very interesting. It has also helped some retail assistants understand their customers' needs more effectively, which has been a positive step towards customer care.

MODEL POLICIES AND PROCEDURES

This section provides a range of model policies and procedures that demonstrate the issues that should be addressed when developing policies. However, it is important to remember that a policy must be correctly implemented, employees must be trained in the requirements of the policy and the impact of the policy must be regularly monitored.

Model equal opportunities policy

This equal opportunities policy represents a statement of the company's general approach towards equal opportunities. It is not intended to form a contractually binding statement.

The Company is committed to ensuring equal opportunities, fairness of treatment, dignity, work-life balance and the elimination of all forms of discrimination in the workplace. One of the key objectives of the policy is for the Company to provide a working environment in which workers feel comfortable and confident that they will be treated with respect and dignity.

It is the Company's stated policy to treat all workers equally and fairly, irrespective of their sex, marital status, trans-gender status, sexual orientation, race, colour, nationality, ethnic origin, national origin, culture, religion, age or disability. A similar policy is adopted towards job applicants. The Company is also committed to ensuring that no policy, procedure, provision, rule, requirement, condition or criterion will be imposed on any worker without justification if it would put that worker at a disadvantage on any of the above grounds. Furthermore, harassment in any form is unacceptable and staff should also familiarise themselves with the Company's anti-harassment policy.

This equal opportunities policy applies to the Company's recruitment and selection practices, employees' terms and conditions of employment (including pay), opportunities for promotion, transfer and training, general treatment at work, disciplinary and grievance procedures, and termination of employment.

Implementation of this policy will be supported by a full programme of communication to ensure that all workers are aware of their responsibilities and rights, and of the Company's commitment to equality.

All staff who have responsibility for recruitment, selection, promotion and/or appraisal, or who supervise other staff, will receive equal opportunities training. Other staff will have the opportunity to attend awareness training in equality and diversity.

The Company will review this policy on a regular basis in order to ensure that individuals are selected, promoted and otherwise treated on the basis of their relevant abilities and merits.

The effectiveness of the policy will be judged by monitoring the numbers and composition (in terms of gender, racial group, age and disability) of:

- successful and unsuccessful job applicants
- staff who receive training
- staff who are promoted
- staff who benefit or suffer detriment as a result of performance assessment
- staff who raise grievances
- staff who are the subject of disciplinary action
- staff who leave the Company.

An annual report containing the result of the monitoring will be prepared and published by the Board.

The overall responsibility for the policy lies with [state name of senior manager]. All workers are, however, expected to act within the spirit and intention of the policy and the law relating to equal opportunities and discrimination at all times. The employer will view any breach of the policy, or any type of discriminatory action against another worker, very seriously. Any worker who breaches the principles of equal opportunity enshrined in this policy will be liable to disciplinary action up to and including summary dismissal.

Any worker who believes they have been the victim of a breach of this policy, or who has witnessed a breach of this policy affecting another worker, should report the matter immediately either to their line manager or to [state name of appropriate contact, for example an HR manager]. Alternatively, a worker who wishes to make a complaint may use the Company's formal complaints procedure.

Model clause covering employees' rights in pregnancy and maternity for insertion into an equal opportunities policy

The Company respects employees' rights not to be subjected to any unfavourable treatment for any reason connected with pregnancy, childbirth or maternity leave. It is therefore the Company's policy to ensure that employees who become pregnant do not suffer any form of detrimental treatment because of pregnancy, an intention to take maternity leave or because they have taken maternity leave. It follows that all employees who become pregnant will be treated fairly and equally in relation to pay, promotion, transfer, training, appraisal, time off work, occupational sick pay, etc.

The Company believes that the promotion of flexible working can increase staff motivation, promote work-life balance and improve performance. It is the Company's policy to endeavour to be flexible on working patterns for all its workers. Flexibility extends to the number of hours that an employee works, the days and start/finish times of those hours, overtime working, shift working and the place of work.

The Company must, however, recognise that the law grants employees who have a minimum of 26 weeks' continuous service and who have parental responsibility for a child under the age of 6 (or under the age of 18 where the child is disabled) the statutory right to request a change to their working pattern. If necessary, therefore, the Company will give priority to requests for flexible working from employees who have the statutory right to request flexible working.

Whenever an employee submits a request for flexible working, full and fair consideration will be given to the request, taking into account the likely effects that the employee's desired working pattern might have on the Company, the work of the employee's department and the employee's colleagues. Agreeing to one employee's request will not therefore set a precedent or create any right for another employee to be granted a similar change to their hours of work or place of work.

Model policy relating to the recruitment, training and retention of disabled workers

It is the Company's policy to support the employment and retention of people with disabilities. This is the case irrespective of whether the individual's impairment is physical or mental. The Company is committed to taking all reasonable steps towards accommodating the needs of disabled workers and job applicants to enable them to be employed, and to continue in employment so long as they are able to do so and wish to do so.

The Company will refrain from making assumptions about the type of work that people with disabilities can or cannot do. Applicants for employment, promotion or transfer will be given full and fair consideration and support. Furthermore, all disabled job applicants who meet the minimum requirements for the job as set out in the job description and employee specification will be guaranteed an interview.

All workers, including those who have a disability, will have equal access to training and opportunities for promotion based solely on their individual merits, taking into account any adjustments that could reasonably be made in the circumstances.

When a worker becomes disabled, or where an existing disability worsens, the Company will do everything it reasonably can to retain the disabled person in employment. If redeployment becomes necessary, the disabled worker will be viewed as a priority within any general redeployment exercise.

In general, the Company will take all reasonably practicable steps to make adjustments to working arrangements, working practices and, where appropriate and feasible, to premises, in order to facilitate the employment or continued employment of a disabled person. The worker will be fully consulted over any proposed adjustments and, where appropriate, expert medical advice will be sought in order that the Company can do its best to support the disabled worker.

Model anti-harassment policy

The Company is committed to ensuring fairness of treatment, dignity, and the elimination of all forms of discrimination, including harassment and bullying, for all its workers. This policy aims to ensure that no worker is subjected to any form of harassment or bullying, and that the Company provides a working environment in which workers feel comfortable and confident that they will be treated with respect and dignity at all times. Harassment and bullying at work are contrary to the interests of the Company because such behaviour is likely to make the victim feel upset, embarrassed, humiliated or intimidated. Such effects will lead to lower levels of motivation and job performance, and may also lead to ill-health.

The Company adopts a zero-tolerance approach towards harassment and bullying. Although managers and supervisors have a particular duty to ensure this policy is adhered to, all workers have an individual responsibility for their own conduct and must comply with both the spirit and the wording of the policy at all times. This will include time spent on the Company's premises and also time spent working for the Company at other locations. This policy applies also to conduct at Company-organised social events.

All workers should be aware that harassment on grounds of sex, trans-gender status, sexual orientation, race, religion and disability are unlawful, and that, additionally, intentional harassment on any grounds constitutes a criminal offence. The Company will be held liable for unlawful harassment, but the individual perpetrator of the harassment may also be convicted of a criminal offence, or may be ordered by an employment tribunal to pay compensation to their victim for unlawful discrimination. There is no limit on the level of such compensation.

The Company will view any type of harassment or bullying perpetrated against another worker very seriously. Any member of staff who acts in breach of this policy will be liable to disciplinary action up to and including summary dismissal.

There is no single definition of what constitutes harassment or bullying. Harassment may take many forms and may be based on sex, trans-gender status, sexual orientation, race, nationality, colour, ethnic origins, national origins, culture, religion, age or disability. Harassment, broadly, is unwanted conduct that violates a person's dignity or creates an uncomfortable working environment for that person. It may be physical, verbal or non-verbal. Harassment may consist of a single serious incident, or may involve persistent behaviour of a particular type or different types.

It is important to understand that the question of whether or not particular behaviour constitutes harassment depends on whether the victim genuinely finds it offensive or otherwise unacceptable, and not how anyone else perceives the same behaviour. Bullying is behaviour that is threatening, intimidating, malicious, abusive or insulting. Often bullying is an abuse of power, position or knowledge and is designed to undermine, humiliate, denigrate or harm the victim. Bullying will have the effect of eroding an individual's confidence and self-esteem, and will cause anger, stress and/or anxiety. Both bullying and harassment can seriously damage working relationships, productivity and morale.

Examples of unacceptable behaviour include (but are not limited to):

- banter, jokes or comments that may be construed as sexually explicit, sexist, racist, homophobic or derogatory on grounds of religion or disability

- calling someone by a name based on sex, race, etc. (for example, calling an Asian employee 'Paki')

- spreading malicious rumours or insulting someone (particularly on grounds of gender, sexual orientation, race, religion or disability)

- ridiculing or demeaning someone

- picking on someone or setting them up to fail

- the display of pin-up calendars or pictures of naked women (or men)

- the display of racist publications

- sexually explicit or racist material displayed on computer screens

- exclusion or victimisation

- overbearing supervision or other misuse of power or position

- unwelcome sexual advances – for instance, touching, standing too close

- displaying offensive pictures

- making threats or comments about job security without foundation

- deliberately undermining a worker by overloading them and then constantly criticising them

- preventing individuals progressing by intentionally blocking promotion or training opportunities.

These behaviours may take place face to face, on the phone or in writing, including e-mail.

(Acknowledgement: ACAS, *Bullying and Harassment at Work: A guide for managers and employers* (ACAS/AL04), from which some of the above points are taken.)

The overall responsibility for this policy lies with [state name of appropriate senior manager].

Model complaints procedure (discrimination and harassment)

The Company is opposed to all forms of unlawful discrimination and harassment and seeks to create and maintain a working environment where all workers are treated with dignity and respect. In order to achieve this aim, the Company has devised this complaints procedure to give employees a means of challenging any unlawful discrimination or harassment that they experience or witness.

All complaints of discrimination or harassment will be treated seriously by the Company and will be dealt with promptly, efficiently and, so far as is possible, in confidence. The main aim of this procedure is to resolve complaints of discrimination or harassment so that the discriminatory treatment is remedied or the harassment stopped.

Any worker may use this procedure if they believe they have:

- been treated unfavourably in contravention of the Company's equal opportunities policy on grounds of sex, trans-gender status, sexual orientation, marital status, race, religion, age or disability
- been subjected to any form of harassment or bullying at work
- witnessed the harassment of a colleague.

Employees who, in good faith, raise a genuine complaint under this procedure will not be subjected to any unfavourable treatment or victimisation as a result of making a complaint.

Any worker who believes that they have been the victim of discriminatory treatment or harassment, or who has witnessed discrimination or harassment, may choose to take either informal or formal action.

Where possible, the worker should talk directly and informally to the person who they believe has discriminated against them or harassed them, and explain clearly their objection to the other employee's actions or conduct. In the case of harassment, the worker should explain clearly what aspect of their colleague's behaviour is unacceptable, or is causing offence, and request that it should stop. It may be that the person whose conduct is causing offence is genuinely unaware that their behaviour is unwelcome or objectionable.

If the worker feels unable to approach the person whose actions or conduct is causing offence, or if they have already done so but to no avail, or if the complaint is one of very serious harassment, they may elect to raise a formal complaint (later).

Alternatively, the complaint can be raised informally with [state name or job title of appropriate contact, eg an HR officer or senior manager], in which case the nominated person will try to assist the employee to find an informal solution to the problem.

The worker may raise the complaint (preferably in writing) with [state name or job title of appropriate person].

The complaint must identify the person who is alleged to have perpetrated discriminatory treatment or harassment, and give specific examples of the actions or conduct that the worker believes constitute discrimination or harassment. Specific incidents should be highlighted, with times and dates, and the names of any witnesses if possible.

The person responsible for dealing with the complaint should act immediately to:

- inform the HR department of the complaint
- investigate the complaint (see later)
- take steps to conciliate if, after discussion, both parties agree this is an acceptable course of action, or
- take formal action if this is appropriate.

In the event of serious allegations of harassment, the manager should consider whether to suspend the alleged perpetrator of the harassment in order to prevent any further contact between the parties until the matter can be fully dealt with (suspension should, however, be done in a way that does not penalise the employee accused of discrimination or harassment, nor prejudge the allegations).

The Company undertakes to investigate all complaints of discrimination and harassment objectively and confidentially. The responsible manager's investigation into the complaint will be handled with due respect for the rights of both the complainant and the alleged perpetrator. Both parties will be separately interviewed as soon as possible and granted the right, if they wish, to be accompanied by a colleague or trade union representative at their interview.

In advance of the interview with the alleged perpetrator of the discrimination/ harassment, the person must be informed in writing of the exact nature of the complaint against them. At the interview itself, the alleged perpetrator must be given a full and fair opportunity to state their side of events, and explain any conduct that forms the basis of the worker's complaint against them.

Following the investigation into the complaint, the responsible manager will produce a written report setting out the findings on the specific complaints made by the worker. This will be done within two weeks of the completion of the interviews. A copy of the report will be given both to the worker and the alleged perpetrator of the discrimination, and a copy placed on the appropriate personnel file(s), but will otherwise be kept confidential. If there are parts of the report that contain statements from third parties (eg other workers) that would identify the third party in spite of their reasonable expectation to the contrary, these parts will not be included in the copies of the report supplied to the worker and the alleged perpetrator.

If, following investigation, it is apparent that the complaint is well-founded, prompt action will be taken to remedy the discrimination or stop the harassment and prevent its recurrence.

The outcome of the investigation into the worker's allegations of discrimination or harassment may be (depending on what is established during the investigation and the interviews) that:

- the complaint is well-founded and the alleged perpetrator of the discrimination or harassment is disciplined or dismissed (in line with the Company's disciplinary procedure)
- the allegations made by the worker are not viewed as discrimination or harassment and no further action is taken
- the worker's complaint is found to be false or malicious, in which case disciplinary action may be taken against them
- standards for future conduct are set, which could involve training.

The Company regards all forms of harassment and bullying as gross misconduct, and any worker found guilty of such behaviour will be liable to disciplinary action up to and including summary dismissal. Disciplinary action will also be taken against any worker found to have made a deliberately false or malicious complaint of discrimination, harassment or bullying.

If the worker who has made the complaint is not satisfied with the outcome, they may appeal in writing to [state name or job title of a more senior manager], setting out the reasons for their dissatisfaction. The appeal must be submitted within two weeks of receipt of the written report from the manager who handled the complaint.

The senior manager responsible for the appeal will convene a hearing with the worker to establish the grounds for their dissatisfaction and explore possible resolutions, having notified them of their right to be accompanied by a colleague or trade union representative at the hearing. The hearing will normally be held within two weeks of receipt of the worker's written appeal.

Following the appeal hearing, the senior manager will reply to the worker within a further two weeks describing any action that they propose to take and the timescale, or informing the worker that the appeal has not been upheld and that no further action will be taken.

If it is not possible to respond within the time periods stated above, the worker will be given an explanation as to the reasons, and asked to agree to a reasonable extension of the timescale.

This will be the final stage of the procedure.

Records will be kept detailing the nature of the allegation of discrimination or harassment, the Company's response, any actions taken, the reasons for them and the outcome. Details of these will be retained on file by the HR manager, who will ensure the records are held in accordance with the Data Protection Act 1998. The HR manager will also be responsible for making arrangements for statistical data to be released about the procedure and its usage for the purposes of monitoring.

TASK

Compare any procedures and policies that you have found in your organisation against these model policies. Have your policies and procedures covered every aspect covered by the model policies? Are there any improvements that you could recommend?

KEY POINTS FROM THIS CHAPTER

- Where proper measures are introduced to prevent discrimination and harassment, they will place the employer in a much stronger position to defend any claims of discrimination taken against them to tribunal.

- Taking measures to deal promptly and effectively with discriminatory conduct when it happens will not remove the employer's liability for the discriminatory act in a general sense, but will help to convince a tribunal that the employer did what was reasonably practicable and necessary to remedy the problem.

- Although there is no legal requirement for employers to put an equal opportunities policy in place, there will be many benefits in doing so.

- Over and above an effective equal opportunities policy and anti-harassment policy, it will be important to have an accompanying complaints procedure, so that workers who are the victims of discrimination or harassment can report any problem and receive support from the employer.

■ Training in equal opportunities matters is especially important for managers, supervisors and anyone else responsible for recruitment and promotion decisions, but ideally it should be given to all staff.

■ Each organisation should have a senior person identified as being responsible for equal opportunities

■ It can be useful to form an equal opportunities committee so that the views of all levels and groups within the organisation can be considered

■ It is essential to monitor equal opportunities within an organisation to determine whether any types of discrimination are occurring.

EXAMPLES TO WORK THROUGH

1   You have been asked to run a one-hour training session on equal opportunities for all line managers in your organisation. Outline the key areas that you would cover in this session.

2   All employees in your organisation have attended a seminar on equal opportunities, and have signed a receipt to say that they have been given a copy of the equal opportunities policy. However, a recent applicant to your organisation has made a claim of sex discrimination to the Employment Tribunals. Her complaint is that she was asked about the arrangements she made for the care of her two young children while she is at work. She claims she was asked whether she had ever had to take time off work to care for them when they were ill. The interviewer has agreed that he asked these questions, and said it was justified because his experience is that women with young children are unreliable employees. Your Managing Director has asked you if the organisation is likely to be found liable for the sex discrimination. What is your advice?

3   A recent analysis of the equal opportunities statistics in your organisation has shown that the profile of ethnic mix within the organisation falls significantly short of the ethnic mix within the locality. What are the possible reasons why this has occurred? What action, if any, should be taken?

References

ADAMS, J. (1965) 'Injustice in social exchange' in Berkowitz, L. (ed), *Advances in Experimental Psychology.* New York: Academic Press.

ARMSTRONG, M. (2002) *Employee Reward.* London: CIPD Publishing.

BOYATZIS, R.E. (1982) *The Competent Manager.* London: John Wiley & Sons.

BROWN, R. (1995) *Prejudice – its social psychology.* Oxford: Blackwell Publishers Ltd.

CIPD (2004) *Diversity: stacking up the evidence.* CIPD Bulletin.

CIPD AND LOVELLS (2003) 'A parent's right to ask: A review of flexible working arrangements'. Report. London: CIPD and Lovells.

COMMISSION FOR RACIAL EQUALITY (CRE) *Racial Equality Impact Assessment,* www.cre.gov.uk

COX, T., JR. (1994) *Cultural Diversity in Organisations: Theory, research and practice.* San Francisco: Berett and Koehler.

DEPARTMENT OF WORK AND PENSIONS (DWP) (1999) *Code of Practice on age diversity in employment.* Nottingham: DWP Publications.

DISABILITY RIGHTS COMMISSION (DRC) (2004) *Code of Practice for the elimination of discrimination in the field of employment against disabled persons.* London: TSO.

EOC (2003) *Code of Practice on Equal Pay,* www.eoc.org.uk

EOC (2004) *Facts about women and men in employment,* www.eoc.org.uk

EOC (2005) www.eoc.org.uk

EQUAL OPPORTUNITIES COMMISSION (EOC) (2001) *The Gender Pay Gap,* www.eoc.org.uk

GOSS, D. (1994) *Principles of Human Resource Management.* London: Routledge.

GOULD, S.J. (1982) A nation of morons. *New Scientist.* 6 May. 349–352.

HERRIOT, P. and SCOTT-JACKSON, W. (2002) Globalisation, Social Identities and Employment. *British Journal of Management.* Vol. 9. 249–257.

HERZBERG, F., MAUSNER, B. and SNYDERMAN, B. (1957), *The Motivation to Work.* New York: Wiley.

HIGGS, D. (2003) *Review of the role and effectiveness of non-executive Directors.* London: DTI.

INTERNATIONAL LABOUR ORGANISATION (ILO) (2004) 'Towards a fair deal for migrant workers in the global economy'. Conference paper, Geneva.

JEHN, K.A. (1995). A multimethod examination of the benefits and detriments of intragroup conflict. *Administrative Science Quarterly.* Vol. 40. 256–282.

KLINK, A. and WAGNER, U. (1999) Discrimination against Ethnic Minorities in Germany: Going Back to the Field. *Journal of Applied Psychology*. Vol. 29, No. 2. 402–423.

LABOUR FORCE SURVEY (2002), http://www.statistics.gov.uk

LABOUR FORCE SURVEY (2003), http://www.statistics.gov.uk

LABOUR FORCE SURVEY (2004), http://www.statistics.gov.uk

LEIGHTON, P. (2004) Discrimination and the law: Does the system suit the purpose? CIPD Executive Briefing.

MACDONALD, L. (2004) *Equality, Diversity and Discrimination: How to comply with the law, promote good practice and achieve a diverse workforce*. London: CIPD.

MACOBY, E. and JACKLIN, C. (1974) *The psychology of sex differences*. Stanford, CA: Stanford University Press.

MACPHERSON (1999) 'The Stephen Lawrence Inquiry. Report of an Inquiry by Sir William MacPherson of Cluny.' Published by The Stationery Office.

MICHENER, H.A., DELAMATER, J.D. and MYERS, D.J. (2004) *Social Psychology*. London:Wadsworth/Thomson.

MODOOD, T., BERTHOUD, R. and LAKEY, J. (1997) *Ethnic Minorities in Britain: Diversity and disadvantage*. London: Policy Studies Institute.

NEISSER, U. et al (1996) Intelligence: Knowns and unknowns. *American Psychologist*. Vol. 51. 77–101.

PAREKH, B.(2000) *Commission on the Future of Multi-Ethnic Britain*.London: Runnymede Trust.

POLZER, J.T., MILTON, L.P. and SWANN, W.B., JR. (2002). Capitalizing on diversity: Interpersonal congruence in small work groups. *Administrative Science Quarterly*. Vol. 43. 296–324.

PRICE, A. (2004) *Human Resource Management in a Business Context*. London: Thomson Learning.

RICHARD, O.C. and JOHNSON, N.B. (2001) Understanding the impact of human resource diversity practice son firm performance. *Journal of Management Issues*. Vol. XIII, No. 2. 177–195.

RICHARD, O.C. and SHELOR, R.M. (2002). Linking top management team age heterogeneity to firm performance: juxtaposing to mid-range theories. *International Journal of Human Resource Management*. Vol. 13. 958–974.

RICHTER, A., VAN DICK, R. and WEST, M. (2004) The relationship between group and organisational identification and effective intergroup relations. Academy of Management Best Conference Paper.

RIKETTA, M. and VAN DICK, R. (2004) Foci of attachment in organisations: A meta-analytic comparison of the strength and correlates of workgroup versus organisational identification and commitment. *Journal of Vocational Behaviour*. 1–19.

ROSS, R. and SCHNEIDER, R. (1992) *From Equality to Diversity: A Business Case for Equal Opportunities*. London: Pitman.

SAYCE, L. (2003) Beyond good intentions. Making anti-discrimination strategies work. *Disability and Society*. Vol. 18, No. 5. 625–633.

SHERIF, M. (1956) Experiments in group conflict. *Scientific American*. Vol. 195. 54–58.

SMITH, K.G., SMITH, K.A. and OLIAN, J.D. (1994). Top management team demography and process: The role of social integration and communication. *Administrative Science Quarterly.* Vol. 39. 412–438.

SMITH, M. (1991) 'Selection in Organisations' in Smith, M. (ed.), *Analysing Organisational Behaviour*. London: Macmillan.

STEETEN, P. (2001) *Globalisation: Threat or Opportunity?* Copenhagen, Copenhagen Business School Press.

STEVENSON, H.W., LEE, S.Y. and STIGLER, J.W. (1986) Mathematics achievement of Chinese, Japanese and American children. *Science*. Vol. 231. 693–699.

STRAW, J.M. (1989) *Equal Opportunities: The Way Ahead*. London: Institute for Personnel Management.

TAJFEL, H. (1970) Experiments in intergroup discrimination. *Scientific American*. Vol. 223. 96–102.

TAYLOR, R. (2002) *Diversity in Britain's Labour Market*. Swindon: Economic and Social Research Council.

TRADES UNION CONGRESS (1966) *Trades unionism*. London: TUC.

TSUI, A.S., EGAN, T.D. and O'Reilly, C.A. (1992). Being different: Relational demography and organizational attachment. *Administrative Science Quarterly*. Vol. 37. 549–579.

TUCKMAN, B. and JENSEN, N. (1977) Stages of Small Group Development Revisited. *Group and Organisational Studies*. Vol 2. 419–427.

TYSON, L. (2003) *The Recruitment and Development of Non-Executive Directors*. London: DTI.

VAN DICK, R. (2004) 'My Job is my Castle: Identification in Organisational Contexts'in COOPER, C.L. and ROBERTSON, I.T. (eds), International Review of Industrial and Organisational Psychology. 171–203. London: John Wiley and Sons.

VAN DICK, R., WAGNER, U. and PETTIGREW, T. (2004) Role of Perceived Importance in Intergroup Contact. *Journal of Personality and Social Psychology*. Vol. 87, No. 2. 211–227.

VAN KNIPPENBERG, D. and HASLAM, S.A. (2003) 'Realising the diversity dividend: Exploring the Subtle interplay between identity, ideology and reality' in Haslam, S.A., van Knippenberg, D. and Platow. M.J. (eds), *Social Identity at work: Developing theory for organisational practice*. 61–77. New York and Hove: Psychology Press.

WATSON, W.E., KUMAR, K. and MICHAELSEN, L.K. (1993) Cultural diversity's impact on interaction processes and performance: Comparing homogeneous and diverse task groups. *Academy of Management Journal*. Vol. 36. 590–602.

WEBBER, S.S. and DONAHUE, L.M. (2001) Impact of highly and less job-related diversity on work group cohesion and performance: a meta-analysis. *Journal of Management*. Vol. 27. 141–162.

WEBSTER, E.C. (1964) *Decision making in the Employment Interview*. Montreal: Industrial Relations Centre, McGill University.

WEST, M.A. (2002). Sparkling fountains and stagnant ponds: Creativity and innovation implementation in work groups. *Applied Psychology: An International Review*. Vol. 51. 355–386.

WILLIAMS, K.Y. and O'REILLY, C.A. (1998) 'Demography and diversity in organizations: a review of 40 years of research' in Staw, B. and Cummings, L. (eds.), *Research in organizational behaviour*. Vol. 20. 77–140. Greenwich, CT: JAI Press.

WOOD, R. and BARON, H. (1992) Psychological testing free from prejudice. *Personnel Management*. December. 34–37.

Index

Also from CIPD Publishing . . .

Developing and Applying Study Skills:

Writing assignments, dissertations and management reports

Donald Currie

Having trouble writing your assignment?

Do you want to improve your study skills and write successful reports?

Help is at hand with this latest title from CIPD Publishing. A practical guide to help you prepare, write and complete assignments, dissertations and management reports. This text looks at the skills required to produce successful documents, how to gain these skills and how and when to use them.

Taking a straight forward, hands-on approach, you can use this book as an ongoing tool to aid you in your studies. It offers guidance on getting the best from lectures, tutorials, seminars, structured learning sessions and group work.

Included throughout the book are exercises, case studies and self-test questions that can help you increase your experience of tackling organisation-based problems, addressing issues, increasing your academic understanding and monitoring your progress.

Order your copy now online at www.cipd.co.uk/bookstore or call us on 0870 800 3366

Donald Currie worked as a personnel officer for more than 15 years before joining the Southampton Institute as a Lecturer in personnel management. In 1990 he was appointed Fellow In Human Resource Management and for more than 10 years led the CIPD Professional Education Scheme. Donald continues to work as a consulatnt to the Southampton Business School, and has been running the CIPD CPP course since 1995.

Published 2005   1 84398 064 9   Paperback   240 pages

The Chartered Institute of Personnel and Development is the leading publisher of books and reports for personnel and training professionals, students, and for all those concerned with the effective management and development of people at work.